Sterility, sterilisation and sterility assurance for pharmaceuticals

Published by Woodhead Publishing Limited, 2013

Woodhead Publishing Series in Biomedicine

Published by Woodhead Publishing Limited, 2013

Published by Woodhead Publishing Limited, 2013

Published by Woodhead Publishing Limited, 2013

The Woodhead/Chandos team responsible for publishing this book:
Publisher: Dr Glyn Jones
Production Editor: Ed Gibbons
Project Manager: Annette Wiseman, RCL
Copy Editor: Jo Egré
Cover Designer: Ian Hutchins

Woodhead Publishing Series in Biomedicine: Number 32

Sterility, sterilisation and sterility assurance for pharmaceuticals

Technology, validation and current regulations

TIM SANDLE

WOODHEAD
PUBLISHING

Oxford   Cambridge   Philadelphia   New Delhi

Published by Woodhead Publishing Limited, 2013

Woodhead Publishing Limited, 80 High Street, Sawston, Cambridge, CB22 3HJ, UK
www.woodheadpublishing.com
www.woodheadpublishingonline.com

Woodhead Publishing, 1518 Walnut Street, Suite 1100, Philadelphia, PA 19102-3406, USA

Woodhead Publishing India Private Limited, G-2, Vardaan House, 7/28 Ansari Road,
Daryaganj, New Delhi – 110002, India
www.woodheadpublishingindia.com

First published in 2012 by Woodhead Publishing Limited
ISBN: 978-1-907568-38-1 (print); ISBN: 978-1-908818-63-8 (online)
Woodhead Publishing Series in Biomedicine ISSN 2050-0289 (print); ISSN 2050-0297 (online)

Typeset by RefineCatch Limited, Bungay, Suffolk, UK
Printed in the UK and USA

This book is dedicated to my wife, Jenny, for her continued support and inspiration

Published by Woodhead Publishing Limited, 2013

Contents

Published by Woodhead Publishing Limited, 2013

List of figures and tables

Figures

Published by Woodhead Publishing Limited, 2013

Tables

Preface

The technology involved in the manufacture of sterile pharmaceuticals, in relation to medical devices, in all aspects of healthcare, and in the production of medical devices, has expanded and developed considerably in the twenty-first century. Such advances include new and innovative methods of sterilisation, through the development and advancement of barrier systems designed to support cleanroom operations. Each of these is focused on eliminating or controlling microbiological contamination.

This book, *Sterility, sterilisation and sterility assurance for pharmaceuticals*, has been written to fill a gap in the current literature. The aim was to produce a book that is applicable to major pharmaceutical production, as well as to small biotechnological operations; and to provide relevant information about medical devices and healthcare. The book balances academic concepts with practical advice, and each chapter includes a mixture of scientific concepts, regulatory expectations and operational advice. The target audience includes microbiologists, engineers, production personnel, R&D scientists, quality assurance staff, and students of pharmaceutical science and pharmaceutical microbiology.

The focus of this book is to examine different means of rendering a product sterile. This is by providing an overview of sterilisation methods including heat, radiation and filtration. Sterilisation technology and the biopharmaceutical manufacturing process are discussed, including aseptic filling, as well as the design of containers and packaging, and addresses the cleanroom environments in which products are prepared. In doing so, the book comprehensively covers sterility, sterilisation and microorganisms, pyrogenicity and bacterial endotoxins, regulatory requirements and good manufacturing practices, and gamma radiation. Other chapters discuss e-beam, dry heat sterilisation, steam sterilisation, sterilisation by gas, vapour sterilisation, and sterile filtration, before the final chapters analyse depyrogenation, cleanrooms, aseptic processing, media simulation, biological indicators, sterility testing, auditing and new sterilisation techniques.

I hope that this book will provide practical assistance and promote an understanding of sterility and sterilisation processes, and that the concepts and thoughts expressed will provide insights to facilitate and stimulate further advances in the field.

Tim Sandle, St Albans, UK
March 2013

Published by Woodhead Publishing Limited, 2013

About the author

Tim Sandle is a chartered biologist and holds a First Class Honours degree in Applied Biology; a Masters degree in Education; and a doctorate from Keele University. He has over twenty-five years experience of microbiological research and biopharmaceutical processing. This includes designing, validating and operating a range of microbiological tests including sterility testing, bacterial endotoxin testing, bioburden and microbial enumeration, environmental monitoring, particle counting and water testing. In addition, he is experienced in pharmaceutical microbiological risk assessment and investigation.

Sandle is a tutor with the School of Pharmacy and Pharmaceutical Sciences, University of Manchester, for the university's pharmaceutical microbiology MSc course. In addition, he serves on several national and international committees relating to pharmaceutical microbiology and cleanroom contamination control (including the ISO cleanroom standards). He is a committee member of the Pharmaceutical Microbiology Interest Group (Pharmig); serves on the National Blood Service advisory cleaning and disinfection committee; and is a member of several editorial boards for scientific journals.

Sandle has acted as a consultant, expert witness and technical advisor to sterile and non-sterile manufacturing facilities, microbiology laboratories, the medical device industry and hospitals. He has undertaken several technical writing and review projects, has written over two hundred book chapters, and peer reviewed papers and technical articles relating to microbiology. This includes editing the book *The CDC Handbook: A Guide to Cleaning and Disinfecting Cleanrooms*; and co-editing the comprehensive books: *Microbiology and Sterility Assurance in Pharmaceuticals and Medical Devices* and *Cleanroom Management in Pharmaceuticals and Healthcare*. He has also delivered papers to over fifty international conferences.

Sandle runs a pharmaceutical microbiology discussion blog (pharmaceutical microbiology online: *http://www.pharmamicroresources. com/*). He can be contacted at: *timsandle@btinternet.com*

Published by Woodhead Publishing Limited, 2013

Introduction

Failure to adequately control any microbial challenge associated with pharmaceutical processing or with a medicinal product intended to be sterile by robust sterilisation, will result in a contaminated marketed product with potential harm to the patient [1]. Sterilisation is therefore of great importance to healthcare and the manufacturers of medical devices and pharmaceuticals. Sterility refers to the total absence of life forms, and sterilisation to the process that renders an item devoid of all life forms. Life forms, in the case, include bacteria, fungi and viruses.

Many types of pharmaceutical preparations are required to be sterile. This relates to the route of administration, particularly for products that are administered by injection (parenteral products, introduced infusion, injection or implantation) or ophthalmic products. The reason for such products is discussed in the first chapter of this book. There are, broadly, two types of sterile medicinal product: those that can be terminally sterilised in their final container and those that require aseptic filling because the act of terminal sterilisation would damage the contents. Within these groups there are a large variety of products and different types of presentation (packaging materials and product size). The need for sterile products applies whether the product is produced by large-scale processing or as a small-scale biotechnological project intended for a clinical trial.

In addition to the product, many items used to develop, process and fill the product are required to be sterile: from large-scale stainless steel vessels, designed to be used again, to small-scale single-use disposable plastic items. Depending upon the design and material type, these are subject to different types of terminal sterilisation.

The process of selecting the appropriate sterilisation method is driven by regulatory, economic and scientific requirements. The regulatory aspects of these are addressed in Chapter 3. In terms of economic considerations, whilst they are no doubt important for modern manufacturing, they fall outside the scope of this book. In considering the scientific and practical aspects, factors to consider include:

Published by Woodhead Publishing Limited, 2013

- whether the product and its packaging fit into an existing sterilisation technology. Ideally, a product will tolerate several different technologies;
- the logistics of transporting the product to and from the site of sterilisation. This is obviously easier when the sterilisation takes place in-house, compared with transporting the product to a contract facility;
- validation requirements to verify that the sterilisation cycle is effective.

Sterilisation is not the same as disinfection. Disinfection is often used erroneously as an interchangeable term for sterilisation; in fact, it is a process that is designed to kill actively growing and vegetative microbial microorganisms to a certain level and it does not, unless the disinfectant is classified as a steriliant, apply to bacterial endsopores. Importantly, disinfection is not a substitute for sterilisation [2]. This book contains a chapter on disinfection. This is in relation to environmental control, which is essential for cleanrooms (the environments in which pharmaceutical processing takes place), and disinfection is of critical importance in the environments where aseptically filled products are produced. This is part of the important emphasis placed upon sterility assurance.

Sterilisation is a science that dates back to times when medics first realised that 'clean' conditions were required for surgery and to the first understanding that microorganisms were the causative agents of infection. Throughout the twentieth century, theories and practices of purification, asepsis, disinfection and sterilisation were put forward and have evolved in tandem with discoveries and developments in the science of microbiology [3]. Methods of sterilisation have not stood still in the twenty-first century either and one chapter in this book is dedicated to other methods of sterilisation, some of which may soon become commonly used techniques in the pharmaceutical or medical device sectors.

This book, then, is about sterility, sterilisation and sterility assurance, as applied to the pharmaceutical and biopharmaceutical sector. The different types of technology, the validation requirements, and the current regulations as required by global medicines agencies, are addressed. Parts of the book will also be of interest to those working in the medical device and healthcare sectors, given that many of the sterilisation technologies and the complexities of their use are the same.

The book is aimed at practitioners across different disciplines, who are either required to process products and materials or to evaluate them. Therefore, it will be of interest to production staff, microbiologists, quality assurance personnel, those working in research and development, and to engineers. The book will also be of interest to students of pharmaceutical science and microbiology, undertaking undergraduate and post-graduate courses. Given the need to cover a range of technologies and applications, the book is only able to provide an introduction to each area and to draw upon case study evidence. The book does, however, outline scientific theory in relation to the each technology and as to what is happening to any contaminating microorganisms, and balances this with the practical application of the technology, covering operation and the validation requirements within the pharmaceutical setting.

The chapters of the book follow a thematic order. The first three chapters cover introductory and contextual material. Chapter 1, a more theoretical chapter, provides an introduction to sterility, sterilisation and sterility assurance. This includes the basics of pharmaceutical microbiology, including a necessary discussion on viability. The Sterility Assurance Level (SAL) concept is also introduced, which is applicable to terminal sterilisation. The different types of sterile products and why sterilisation is important are also described.

Chapter 2 discusses a related area to sterilisation: pyrogens and endotoxins. There is an important point here: a product may be rendered sterile but it can still cause harm to the patient. This is because the by-products of microorganisms (toxins) can be resistant to many standard sterilisation cycles. To eliminate fever-causing toxins such as endotoxins, depyrogenation is required.

The regulatory requirements for pharmaceutical products are very detailed and further complicated by differences between the global regulatory agencies, including the US Food and Drug Administration (FDA) and the various national bodies under the European Medicines Agency (EMA). To this end there are pharmacopeial chapters in the ISO standards and ICH guidances. Chapter 3 provides a road map for the understanding of regulations and standards pertaining to pharmaceutical manufacturing.

Chapters 4 to 9 outline methods of terminal sterilisation where microorganisms are affected by a process that either destroys them or inactivates them. Chapter 4 looks at gamma radiation and Chapter 5 at electron beam radiation. These two radiation processes have similarities and differences and are applicable to different situations and suited to different materials, in relation to speed of processing, degree of penetration and for their validation requirements.

Chapters 6 and 7 look at sterilisation by heat. Chapter 6 examines dry heat sterilisation (as distinct from depyrogenation by heat) and Chapter 7 reviews the more widely used moist heat (or steam) sterilisation, of which the ubiquitous autoclave is the most widely used example. Dry heat sterilisation technology is less destructive to many materials than steam, which can be corrosive to metal objects and damaging to certain glass surfaces. However, often the heating and cooling times of dry heat sterilisers are lengthy [4]. Steam sterilisation is performed under high pressure at temperatures that range from 121–140°C, which is lower than temperatures required for dry heat sterilisation and the sterilisation times are often shorter [5]. Given the prominence of these methods, considerable emphasis is given to their validation requirements.

Chapters 8 and 9 look at sterilisation by gas of vapour. Chapter 8 casts an overview over sterilisation by gas (ethylene oxide, chlorine dioxide and ozone), whilst Chapter 9 considers the more specialist area of vapour phase hydrogen peroxide. Whilst the leading gas, ethylene oxide, is used as an alternative to gamma radiation [6], hydrogen peroxide vapour is generally used for the surface sanitisation of pharmaceutical isolators [7].

Chapter 10 moves on to a different type of sterilisation by addressing filtration. Filtration concerns the rendering of a liquid or gas as sterile by the physical removal of microorganisms. Filtration processes can be complicated and the validation is dependent upon the type of material being filtered and its physical properties.

Chapter 11 concludes the discussion on methods of sterilisation that can be considered as 'terminal sterilisation' methods, by considering alternative and emerging methods of sterilisation. Caution is required at this point, for 'new' is often a marketing description for the latest outcome in a gradual development and refinement of an existing process. It also stands that some technologies will not be taken up on a wide scale due to their cost or operational complexities. Of those which might have a more prominent role in a future book on sterilisation are X-rays and plasma gas.

Chapter 12 represents an interregnum, moving beyond classical sterilisation and looking at depyrogenation. The chapter looks at the methods for the removal or the destruction of endotoxins. Whilst various methods are considered, the focus of the chapter is upon the most widely used method of depyrogenation by dry heat. The chapter expands the discussion through a case study.

Chapter 13 moves towards aseptic filling and processes applicable to medicinal products that cannot be terminally sterilised. The supporting environment, in which aseptically filled products (and some terminally sterilised products) are prepared and filled, such as cleanrooms and barrier systems, is considered. Of the barrier systems, the most effectively controlled environment is provided by the isolator.

Published by Woodhead Publishing Limited, 2013

Chapter 14 looks at the complexities surrounding aseptic filling in general, and outlines why this is the most difficult of processes and the type most at risk from microbial contamination. A comprehensive overview of aseptic product manufacturing is provided.

Chapter 15 continues with the aseptic filling theme and considers the validation of filling through the use of media simulation trials. Guidance is provided for selecting the criteria to monitor for when establishing a media filling protocol and on constructing a matrix approach for the selection of media fill parameters based on 'worst case' conditions.

Chapter 16 addresses an important part of the microbiological control of cleanrooms by examining cleaning and disinfection and should be read in conjunction with Chapter 13. Emphasis is placed upon the validation of disinfectants, from suspension tests through to the consideration of different surfaces and field trials. The chapter also discusses the differences between US and European norms.

The validation of most, but not all, sterilisation processes requires a biological control to supplement physical measurements. This is particularly important for sterilisation by heat. For this, biological indicators (spore populations) of bacteria of a known resistance are used. Chapter 17 explains the key criteria for biological indicators and outlines how they are used and how their resistance is assessed.

Chapters 18 and 19 address the Sterility Test. The Sterility Test remains, in many instances, a key release test and remains mandatory for all aseptically filled medicinal products. Chapter 18 examines the way in which the test is conducted, including practical aspects, whilst Chapter 19 provides guidance for the investigation of Sterility Test failures. This includes the importance of risk in assessing the pharmaceutical process and the genotypic identification of the microbial contaminant.

Chapter 20 concludes with the auditing of sterile processing. As the chapter outlines a framework for the auditing of sterilisation, it addresses key concepts of sterility assurance and as such links to some of the theoretical constructs discussed in Chapter 1 and some of the pertinent regulatory issues presented in Chapter 3.

With the conclusion, the book completes its purpose in providing a single-volume overview of sterility, sterilisation and sterility assurance as applicable to the pharmaceutical sector. It weaves together the reasons for and importance of sterile products with the methods that render products sterile or measures which provide clean conditions for the aseptic dispensing of medicines, and addresses the controls and standards necessary to provide sterility and quality assurance and thus the confidence that a sterile product has been produced.

I.1 References

1. Sandle, T. and Saghee, M.R. (2011), 'The essentials of pharmaceutical microbiology', in: Saghee, M.R., Sandle, T. and Tidswell, E.C. (eds), *Microbiology and Sterility Assurance in Pharmaceuticals and Medical Devices*, New Delhi: Business Horizons, pp. 1–30.
2. Gaughran, E.R.L. and Kereluck, K. (eds) (1977), *Sterilization of Medicinal Products*, New Brunswick, NJ: Johnson & Johnson.
3. Halls, N.A. (1994), *Achieving Sterility in Medical and Pharmaceutical Products*, New York: Marcel Dekker Inc, pp. 109–21.
4. Wood, R.T. (1993), 'Sterilization with dry heat', in: Morrissey, R.F. and Phillips, G.B (eds), *Sterilization Technology: A Practical Guide for Manufacturers and Users of Health Care Products*, New York: Van Nostrand Reinhold, pp. 81–119.
5. Joslyn, L.J. (1991), 'Sterilization by heat', in: Block, S.S. (ed.), *Disinfection, Sterilization, and Preservation*, 4th edition, Philadelphia, PA: Lea and Febiger, pp. 495–526.
6. Burgess, D.J. and Reich, R.R. (1993), 'Industrial ethylene oxide sterilization', in: Morrissey, R.F. and Phillips, G.B. (eds), *Sterilization Technology: A Practical Guide for Manufacturers and Users of Health Care Products*, New York: Van Nostrand Reinhold, pp. 152–95.
7. Rickloff, J.R. and Graham, G.S. (1989), 'Vapor phase hydrogen peroxide sterilization', *Journal of Healthcare Materiel Management*, 7(5): 45–8.

Sterility, sterilisation and microorganisms

DOI: 10.1533/9781908818638.1

Abstract: This chapter provides an introduction to the main themes of this book. It examines the theory of sterility and how it is a concept of probability. Microorganisms and viability in relation to sterility and sterilisation are considered. The discussion of microorganisms highlights the limitations both with environmental assessments (due to the presence of so-called viable but non-culturable microorganisms) and with the Sterility Test (limited by the sample size and growth based factors). With sterilisation, and returning to the theme of sterility as a probabilistic idea, this chapter examines the Sterility Assurance Level (SAL) in relation to terminal sterilisation and contrasts this quantitative assessment with aseptic processing, which is reliant upon environmental controls.

Key words: sterility, sterilisation, Sterility Assurance Level, terminal sterilisation, aseptic processing, viability, viable but non-culturable, Sterility Test, pharmaceutical science, dosage forms, good manufacturing practice, sterile bulk manufacturing, quality assurance.

1.1 Introduction

Injections, infusions and pharmaceutical forms for application to eyes and mucous membranes must meet the requirement to be sterile. This is because certain medicines, such as peptides, proteins and many chemotherapeutic agents, would be inactivated in the gastrointestinal tract if they were given by mouth. Thus, most types of sterile products are administered by injection [1].

The development and production of such sterile medicinal products, from large-scale pharmaceutical processing to small-scale biotechnology, with medicines made on a named patient basis prepared within a hospital pharmacy to the processing of sterilised components, is arguably the most difficult and important facet of the preparation of pharmaceutical medicines. This is not necessarily due to the formulation of the products but because the medicines, due to their route of administration, are required to be sterile at the point where they are administered to the patient. If medicines are not sterile, this could lead to patient harm or even death. It is not possible to determine to what extent a non-sterile product would affect an individual patient. This is because people are unique in relation to form and physiology, and also because the context of administration and treatment will vary widely between individuals. Nonetheless, a contaminated product, especially one administered intravenously (via a vein) or intrathecally (via the brain or the spinal cord), is likely to cause harm.

The most effective means of reducing the risk of infection is the provision of a sterile product together with the complete prevention of microbial ingress up to and including the time of administration to the patient. This includes using sterile items to administer the drug (i.e. a sterile syringe and needle) and to administer the drug under clean conditions, using trained medical or nursing practitioners.

In addition to the medicinal product, the various components required for the production and development of sterile products are equally as important. These too need to be sterile, whether they are large stainless vessels subjected to steam sterilisation using an autoclave, or packaging or ready-assembled sterile disposable kits, which have been sterilised using radiation or gas.

A further area in which sterilisation applies is to medical devices, which cover a large spectrum of items including instruments, apparatus, implants, *in vitro* reagents and any articles that are used to diagnose, prevent or treat disease or other conditions. Medical devices do not achieve these purposes through chemical action within or on the body, unlike medicines [2].

Each of these various elements, which combine to create a sterile product or item, relate to the industrial process of sterile manufacturing. Sterile manufacturing itself is a continuum that stretches from development to manufacturing, to finished product, to marketing and distribution, and to utilisation of drugs and biologics in hospitals, as well as in patients' homes. Although the terms 'sterile manufacture' or 'aseptic manufacturing' are widespread, there is no generic approach to the manufacturing of sterile products. Each plant or process will differ in relation to the technologies, products and processing steps. The common point is that a product is produced which is sterile and where there is no risk of contamination until the contents of the outer packaging are breached (i.e. through the injection of a needle through a bung of a product vial).

Sterility and production of sterile products are relatively new concepts in the history of human development. Unhealthy practices were part and parcel of the medical profession until the late 1800s, when the germ theory of disease gained credibility by explaining the increased cases of illnesses within hospital settings (notably the work of Lord Joseph Lister and aseptic methods in surgery, including the use of carbolic acid from 1867) [3]. Throughout the 1880s and 1890s, antiseptic surgical dressings and other forms of sterilisation such as dry-heat and steam pressure, were introduced to the medical field. For example, Ernst von Bergmann introduced the autoclave in the 1870s, a device used to sterilise surgical instruments [4] and in the 1920s the wide-scale production of sterile syringes and needles began [5]. Since these early beginnings, hygienic practices and sterilisation methods have been used and developed to decrease the spread of disease and infections [6]. For example, increased development in technology led to the first use of ethylene oxide gas as a hospital sterilant in 1940, radiation sterilisation in 1956 and gamma radiation sterilisation in 1964.

As a way of introducing the reader to many of the concepts, terms and ideas outlined in this book, this chapter explores the theory of sterility, the objectives of sterilisation and microbiological concepts such as viability. Presenting such material without veering too much to the abstract or leaning too heavily upon the theoretical is not possible. However, if the reader gains familiarity with these terms (or, depending upon their experience, using this chapter as an aide-mémoire), this will help them to understand and contextualise many of the more practical based chapters that are to follow.

1.2 Sterility

1.2.1 Defining sterility

Sterility can be defined as 'the absence of all viable microorganisms'. Therefore, something would be deemed sterile only when there is complete absence of viable microorganisms within it. Sterility is an absolute term. Either something is sterile or it is not. There is no such thing as 'slightly sterile' or 'almost sterile'.

Microorganism refers to a living entity, only visible through a microscope, which comprises a single cell (unicellular), cell clusters or multicellular relatively complex organisms. Microorganisms includes bacteria (prokaryotes), fungi (eukaryotes) and viruses in various states (notably, not all microbiologists consider viruses to be living) [7]. The prokaryotes, bacteria and archaea are the most diverse and abundant group of organisms on Earth [8]. They are found in sea water, soil, air, animals' gastrointestinal tracts, hot springs and even in rocks deep within the Earth's crust. Fungi too are found in a diverse range of habitats. As eukaryotic organisms, fungi are more complex organisms than bacteria. Many types of bacteria and fungi are found within the environments where medicinal products are processed, being carried into the areas through air-streams, via equipment, and by people. Chapter 13 looks at the sources of microbial contamination within cleanrooms.

From the above definition of sterility, sterilisation can be taken to mean the use of a physical or chemical procedure to destroy all microbial life, including highly resistant bacterial endospores. This destruction of bacterial spores means that sterilisation is a complete process for the destruction of life, unlike disinfection which refers to the reduction of a microbial population by destruction or inactivation.

Importantly, this simple definition refers to microorganisms that are 'viable', that is bacteria, fungi and viruses that are capable of reproducing under the correct conditions. However, it does not refer to the absence of microbial by-products. By-products include toxins which may cause harm, such as endotoxins, exotoxins or enterotoxins. These can be released by microorganisms as they function or when they die; several toxins are resistant to many types of sterilisation (e.g. for endotoxins, a depyrogenation process is required, as set out in Chapter 12).

Furthermore, the term 'sterile' does not extend to other aspects of the formulation that might cause patient harm, such as the presence of particulates or chemical impurities. Moreover, something which is sterile, such as a liquid in a bottle, is only sterile at a point in time; something which has been rendered sterile can become non-sterile if there is ingress of microorganisms (i.e. a crack in the bottle allowing microbial ingress). Thus, something which has been rendered sterile is subject to the possibility of becoming non-sterile under certain conditions [9].

Whilst the author regards the definition of sterility, 'the absence of all viable microorganisms', as essentially correct, the evidence that something

Published by Woodhead Publishing Limited, 2013

is sterile can only be considered in terms of probability. This is because absolute sterility can only be proved by testing every single item produced (and with technology that will give an undisputable result). However, the act of testing destroys the very item which is required for administration to the patient, so sterility cannot be proven empirically.

Therefore, the concept of what constitutes 'sterile' is measured as a probability of sterility for each item to be sterilised [10]. Probability can be considered in relation to components that are sterilised and to products that can be terminally sterilised in relation to the concept called the Sterility Assurance Level (SAL). Importantly, the SAL concept cannot be applied to aseptically filled products. With these products, the probability of sterility or non-sterility is the product of environmental controls (from clean air devices and cleanrooms), product filtration, sterilised components, personnel behaviours and gowning.

Before considering this notion of probability and the SAL further, it is important to consider the concepts of 'viable microorganisms' and 'viability'.

1.2.2 Microorganisms and viability

Viability is itself a difficult concept and microbiologists periodically debate the issue of whether or not 'dead means dead'. Our understanding of viability is also limited by what we can see, and to see microorganisms is still very reliant upon the use of growth media [11]; it is easier to demonstrate that a microorganism is dead than it is to demonstrate that it is alive [12]. The limitation is that microbial cells may exist in 'cryptobiotic' [13], 'dormant' [14], 'moribund' [15] or 'latent' [16] states. The inference of this is that although we can recognise and predict the likely number of microbial species using modern genotypic-based technologies, it remains that only a small percentage of these microorganisms are culturable [17]. Indeed it has been estimated that only between 1% and 5% of all microorganisms are culturable using established collection methods, agars and incubation conditions [18, 19]. The reason for this is because the culturing of the majority of all species of microorganisms is dependent upon sophisticated, artificial simulation of natural habitats, which closely and necessarily reproduce their natural environment [20].

Therefore, within the manufacturing environment for pharmaceuticals and medical devices, it is probable that a diverse spectrum of microorganisms exists, many of which may not be recoverable or culturable on traditional growth supportive media. Under non-ideal conditions, microorganisms may resort to a state often described as 'viable but non-culturable' (VBNC) [21] or alternatively, as 'active but non-culturable' (ABNC) [22]. In these states, bacterial cells retain certain features of viable cells, such as cellular integrity and measureable metabolic activity, yet will not culture.

This has implications for the monitoring of the environment (which impacts especially on aseptic filling), assessing the bioburden of a load prior to sterilisation, assessing the microbial content of a product prior to final filtration, and using the Sterility Test. The implications place greater emphasis upon the need for sterilisation processes that are consistent, reproducible, and which have a degree of 'overkill' built into them.

For certain products, prions are a risk and require a separate mention to microorganisms. Prion diseases, such as Creutzfeldt–Jakob disease (CJD), are a group of degenerative brain diseases that have received much attention during the past few years. They occur in animals (dogs, cows and primates) as well as humans and are rapidly fatal once symptoms develop. In humans, CJD remains rare, with an incidence of less than one per million in the general population. CJD poses a unique infection prevention problem because prions, which are protein-containing infectious agents, can survive recommended heat or high-pressure steam sterilisation processes [23]. In addition, chemical disinfectants, including sterilants such as glutaraldehydes and formaldehyde, are not strong enough to eliminate prion infectivity on contaminated instruments and other items. Therefore, surgical instruments and other critical devices contaminated with high-risk tissue (i.e. brain, spinal cord and eye tissue) from patients with known or suspected CJD require special treatment. Heat-resistant instruments and other devices should first be decontaminated by placing them in a gravity displacement sterilizer at 121 °C for 1 hour, or in a pre-vacuum sterilizer at 134 °C for 18 minutes [24]. Alternatively, contaminated instruments and other devices can be soaked in 1 N sodium hydroxide (NaOH) for 1 hour [25].

1.3 Sterility Assurance and the Sterility Assurance Level (SAL)

The manufacture of sterile products involves the philosophy and application of sterility assurance. Sterility assurance, as a broad term, refers to the philosophy of protecting a sterile product throughout its manufacturing life in relation to controls and practices. It is not synonymous with the SAL, although the reduction of the two concepts is, unfortunately, too common. The term 'sterility assurance' is a combination of two words with the following definitions:

■ *Sterility* – state of being free from viable microorganisms; and

■ *Assurance* – a positive declaration intended to give confidence.

Sterility assurance concerns the wider aspects of Good Manufacturing Practice (GMP), which are designed to protect the product from contamination at all stages of manufacturing (from incoming raw materials through to finished products) and thus it forms an integral part of the quality assurance system.

A quantitative assessment of the sterility assurance can be provided through the SAL, a term used to describe the probability of a single unit being non-sterile after a batch has been subjected to the sterilisation process, or the probability of a single viable microorganism surviving on or in an item after sterilisation [26]. Importantly, the SAL concept was developed for sterilisation processes and should be limited to terminal sterilisation, thus it cannot, as a probabilistic concept, be applied to aseptic manufacture; whilst certain literature attempts to do so, such attempts should be avoided for they are scientifically inaccurate.

A second important point is that the SAL is not exactly a definition of the assurance of 'sterility'; rather it is the probability of 'non-sterility' [27]. SALs are used to describe the probability that a given sterilisation process has *failed* to destroy all of the microorganisms. This is why the term is defined as the probability of a treated item remaining contaminated by one or more viable microorganisms and not, as sometimes misreported, the probability of successful sterilisation.

The reason that sterilisation is discussed in terms of probability is because it is impossible to prove that all microorganisms have been destroyed. This is because:

1. Microorganisms could be present but undetectable, simply because they are not being incubated in their preferred environment; and

2. Microorganisms could be present but undetectable, because their existence has never been discovered.

SALs can be used to estimate the microbial population that was destroyed by the sterilisation process. Each log reduction (10^{-1}) represents a 90% reduction in the microbial population. So a process shown to achieve a '6-log reduction' (10^{-6}) will reduce a population from a million microorganisms (10^6) to very close to zero (theoretically). The same logic can apply to containers as to microorganisms. For example, an SAL of 10^{-6} expresses probability of survival, that is, there is one chance in 10^6 that any particular container out of 10^6 containers would theoretically not be sterilised by the process [28].

SAL is demonstrated through validation using innocuous bacterial endospores (biological indicators). The assumption is that the inactivation of such highly resistant microorganisms encompasses all less resistant organisms, including most pathogens [29]. The use of biological indicators is discussed in relation to moist heat terminal sterilisation (Chapter 7) and in general (Chapter 17).

In assigning a quantitative value, an SAL of 10^{-6} takes a lower value but provides a greater assurance of sterility than an SAL of 10^{-3} [30]. Furthermore, the SAL is normally expressed as 10^{-n}. For example, if the probability of a spore surviving were one in one million, the SAL would be 10^{-6}. The reader will note that the SAL is a fraction of 1 and therefore carries a negative exponent (so the 6-log reduction is written as 10^{-6} rather than 10^6). However, the reader should be aware that SAL refers to individual items of product and not to a batch of product.

This theoretical reduction in microbial population also assumes that [31]:

- a single species of microorganism is present on or in each product;
- there is a homogenous microbial population;
- the population has a mono-dispersal distribution on the surfaces to be sterilised, i.e. there is no clumping;
- the exclusion of multi-nucleate spores (e.g. ascospores) or microorganisms.

For many years, an SAL of 10^{-6} has represented the sterilisation standard for invasive and implantable devices and medicinal products administered by injection. In practice, many processes use 'overkill cycles', which assure an even lower probability that a device will be non-sterile [32].

1.4 Sterility testing

A common means to assess the effectiveness of sterility for medicinal products is the Sterility Test. The Sterility Test is less common for the sterilisation of consumables where a terminal sterilisation process is used. Here the product bioburden is assessed prior to sterilisation and compared to validation cycles for the microorganisms found in relation to the population and resistance of the microorganisms to the sterilisation process. For medicinal products that can be terminally sterilised, parametric release is often used in lieu of the Sterility Test (see Section 1.5 on 'Parametric release').

For aseptically filled products, and some terminally sterilised products, the Sterility Test is a regulatory requirement (as per the US Food and Drug Administration (FDA) and the European Medicines Agency (EMA)). All pharmacopoeial tests for sterility have been traditionally growth based. Despite the emergence of some rapid sterility tests, the regulatory body guidance and individual national legislations mandate a growth-based test to prove sterility [33].

Despite the requirement to conduct the Sterility Test on a representative batch size, it remains that it is a flawed test on a number of levels. The first relates to the very small sample size tested. Testing any pharmaceuticals and medical devices to a level of statistical significance would require a sample size that would be practically and economically unsustainable. Second, the microbial challenge to the manufacture of pharmaceuticals and medical devices includes microorganisms, which by virtue of their fastidious nature or physiological prerogative, will not grow on growth medium [34]. There is growing evidence that microorganisms in forms that will not necessarily replicate retain their propensity and have been proven to cause disease [35]. The Sterility Test is discussed in further detail in Chapter 18.

1.5 Parametric release

Products that can be terminally sterilised can be subject to parametric release without undertaking finished product testing. The European Organisation for Quality defines parametric release as:

> A system of release that gives the assurance that the product is of the intended quality based on information collected during the manufacturing process and on the compliance with specific GMP requirements related to Parametric Release.

Importantly, the organisation must demonstrate the capability of the sterilisation agent to penetrate to all relevant parts of the product [36].

Parametric release assumes that a robust sterility assurance system is in place, consisting of:

- good product design;
- the company having knowledge of and control of the microbiological condition of starting materials and process aids (e.g. gases and lubricants);
- good control of the contamination of the process of manufacture to avoid the ingress of microorganisms and their multiplication in the product. This is usually accomplished by cleaning and sanitation of product contact surfaces, prevention of aerial contamination by handling in cleanrooms or in isolators, use of process control time limits and, if applicable, filtration stages;
- systems for the prevention of mix ups between sterile and non-sterile product streams;
- maintenance of product integrity;
- a robust and consistent sterilisation process;
- the totality of the Quality System that contains the sterility assurance system, e.g. change control, training, written procedures, release checks, planned preventative maintenance, failure mode analysis, prevention of human error, validation and calibration.

1.6 Sterile products

There are two main groups of sterile products, related to the way in which they are treated (or not) after filling the final container (i.e. a bag, vial or syringe). The distinction is between products that can be terminally sterilised in their final container and those that cannot due to the effect of the sterilisation process upon the product. For example, some protein-based products cannot be subjected to heat. Products that cannot be subjected to terminal sterilisation are aseptically filled and rely on the pre-sterilisation of the components and bulk product before being aseptically filled within a cleanroom. For these processes, there are different, and higher, levels of risk.

The regulatory bodies, such as the FDA and European regulators, favour terminal sterilisation, and in the development of new sterile dosage forms, the EU regulations demand that a decision tree is followed whereby the new dosage must be proven to be unable to withstand various defined processes of terminal sterilization before it is allowed to be manufactured aseptically. It is important that the organisation has selected the appropriate method of sterile manufacturing and is aware of

Published by Woodhead Publishing Limited, 2013

why that method is in place. The preparation of sterile products up to the filling and sterilisation of the final product are broadly similar. The two types of sterile product are examined further below.

1.6.1 Terminal sterilisation

Both the FDA guidance on aseptic filling (2004) and the *European Pharmacopoeia* (section 5.1.1) state that of the methods of sterile manufacture, a process in which the product is sterilised in its final container (terminal sterilisation) is the preferred method [37]. This is not suitable for all types of products, so filtration through a bacteria-retentive filter and aseptic processing is used.

Terminal sterilisation involves filling and sealing product containers under high-quality environmental conditions. This means that non-parenteral products that are to be terminally sterilised may be filled in an EU GMP Grade C/ISO 14644 class 8 area (for details of cleanroom grades, see Chapter 13). Parenteral products can be filled under the same conditions if the process or product does not pose a high risk of microbial contamination. Examples of high-risk situations include slow filling operations, the use of wide-necked containers or the exposure of filled containers to the environment for more than a few seconds before sealing. In these cases, products are filled in an aseptic area with at least an EU GMP Grade B/ISO 14644 class 7 environment or in an EU GMP Grade A/ISO 14644 class 5 zone, with at least an EU GMP Grade C/ISO class 8 background, prior to terminal sterilisation.

Products are filled and sealed in this type of environment to minimise the microbiological content of the in-process product and to help ensure that the subsequent sterilisation process is successful. It is accepted that the product, container and closure will probably have low bioburden but they are not sterile. The product in its final container is then subjected to a terminal sterilisation process such as heat or irradiation. As terminally sterilised drug products, each product unit undergoes a single sterilisation process in a sealed container. The assumption is that the bioburden within the product can be eliminated by the sterilisation process selected [38].

Product formulation is undertaken at EU GMP Grade C/ISO 14644 class 8 or EU GMP Grade D/ISO 14644 class 9 environments. For some higher risk products, pre-filtration through a bacteria retentive filter may be advisable in such cases, particularly where there is a high bioburden. It is up to the pharmaceutical organisation to define the level of risk and to justify this to an inspector.

1.6.2 Aseptic filling

Aseptic manufacturing is used in cases where the drug substance is unstable when subjected to heat (thus sterilisation in the final container closure system is not possible) or where heat would cause packaging degradation. Aseptic filling is arguably the most difficult type of sterile operation. This is because the end product cannot be terminally sterilised and so there are far greater contamination risks during formulation and filling. With aseptic processing there is always a degree of uncertainty, particularly because of the risk posed by personnel to the environment in which filling takes place.

In aseptic manufacturing, the dosage form and the individual components of the containments system are sterilised separately and then the whole presentation is brought together by methods that ensure that the existing sterility is not compromised. Sterility is normally achieved through sterile filtration of the bulk using a sterilising grade filter (with a pore size of 0.2 μm or smaller) in sterile container closure systems and working in a clean area [39]. This is undertaken in an EU GMP Grade C/ISO 14644 class 8 cleanroom environment. The container and closure are also subject to separate sterilisation methods. The sterilised bulk product is filled into the containers, stoppered and sealed under aseptic conditions (under EU GMP Grade A/ISO 14644 class 5 air) within an EU GMP Grade B/ISO 14644 class 7 cleanroom, unless filling is undertaken within a barrier system.

To assist with aseptic processing, engineering and manufacturing technology throughout all industries has evolved considerably. In the context of sterile and aseptic manufacture of pharmaceutical and medical devices, blow-fill-seal (BFS), pre-filled syringe filling, restricted access barrier systems (RABS) and isolator technologies represent the main developments. Aseptic processes that exclude human intervention (i.e. robotics or barrier systems) present a considerably lower risk than operations that consist of filling machines under unidirectional airflow devices, where there is a need for periodic human intervention. With isolator systems, the background environment in the cleanroom can be at EU GMP Grade C/ISO 14644 class 8, based on an appropriate risk assessment. There are additional risk considerations for isolators, in that the decontamination procedures should be validated to ensure full exposure of all isolator surfaces to the chemical agent. Aseptic filling is the subject of Chapter 14.

1.6.3 Blow-fill-seal technology

Blow-fill-seal (BFS) technology is a type of aseptic filling but one at a theoretical lower risk compared with conventional filling. BFS is an automated process where containers are formed, filled and sealed in a continuous operation without human intervention. This is performed in an aseptic enclosed area inside a machine. The technology can be used to aseptically manufacture certain pharmaceutical liquid dosage forms.

BFS operations are undertaken under EU GMP Grade A/ISO 14644 class 5 conditions with the background environment at EU GMP Grade C/ISO 14644 class 8. Where BFS equipment is used for the production of products that are terminally sterilised, the operation can be carried out within an EU GMP Grade D/ISO 14644 class 9 background environment, if appropriately risk assessed [40].

1.7 Sterilisation

Although there are a wide variety of mechanisms and processes by which a pharmaceutical or medical device might be rendered free from microorganisms (i.e. sterile), they may be grouped into three main categories [41]:

1. *Physical removal* – the complete removal of all microorganisms to achieve a physical absence of microorganisms (i.e. filtration);

2. *Physical alteration* – including physical destruction and disintegration of microorganisms, altering, changing or deforming the physical cellular or biochemical architecture to destroy all physiological functionality;

3. *Inactivation* – the permanent disruption of critical biochemical and physiological properties, potential and the microorganisms propensity (whether active or latent) to realize a clinical condition, thus ensuring impotency for generating an infection. For complete assurance of inactivation, the microorganisms must therefore be essentially 'killed', with no residual metabolic activity.

From these important concepts, primary methods of sterilisation consist of the following four main categories:

1. high temperature/pressure sterilisation (by dry heat or moist heat);

2. chemical sterilisation (i.e. gassing using ethylene oxide);

3. filtration;

4. radiation sterilisation (i.e. gamma).

These different methods are each the topic of individual chapters within this book.

All forms of sterilisation have negative effects on a wide variety of packaging materials, and sometimes on the item or product itself. These effects can vary from material to material and between the different packaging components. Sterilisation can affect polymers, seal strength, label and box adhesion, corrugated and paperboard strength, and material colour. The selection of the sterilisation method is therefore of considerable importance.

1.8 Factors affecting sterilisation

There are a number of factors that affect the success or otherwise of a sterilisation process. These are outlined below.

1.8.1 Number and location of microorganisms

If all other conditions remain constant, the larger the number of microorganisms then the longer the sterilisation process is required to run, in order to destroy all of microorganisms present. Reducing the number of microorganisms that must be inactivated through meticulous cleaning and disinfection, or by assembling components within classified cleanrooms, increases the margin of safety when the sterilisation process is applied [42].

In terms of the location of microorganisms, research has shown that aggregated or clumped microbial cells are more difficult to inactivate than mono-dispersed cells. Microorganisms may also be protected from poor penetrating sterilisation methods by the production of thick masses of cells and extracellular materials, or biofilms [43]. It has also been shown that products which have crevices, joints and channels are more difficult to sterilise than flat-surfaced equipment, because penetration of the sterilising agent to all parts of the equipment is more difficult [44].

1.8.2 Innate resistance of microorganisms

Microorganisms vary greatly in their resistance to sterilisation processes. Intrinsic resistance mechanisms in microorganisms vary. For example, spores are generally the most resistant to sterilisation processes, because the spore coat and cortex act as a barrier. Implicit in all sterilisation strategies is the consideration that the most resistant microbial sub-population controls the sterilisation time. That is, to destroy the most resistant types of microorganisms (bacterial spores), the user needs to employ exposure times and a concentration or dose needed to achieve complete destruction [45].

1.8.3 Physical and chemical factors

Several physical and chemical factors also influence sterilisation processes, especially temperature and relative humidity. For example, relative humidity is the single most important factor influencing the activity of gaseous sterilants, such as ethylene oxide, chlorine dioxide and formaldehyde [46]; whereas achieving a certain temperature is critical for the operation of an autoclave.

1.8.4 Organic and inorganic matter

Organic matter, such as serum or blood, can interfere with the antimicrobial activity of sterilisation processes by interfering with the chemical reaction between the certain sterilants and the organic matter, resulting in less of the active sterilant being available for attacking microorganisms. The effects of inorganic contaminants on the sterilisation process can afford protection to microorganisms, thereby limiting the potential effectiveness of the sterilisation process [47].

1.8.5 Duration of exposure

Items must be exposed to the sterilisation process for an appropriate minimum time. Most sterilisation processes have minimum cycle times, established during validation runs.

1.8.6 Storage

All sterile items should be stored in an area and manner whereby the packs or containers will be protected from dust, dirt, moisture, animals and insects. The shelf life of sterilisation depends on the following factors:

- quality of the wrapper or container;
- number of times a package is handled before use;
- number of people who have handled the package;
- whether the package is stored on open or closed shelves;
- condition of storage area (e.g. humidity and cleanliness);
- use of plastic dust covers and method of sealing.

1.9 Risk assessment

When considering any type of sterile manufacturing, the essential risk must never be forgotten: that the objective is to avoid the contamination of the product by microorganisms or microbial by-products (i.e. endotoxins). It is also important to focus on the most common sources of contamination [48]:

- *Air* – air is not a natural environment for microbial growth (it is too dry and absent of nutrients), but microorganisms such as *Bacillus, Clostridium, Staphylococcus, Penicillin* and *Aspergillus* can survive. To guard against this, products and sterile components must be protected with filtered air supplied at sufficient volume.

- *Facilities* – inadequately sanitised facilities pose a contamination risk. Furthermore, poorly maintained buildings also present a risk such as potential fungal contamination from damp or inadequate seals. The design of buildings and the disinfection regime are thus of importance.

- *Water* – the presence of water in cleanrooms should be avoided. Water is both a growth source and a vector for contamination.

- *Incoming materials* – incoming materials, either as raw materials (which will contain a level of bioburden) or packaged materials, present a contamination risk if they are not properly controlled. Paper and cardboard sources in particular present a potential risk.

- *People* – people are the primary source of contamination within cleanrooms. People generate millions of particles every hour from activities of breathing, talking and body movements, where particles are shed from hair, skin and spittle. Many of these particles will be carrying microorganisms. As such, a considerable proportion of this book is concerned with the control and training of personnel [49].

These factors should be borne in mind when designing different sterilisation processes.

1.10 Conclusion

This chapter has provided an introduction to sterility and sterilisation. It has outlined basic pharmaceutical microbiology in relation to the ways by which microorganisms can survive within processing environments and thereby present a risk to sterilisation or aseptic filling. It is explained further that sterility is an absolute term, but equally one that is difficult to prove and thus can only be understood in terms of risk and probability. For terminally sterilised products and sterilisation processes, the sterility assurance concept is useful. However, this concept cannot be applied to aseptic filling and instead there is a strong reliance upon environmental controls.

In introducing these terms and ideas, this chapter provides a framework within which the other chapters, outlining different facets of sterilisation or different sterilisation methods, should be considered. The reader is encouraged to return to this chapter from time to time to act as a refresher and to provide a note of caution: sterility and sterilisation are not straightforward concepts and microbial risks are ever present.

1.11 References

1. Akers, M.J. (2010), 'Introduction, scope, and history of sterile products', in: Akers, M.J. (ed.), *Sterile Drug Products*, London: Informa Healthcare.
2. Sandle, T. and Saghee, M.R. (2012), 'Application of sterilization by gamma radiation for single-use disposable technologies in the biopharmaceutical sector', *Pharmaceutical Technology*, Supplement: *Bioprocessing and Pharmaceutical Manufacturing*, May: SS20–7.
3. Ramstorp, M. (2000), *Introduction to Contamination Control Technology*, Weinheim: Wiley-VCH, pp. 1–17.
4. Blair, J.S.G. (2006), 'Ernst Von Bergmann', *Journal of the Royal Army Medical Corps* (England), 152(2): 108–9.
5. Anon. (2011), *Syringe and Needle History*, Franklin Lakes, NJ: Beckton and Dickinson. Available from: *http://www.ahrn.net/library_upload/uploadfile/file2376.pdf*
6. Faria, M.A. Jr. (2002), 'Medical history – Hygiene and sanitation', *Medical Sentinel*, 7(4): 122–3.
7. Madigan, M. and Martinko, J. (eds) (2006), *Brock Biology of Microorganisms*, 13th edition, London: Pearson Education, p. 1096.

8. Whitman, W., Coleman, D. and Wiebe, W. (1998), 'Prokaryotes: The unseen majority', *Proceedings of the National Academy of Sciences, USA*, 95(12): 6578–83.

9. Sandle, T. and Saghee, M.R. (2011), 'The essentials of pharmaceutical microbiology', in: Saghee, M.R., Sandle, T. and Tidswell, E.C. (eds), *Microbiology and Sterility Assurance in Pharmaceuticals and Medical Devices*, New Delhi: Business Horizons, pp. 1–30.

10. Favero, M.S. (2001), 'Sterility assurance: Concepts for patient safety', in: Rutala, W.A. (ed.). *Disinfection, Sterilization and Antisepsis: Principles and Practices in Healthcare Facilities*. Washington, DC: Association for Professional in Infection Control and Epidemiology, pp. 110–9.

11. Amann, R.I., Ludwig, W. and Schleifer, K.H. (1995), 'Phylogenetic identification and *in situ* detection of individual microbial cells without cultivation', *Microbiological Reviews*, 59: 143–69.

12. Davey, H.M., Kell, D.B., Weichart, D.H. and Kaprelyants, A.S. (2004), 'Estimation of microbial viability using flow cytometry', *Current Protocols In Cytometry*, 11: 11.3.1–21.

13. Keilin, D. (1959), 'The problem of anabiosis or latent life: History and current concepts', *Proceedings of the Royal Society, Series B*, 150: 149–91.

14. Kaprelyants, A.S. and Kell, D.B. (1993), 'Dormancy in stationary-phase cultures of *Micrococcus luteus*: Flow cytometric analysis of starvation and resuscitation', *Applied and Environmental Microbiology*, 59: 3187–96.

15. Postgate, J.R. (1967), 'Viability measurements and the survival of microbes under minimum stress', *Advances in Microbial Physiology*, 1: 1–23.

16. Wayne, L.G. (1994), 'Dormancy of *Mycobacterium tuberculosis* and latency of disease', *European Journal of Clinical Microbiology and Infectious Diseases*, 13: 908–14.

17. Hunter-Cevera, J. (1998), 'The value of microbial diversity', *Current Opinion in Microbiology*, 1: 278–85.

18. Anderson, T-H. (2003), 'Microbial eco-physiological indicators to assess soil quality', *Agricultural Ecosystems and Environment*, 98: 285–93.

19. Torsvik, V.G., Golsor, J. and Daae, F. (1990), 'High diversity in DNA of soil bacteria', *Applied and Environmental Microbiology*, 56: 782–7.

20. Kaeberlein, T., Lewis, K. and Epstein, S.S. (2002), 'Isolating "uncultivable" microorganisms in pure culture in a simulated natural environment', *Science*, 296: 1127–9.

21. Weichart, D. (1999), 'Stability and survival of VBNC cells – Conceptual and practical implications', in Bell, C.B-G. (ed.), *Proceedings of the 8th International Symposium on Microbial Ecology*. Halifax, Canada: Atlantic Canada Society for Microbial Ecology.

22. Kell, D.B., Kaprelyants, A.S., Weichert, D.H., Harwood, C.R. and Barer, M.R. (1998), 'Viability and activity in readily culturable bacteria: A review and discussion of the practical issues', *Antonie van Leeuwenhoek*, 73: 169–87.

23. Holman, R.C., Khan, A.S., Belay, E.D. and Schonberger, L.B. (1996), 'Creutzfeldt–Jakob disease in the United State, 1979–1994: Using national mortality data to access the possible occurrence of variant cases', *Emerging Infectious Diseases*, 2(4): 333–7.

24. Rutala, W.A. and Weber, D.J. (2001), 'Creutzfeldt–Jakob disease: recommendations for disinfection and sterilization', *Clinical Infectious Diseases*, 32(9): 1348–56.

25. Abrutyn, E., Goldman, D.A. and Scheckler, W.E. (eds) (1998), *Saunders Infection Control Reference Service*, Philadelphia, PA: W.B. Saunders & Co., pp. 569–70.

26. International Organization for Standardization (2006), *Sterilization of Health Care Products, Vocabulary*, ISO/TS 11139:2006, Geneva: ISO.

27. Halls, N.A. (1994), *Achieving Sterility in Medical and Pharmaceutical Products*, New York: Marcel Dekker, Inc.

28. Berube, R., Oxborrow, G.S. and Gaustad, J.W. (2001), *Sterility Testing: Validation of Sterilization Processes and Sporicide Testing in Disinfection, Sterilization and Preservation*, 5th edition, Block, S.S. (ed.), Philadelphia, PA: Lippincott Williams & Wilkins, p. 1361.

29. Baird, R.M. (1999), 'Sterility assurance: Concepts, methods and problems', in: Russell, A.D., Hugo, W.B. and Ayliffe, G.A.J. (eds), *Principles and Practice of Disinfection, Preservation and Sterilization*, 3rd edition, Oxford: Blackwell Science, pp. 787–99.

30. Stumbo, C.R. (1973), *Thermobacteriology in Food Processing*, 2nd edition, Orlando, FL: Academic Press, Inc, p. 130.

31. Mosley, G.A. (2003), 'Microbial lethality: When it is log-linear and when it is not!' *Biomedical Instrumentation & Technology*, 37(6): 451–4.

32. Pflug, I.J. (2003), *Microbiology and Engineering of Sterilization Processes*, 11th edition, Minneapolis: Environmental Sterilization Services.

33. Tidswell, E.C., Khorzad, A. and Sadowski, M. (2009), 'Novel and emerging sterilization technologies', *European Pharmacology Review*, 5: 11–21.

34. Bryce, D.M. (1956), 'Tests for sterility of pharmaceutical preparations; the design and interpretation of sterility tests', *Journal of Pharmacy and Pharmacology*, 8: 561.

35. Sandle, T. (2011), 'Sterility test requirements for biological products', *Pharmaceutical Microbiology Forum Newsletter*, 17(8): 5–14.

36. PIC/S (2007), *Recommendation on Guidance for Parametric Release. Pharmaceutical Inspection Convention and Pharmaceutical Inspection Co-operation Scheme*, Brussels. Available from: *http://www.picscheme.org/ pdf/24_pi-005-3-parametric-release.pdf*

37. Sirch, E.C. (2002), 'Isolatortechnik in der pharmazeutischen Industrie: GMP-/FDA-gerechte aseptische Produktion', *Pharma Technologie Journal*, 1082: 106–25.

38. Agallocco, J. (2011), 'Process selection for sterile products', in: Saghee, M.R., Sandle, T. and Tidswell, E.C. (eds), *Microbiology and Sterility Assurance in Pharmaceuticals and Medical Devices*, New Delhi: Business Horizons, pp. 603–14.

39. Meltzer, T.H. (1987), *Filtration in the Pharmaceutical Industry*, New York: Marcel Dekker, Inc.

40. Bradley, A., Probert, S.C., Sinclair, C.S. and Tallentire, A. (1991), 'Airborne microbial challenges of blow/fill/seal equipment: a case study', *Journal of Parenteral Science and Technology*, 45: 187–92.

41. Tidswell, E. (2011), 'Sterility', in: Saghee, M.R., Sandle, T. and Tidswell, E.C. (eds), *Microbiology and Sterility Assurance in Pharmaceuticals and Medical Devices*, New Delhi: Business Horizons, pp. 589–602.

42. Block S.S. (2001), *Disinfection, Sterilization, and Preservation*, Philadelphia, PA: Lippincott Williams & Wilkins.

43. LeChevallier, M.W., Cawthon, C.D. and Lee, R.G. (1988), 'Inactivation of biofilm bacteria', *Applied and Environmental Microbiology*, 54: 2492–9.

44. Russell, A.D., Hugo, W.B. and Ayliffe, G.A.J. (1999), *Principles and Practice of Disinfection, Preservation and Sterilization*, Oxford: Blackwell Scientific Publications.

45. Russell, A.D. (2001), 'Principles of antimicrobial activity and resistance', in: Block, S.S. (ed.), *Disinfection, Sterilization, and Preservation*, Philadelphia, PA: Lippincott Williams & Wilkins, pp. 31–55.

46. Rutala, W.A. (1999), 'Selection and use of disinfectants in healthcare', in: Mayhall, C.G. (ed.), *Infection Control and Hospital Epidemiology*, Philadelphia, PA: Lippincott Williams & Wilkins, pp. 1161–87.

47. Muscarella, L.F. (1995), 'Sterilizing dental equipment', *Nature Medicine*, 1: 1223–5.

48. Reinmüller, B. (2001), 'People as a contamination source – Clothing systems', in: Anon., *Dispersion and Risk Assessment of Airborne Contaminants in Pharmaceutical Cleanrooms*, Royal Institute of Technology, Building Services Engineering, Bulletin No. 56, Stockholm, August, pp. 54–77.

49. Sharp, J., Bird, A., Brzozowski, S. and O'Hagan, K. (2010): 'Contamination of cleanrooms by people', *European Journal of Parenteral and Pharmaceutical Sciences*, 15(3), 73–81.

Published by Woodhead Publishing Limited, 2013

Pyrogenicity and bacterial endotoxin

DOI: 10.1533/9781908818638.21

Abstract: This chapter examines pyrogens (substances which induce fever in mammals) and the most common type of pyrogen found within pharmaceutical manufacturing processes: bacterial endotoxin. Why pyrogenic substances are of concern, and especially to sterility, is outlined. The chapter proceeds to examine the most ubiquitous pyrogen – bacterial endotoxin – and describes the primary assays used for its detection. It concludes by considering the main source of endotoxin in processing areas, water, and some of the control measures required for endotoxin control.

Key words: pyrogens, bacterial endotoxin, *Limulus* Amebocyte Lysate test, fever, lipopolysaccharide, coagulation, clotting, water, pharmaceutical processing.

2.1 Introduction

Sterile drug products are not only at risk from viable microorganisms, but microbial toxins can also pose a significant risk to patients, particularly if toxins are injected into the blood stream. There are a range of microbial toxins (endotoxins, exotoxins and enterotoxins) with different immunological effects, with endotoxins being of greatest concern to sterile drug products.

Pyrogens are substances which, when injected into the mammalian body, will cause a variety of symptoms, the most recognisable of which is an increase in core body temperature [1]. With microbial pyrogenic substances, such as endotoxin, there is an association with pyrogens and dead microbial cells. Although endotoxin is shed naturally by living cells, it is released in higher quantities when a cell undergoes lysis. Therefore, a drug product or component may be 'sterile' (i.e. contain no viable microorganisms) but at the same time be pyrogenic (because it contains cellular by-products).

Due to these concerns, pharmaceutical products which are injected into the human body are tested for pyrogenic substances. The most common, and arguably most important test, is for a pyrogenic substance called bacterial endotoxin [2]. This is because endotoxin is by far the most common pyrogenic substance found in pharmaceutical facilities, although it is important to distinguish that endotoxin is a pyrogen, but not all pyrogens are endotoxin.

The pathological effects of endotoxin, when injected, are a rapid increase in core body temperature followed immediately by severe shock, often followed by death before the cause is even diagnosed. However, there needs to be large quantities of endotoxin within the human body for this to occur and the endotoxin needs to be injected into the blood stream (the presence of endotoxins in the blood is called endotoxemia) [3]. Bacterial endotoxin is the lipopolysaccharide (LPS) component of the cell wall of Gram-negative bacteria. It is pyrogenic and is a risk to patients who are administered intravenous and intramuscular preparations. The primary test for bacterial endotoxin is the *Limulus* Amebocyte Lysate (LAL) test [4], although there are alternative assays.

This chapter provides an overview of pyrogens and bacterial endotoxin, describes the LAL test and other assays for endotoxin, and outlines the primary risks of pyrogenic contamination in the manufacture of sterile drug products. Pyrogens are removed from pharmaceutical processes through a process called depyrogenation (Chapter 12).

2.2 Pyrogenicity

The term pyrogen is derived from the Greek word pyrexia. Pyrogens can be either internal (endogenous) or external (exogenous) to the body. All endogenous pyrogens are cytokines, molecules that are a part of the innate immune system (e.g. interleukin 1 (α and β) and interleukin 6 (IL-6)). Exogenous pyrogens can enter the blood stream via injection of pharmaceutical preparations (parenteral products). The most common type is bacterial endotoxin. Although a 'pyrogen' is introduced into the body as an exogenous agent, its presence causes the release of endogenous factors, that is, the immunological response within the body is the same [5].

In the early days of the pharmacopoeia, drug substances were classed as apyrogenic or pyrogenic based, from 1942 and until the 1980s, solely on the 'pyrogen test', whereby a quantity of the drug was injected into three rabbits and the temperature response of the rabbits was noted. The rabbit pyrogen test was first described by Florence Seibert in 1925 [6].

The rabbit test is no longer widely used and has been largely been replaced, for the testing of parenteral drug products, by the LAL test, particularly within Europe under the requirements of the European Pharmacopoeia Commission [7] and the European Medicines Agency [8]. The LAL test is a method of the Bacterial Endotoxin Test (BET) for detecting the presence, and to go some way to determining the level, of Gram-negative bacterial endotoxins in a given sample or substance. Current editions of the *Pharmacopoeia* carry statements to the effect that where the term apyrogenic or pyrogen-free is used, it should be interpreted as meaning that samples of the product will comply with a limit for bacterial endotoxin.

It was not until the early twentieth century that an understanding began to emerge in which bacteria could be classified into pyrogenic and non-pyrogenic types, correlatable to their Gram stain. Gram staining is a method of differentiating bacterial species into two large groups (Gram-positive and Gram-negative). It is based on the chemical and physical properties of their cell walls. Primarily, it detects peptidoglycan, which is present in a thick layer in Gram-positive bacteria. A Gram-positive results in a purple/blue colour, while a Gram-negative results in a pink/red colour.

Gram-negative bacteria were found to be pyrogenic, Gram-positive bacteria were generally not and killed cultures of Gram-negative bacteria were comparable to live cultures in their ability to induce fevers. It was found that the injection of living or killed Gram-negative cells into experimental animals caused a wide spectrum of non-specific pathophysiological reactions, such as fever, changes in white blood cell counts, disseminated intravascular coagulation, hypotension, shock and death.

Thus, by the 1920s it was apparent that sterility in parenteral pharmaceuticals could be no guarantee of non-pyrogenicity, and that if pyrogenicity was to be avoided, it was imperative to avoid bacterial contamination at every stage of manufacture of parenteral pharmaceuticals.

In recognition that the causative agent of pyrogenicity was filterable and heat stable, efforts were applied to identify its chemical composition.

Trichloracetic acid and phenol-water extractions of bacteria were found to be effective in isolating the pyrogenic element from bacteria. These extracts were chemically identifiable as LPS, or what is commonly described as bacterial endotoxin.

2.3 Endotoxin

The structural rigidity of the bacterial cell wall is conferred by a material called peptidoglycan (also known as murein) [9]. It is a polymer consisting of sugars and amino acids that forms a mesh-like layer outside the plasma membrane of bacteria, forming the cell wall.

In Gram-positive bacteria, peptidoglycan is present as a thick layer that is outermost in the cell wall. In Gram-negative bacteria, the peptidoglcan is only a thin layer and is not the outermost layer. Gram-negative bacteria are sometimes described as having a cell envelope rather than a cell wall. The term envelope better describes the loosely attached layer of material called LPS, which is located outside a thin structural layer of peptidoglycan (Figure 2.1).

The outer layer of this LPS envelope forms a permeable barrier, effective against the diffusion of exo-enzymes into the external environment [10]. This is an evolutionary feature which has arisen to allow Gram-negative bacteria to survive and increase in numbers in environments such as water in which there are only low concentrations of organic nutrients. LPS is pyrogenic [11] and bacterial endotoxin is a synonym for LPS.

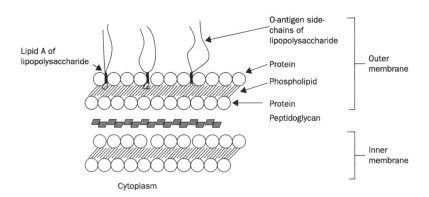

Figure 2.1 Diagram of the outer bacterial cell wall (from Creative Commons Library)

Although intimately associated with the cell envelope of Gram-negative bacteria, LPS is constantly shed by the bacteria into the environment, much like the shedding of the outer layers of human skin. When Gram-negative bacteria die and lyse, all of their LPS is shed into the environment.

Furthermore, when bacterial cells are lysed by the immune system, fragments of membrane containing lipid A are released into the circulation, causing fever, diarrhoea and possible fatal endotoxic shock (also called septic shock) [12]. There are some other substances which are also pyrogenic, but they are unusual and are extremely rarely found associated with pharmaceutical preparations.

LPS has three distinct chemical regions (Figure 2.2).

- an inner core called Lipid A;

- an intermediate polysaccharide layer;

- an outer polysaccharide side chain.

Lipid A is a powerful biological response modifier that can stimulate the mammalian immune system. Thus lipid A, embedded in the bacterial outer membrane, is responsible for pyrogenicity.

Endotoxin presents a risk to pharmaceutical processing due to its primary source, water, and it being filterable and unaffected by steam sterilisation. Thus the control of water is of great importance (as addressed later in this chapter), as are processes of depyrogenation (Chapter 12).

2.4 The LAL test

The principle of the LAL test is a reaction between LPS and a substance ('clottable protein') contained within amoebocyte cells derived from the blood of the horseshoe crab (of which *Limulus polyphemus* is the most commonly used species[1]). The reaction is specific. The reaction of the horseshoe crab to endotoxin (the formation of a clot) has been known since the 1950s [13]. The clotting mechanism of the blood of the crab is designed to prevent the spread of bacterial contamination throughout its biochemical system (haemolymph). When the endotoxin of Gram-negative bacteria contacts with the crab's amebocytes, a series of enzymatic reactions begin. The pathway alters amebocyte coagulogen into a fibrinogen-like clottable protein, which forms a coagulin gel [14].

LAL is an aqueous extract obtained after lysis of blood cells (amoebocytes) from horseshoe crabs. When endotoxin comes into

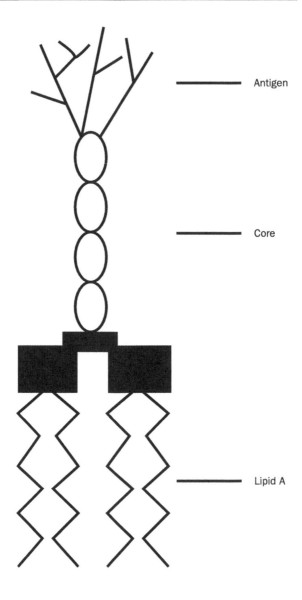

LIPOPOLYSACCHARIDE

Figure 2.2 Diagram of LPS

contact with LAL, it initiates a series of enzymatic reactions that result in the activation of a pathway to the production of at least three serine protease zymogens (Factor C, Factor B and pro-clotting enzyme). This pathway alters amoebocyte coagulogen (an invertebrate fibrinogen-like

Published by Woodhead Publishing Limited, 2013

clottable protein) to form coagulin gel. Serine proteases are enzymes that cleave peptide bonds in proteins, in which serine serves as the nucleophilic amino acid at the active site. They are found in humans as well as in the horseshoe crab (and indeed in all mammals). In humans,[1] they are responsible for co-ordinating various physiological functions, including digestion, immune response, blood coagulation and reproduction. It is the blood coagulation reaction that is so similar in humans and the horseshoe crab [15].

The reference LAL test in the pharmacopoeias is called the gel clot (or gelation) and is conducted on the end-point principle (it became a licensed test in 1973). The description of the test and the necessary validation and accompanying controls is detailed in both the United States and European pharmacopoeia (harmonised since 1999). The LAL reagent used for the gel-clot is supplied with an identified sensitivity or label claim (lamda or λ), for example, 0.03 endotoxin units (EU) per mL. This means that when mixed with an equal volume of the material under test, a gel or clot will form if the material contains 0.03 EU per mL or greater. By using product dilutions, the test can provide semi-quantitative estimates of the endotoxin level in a given sample.

The unit of measurement for the LAL test is the Endotoxin Unit (EU), expressed as EU per mL or mg. These are a measure of the activity of the endotoxin. Endotoxins differ in their biological activity or potency; the pyrogenicity or LAL reactivity of one endotoxin preparation may be very different from that of another of the same weight. Conversely, two endotoxin molecules may be of different sizes and different weights but may have the same reactivity in an LAL test. The potency of an endotoxin determined with one LAL reagent lot may differ from that determined with another lot. Expressing endotoxin concentrations in EUs avoids the issues of different potencies of different endotoxins and allows microbiologists to compare results of different LAL tests performed in different laboratories.

Some pharmacopoeia use the term IU (International Unit), although the units are equivalent based on an international reference standard. The standard, called RSE (Reference Standard Endotoxin), is manufactured from a specific strain of *Escherichia coli* bacteria [16].

Acceptable endotoxin limits are set for pharmaceutical products or ingredients (such as Water-for-Injections, which has a limit of not more than 0.25 EU/mL), or limits are set for products using a standard equation based on the maximum allowable dose per adult. Because the dose varies from product to product, the endotoxin limit is expressed as K/M. K is 5.0 EU/kilogram (kg), which represents the approximate threshold pyrogen dose for humans. That is the level at which a product is judged to be pyrogenic or non-pyrogenic. M represents the maximum human dose per kg that would be administered in a single 1 hour period, whichever is larger. If a product is labelled for intrathecal injection, then K is 0.2 EU/kg.

Following the adoption of the gel-clot test, the 1990s saw the introduction onto the market of more sensitive, rapid and semi-automated LAL test methods: the turbidimetric and chromogenic, described as the kinetic methods because the rate of reaction is proportionate to the amount of endotoxin present [17]. With these methods, the test sensitivity is determined by the lowest point of the standard curve used with each assay [18]. With these assays, changes in turbidity and colour are discernable by spectrophotometers.

Two concerns in relation to using the LAL test are the presence of interfering factors, which can lead to inhibition or enhancement of endotoxin and the over-dilution of samples, so that a false negative is obtained, underestimating the quantity of endotoxin present in the sample [19]. These risks are avoided through, in the case of interfering factors, the use of positive sample controls, where samples are challenged with a known quantity of endotoxin and the recovery calculated; and with over-dilution, the use of a formula to calculate the Maximum Valid Dilution (MVD). Tests are additionally run against a standard series of expected endotoxin concentrations and negative controls. Negative controls consist of samples of LAL reagent water containing no detectable endotoxin to which LAL reagent is added. Their purpose is to assure that the test system does not give a signal in the absence of endotoxin and to verify that the reagents are not contaminated.

2.5 Alternative assays

Later developments with the LAL test have seen the growing use of recombinant lysates, due to concerns with the prolonged ecological and economic use of horseshoe crabs. Other methods have also been developed, such as ELISA (Enzyme-Linked Immunosorbent Assay) based methods. With these methods, endotoxin is bound to a phage protein and detected by recombinant Factor C (rFC) and quantified through the detection of a fluorescence substrate.

An alternative to both the LAL test and the classic rabbit pyrogen test is the Monocyte Activation Test (MAT). The basis of the MAT is that pyrogens stimulate monocytes to produce cytokines (IL-6, TNF-a) or lead to the formation of metabolites (neopterin, nitrite) from cytokine-inducible pathway cells, which can then be measured in the supernatants of the cultured cells by ELISA methods (IL-6, TNF-a, neopterin). Thus, the test can detect non-endotoxin pyrogens as well as endotoxins [20]. Whilst the method is limited by the need of blood from donors and the variability from one donor to another, it is described in the *European Pharmacopoeia*, which confers it legitimacy (chapter 2.6.30: Monocyte-activation Test). pharmacopoeia

2.6 Water: the source of endotoxins in pharmaceutical manufacturing

Having outlined above the risks associated with pyrogens and the primary tests for their detection, this section addresses the main sources of pyrogens in the manufacture of sterile pharmaceutical and biopharmaceutical products: water. Given that the most ubiquitous types of pyrogens are endotoxins, the focus is on sources of bacterial endotoxin.

Although all bacteria have some associated endotoxin, the most potent source is from Gram-negative bacteria. Endotoxins may be shed from viable bacteria during growth, or they may be associated with non-viable bacteria. The most common habitat for Gram-negative bacteria is water, where they have evolved to be able to survive and increase in numbers with minimal nutritional support and to be able to adapt their metabolism to metabolise complex organic macromolecules that other bacteria cannot.

In any form of pharmaceutical manufacture, water is one of the most serious potential sources of microbiological contamination. Water cannot be totally excluded from sterile products manufacturing facilities. The primary focus on endotoxin control in pharmaceutical manufacture is on controlling it at its source – water. If endotoxin is not controlled at its source, it has the potential to create difficulties throughout manufacture to the finished product, potentially leaving no recourse but final product batch rejection. Endotoxin is practically impossible to remove terminally from pharmaceutical dosage forms.

The measures taken to control contamination from water in sterile manufacturing facilities can be seen as measures taken to minimise the risk of endotoxin contamination of products. Water is used in pharmaceutical processing for the following purposes:

- 'ingredient' water for aqueous sterile products;
- water supplied for cleaning of product contact equipment and components;

- water supplied to laundries;
- water supplied for hand washing;
- steam supplies to autoclaves, SIP systems, etc.

The pharmacopoeia deal with the ingredient, water, in two monographs, *Purified Water* and *Water for Injection* (WFI). To comply with the FDA requirements, WFI may be prepared by distillation or by reverse osmosis. For Europe, WFI can only currently be produced from distillation. With distillation, LPS has a molecular weight of more than 100,000 Daltons [21], heavy enough to be left behind when water is rapidly boiled off, as in a still.

Where water has an endotoxin limit it does not mean that it will automatically comply with that limit. Suitably controlled means of preparation, storage and distribution must be employed to ensure that the limits are complied with at point of use. Systems and user points require monitoring to demonstrate that the level of endotoxin in water is below the maximum permitted level of 0.25 EU/mL.

WFI as prepared by distillation will comply, if sampled directly from the preparation point and not contaminated in sampling or testing. However, it is immediately fed to a storage tank and pumped round a distribution system where, at least in theory, microbiological contamination may be lurking and shedding endotoxin.

When used in bulk for manufacturing purposes, the pharmacopoeia also apply a microbiological limit to WFI, at not more than 10 cfu (colony-forming units) per 100 mL. This limit does not tie in with the endotoxin specification. The amount of endotoxin associated with Gram-negative bacteria is thought to be around 10–15 g per bacterium. The first batch of RSE titrated at $1\,EU = 2 \times 10^{-10}\,g$. Therefore the endotoxin limit of 0.25 EU/ml for WFI can be understood to correspond to $5 \times 10^{-11}\,g/ml$ or about $10^{>4}$ bacteria/ml. Despite there being a great deal of uncertainty about these figures, and that Gram-negative bacteria not only have associated endotoxin but also shed endotoxin continuously, and that Gram-positive bacteria are generally not very endotoxic, it is apparent that water that meets the limit for endotoxin may exceed the limit for viable microorganisms.

The means of controlling the development of Gram-negative (and other) microorganisms in water storage and distribution systems are [22–24]:

- Smooth internal surfaces in tanks and pipe-work. Microorganisms adhere less well to smooth surfaces than to rough surfaces. Pipe joints and welds can disrupt smoothness.

Published by Woodhead Publishing Limited, 2013

- Continuous movement of the water in tanks and rapid flow in pipe-work. Where shear forces are involved, microorganisms adhere poorly to surfaces. Where there is no movement of the water, there is no shear. Shear increases with speed of flow.

- Avoidance of areas where water can remain stagnant. These include 'dead legs' – water may stagnate in branch pipes. If the length of the branch is too long, it will not allow the turbulence of the flowing main to disturb the contents of the branch pipe. FDA have defined 'dead legs' according to their dimensions in the 1993 *Guide to Inspection of High Purity Water Systems*, but fundamentally the principle is to always minimise the length of branch pipes.

  Water can also remain stagnant in valves, particularly at user points and even more particularly at user points that are not in frequent and regular use. This is counteracted by use of so-called hygienic or 'zero dead leg' valves which, although significantly better than many alternatives (i.e. ball valves), should not lead to a sense of false security, for such a valve design can harbour endotoxin-shedding biofilms.

- Ring mains should be sloped (have 'drop') from point of origin to point of return, to ensure that systems are completely drainable.

- Avoidance of leakage. Water leaks can cause bridging of water to the external environment through which bacteria may enter the system. Storage tanks should be equipped with a filter on their air vents to prevent airborne microbiological ingress. They may even be held under a 'blanket' of an inert gas such as nitrogen.

- High temperature storage and distribution. The risks of endotoxin-shedding biofilms are considered to be so consequential that the regulatory bodies require the temperature of storage and distribution to be maintained at higher than 75°C. However, it should be considered that 75°C is too high a temperature for most pharmaceutical formulation purposes and will scald personnel coming into contact with it. In practise, user points are generally equipped with some form of cooling mechanism. It is important to emphasise that heat exchangers used for this purpose may be a source of endotoxin and bacterial contamination and may thus cancel out many of the benefits of high temperature circulation.

2.7 Conclusion

This chapter has provided an introduction to pyrogens and the most common type found in pharmaceutical facilities, bacterial endotoxin.

The primary method for detecting endotoxin, the LAL test, has also been outlined. The risks of endotoxin to pharmaceutical processing and some of the control measures in place to reduce the risk of endotoxin contamination were examined. The aim of the chapter was to provide an introduction to this important subject and to emphasise that 'sterility' does not necessarily mean that a product is safe under circumstances where microbial by-products, such as endotoxin, present a risk.

2.8 Note

1. The other main alternative, used more often in Japan, is *Tachypleus tridentatus*.

2.9 References

1. Dinarello, C. (2004), 'Infection, fever, and exogenous and endogenous pyrogens: Some concepts have changed', *Journal of Endotoxin Research*, 10: 201–22.
2. Twohy, C.W., Duran, A.P. and Munson, T.E. (1984), 'Endotoxin contamination of parenteral drugs and radiopharmaceuticals as determined by the *Limulus* amebocyte lysate method', *Journal of Parenteral Science and Technology*, 38: 190–201.
3. Hurley, J.C. (1995), 'Endotoxemia: Methods of detection and clinical correlates', *Clinical Microbiology Reviews*, 8(2): 268–92.
4. Guy, D. (2003), 'Endotoxins and Depyrogenation', in: Hodges, N. and Hanlon, G. (eds), *Industrial Pharmaceutical Microbiology: Standards and Controls*, Passfield, UK: Euromed Communications, pp. 12.1–15.
5. Boron, W.F. and Boulpaep, E.L. (2003), *Medical Physiology: A Cellular and Molecular Approach*, London: Elsevier/Saunders.
6. Seibert, F.B. (1925), 'The cause of many febrile reactions following intravenous injection', *American Journal of Physiology*, 71: 621–51.
7. European Pharmacopoeia Commission. *European Convention on the Use of Animals for Experimental and Other Scientific Purposes*, and with EU Directive 86/609/EC.
8. European Medicines Agency (2009), Guideline of the replacement of rabbit pyrogen testing by an alternative test for plasma derived medicinal products, London: European Medicines Agency.
9. Novitsky, T.J. (1984), 'Discovery to commercialization: The blood of the horseshoe crab', *Oceanus*, 27: 13–18.
10. Madigan, M.T., Martinko, J.M., Dunlap, P.V. and Clark, D.P. (2009), *Brock Biology of Microorganisms*, 12th edition, San Francisco, CA: Pearson/Benjamin Cummings.

11. Raetz, C.R.H. (1990), 'Biochemistry of endotoxins', *Annual Review of Biochemistry*, 59: 129–70.
12. Rudbach, J.A., Akiya, F.I., Elin, R.J., Hochstein, H.D., Luoma, M.K., *et al.* (1979), 'Preparation and properties of a national reference endotoxin', *Journal of Clinical Microbiology*, 3(10): 21–5.
13. Brandberg, K., Seydel, U., Schromm, A.B., Loppnow, H., Koch, M.H.J., *et al.* (1996), 'Conformation of Lipid A, the endotoxic center of bacterial lipopolysaccharide', *Journal of Endotoxin Research*, 3(3): 173–8.
14. Bang, F.B. (1956), 'A bacterial disease of limulus polyphemus', *Bulletin of JohnsHopkins Hospital*, 98(5): 325–51.
15. Cooper, J.F. and Williams, K. (2007), 'Pyrogenicity Case Studies', in: Williams, K. (ed.), *Endotoxins: Pyrogens, LAL Testing and Depyrogenation*. New York: Informa Healthcare.
16. Rudbach, J.A., Akiya, F.I., Elin, R.J., Hochstein, H.D., Luoma, M.K., *et al.* (1979), 'Preparation and properties of a national reference endotoxin', *Journal of Clinical Microbiology*, 3(10): 21–5.
17. McCullogh, K.C. and Weider-Loeven, C. (1992), 'Variability in the LAL test: comparison of three kinetic methods for the testing of pharmaceutical products', *Journal of Parenteral Science and Technology*, 46(93): 69–72.
18. Sandle, T. (2001), 'Performance characteristics of automated LAL tests', *Pharmaceutical Microbiology Interest Group News*, 4: 3–6.
19. Moser, K. (2009), 'Playing hide and seek with endotoxin', *Associates of Cape Cod LAL User Group Newsletter*, 3(2): 1–5.
20. Hartung, T., Aaberge, I., Berthold, S., Carlin, G., Charton, E., *et al.* (2001), 'Novel pyrogen tests based on the human fever reaction. The report and recommendations of eCVAM Workshop 43', European Centre for the Validation of Alternative Methods. *Alternatives to Laboratory Animals*, 29: 99–123.
21. Mayer, H., Tharanathan, R.N. and Weckesse, J. (1985), 'Analysis of lipopolysaccharides of gram-negative bacteria', *Methods in Microbiology*, 18: 157–207.
22. Levin, J., Buller, H.R., ten Cate, J.W., van Deventer, S.J.H. and Sturk, A. (1988), Bacterial endotoxins. *Pathophysiological effects, clinical significance, and pharmacological control*, vol. 272, New York: Alan R. Liss, Inc.
23. Blanden, P.D., James, J.B., Krygier, V. and Howard, G. Jr. (1991), 'Comparison of bacterial and endotoxin retention by charge-modified sterilizing grade filters during intermittent long-term use', *Journal of Parenteral Science and Technology*, 45(5): 229–32.
24. Sweadner, K.J., Forte, M. and Nelse, L.L. (1977), 'Filtration removal of endotoxin (pyrogens) in solution in different states of aggregation', *Applied and Environmental Microbiology*, 34: 382–5.

3

Regulatory requirements and Good Manufacturing Practices (GMP)

DOI: 10.1533/9781908818638.35

Abstract: The proper sterilisation of medical devices, surgical instruments, supplies and equipment utilised in direct patient care and surgery, together with the preparation of medicinal products that are required to be filled aseptically, is a critical aspect of the modern health care delivery system and directly impacts patient safety. To ensure this, international standards together with an overarching regulatory framework are essential. The various sources and types of standards and guidance applicable to sterilisation and to the manufacture of sterile products are introduced. The regulatory approach, with a focus on European regulatory and the US FDA, is outlined. Many of the standards have the objective of describing or advancing Good Manufacturing Practice (GMP) and the centrality of GMP to quality systems is emphasised. In order to place current standards in context, the origin of GMP in the wake of infamous medical incidents are discussed.

Key words: sterility, standards, regulations, inspections, FDA, MHRA, EMA, ICH, CFR, pharmacopoeia, ISO, Good Manufacturing Practice.

3.1 Introduction

Sterile processing is one of the most regulated areas within healthcare, due to the potential risk to patients, either directly from the developed drug or through an associated reagent or medical device. If the medicine is contaminated with microorganisms, then the patient may become ill or even die [1]. A pertinent example of the damage caused by contaminated medicines was seen with the New England Compounding Center (NECC), which has been the most serious case of a contaminated sterile product in recent years.

In October 2012, an outbreak of fungal meningitis was reported in the United States. The US Centers for Disease Control and Prevention (CDC) traced the outbreak to fungal contamination in three lots of medication used for epidural steroid injections. The medication was packaged and marketed by the NECC, a compounding pharmacy in Framingham, MA. Due to a failure to follow Good Manufacturing Practice (GMP), most notably due to inadequate control and validation of a steam sterilising autoclave, several lots of medicine became contaminated with the environmental fungi. According to the US Food and Drug Administration (FDA), records suggested that NECC had failed to sterilize products for even the minimum amount of time necessary to ensure sterility.

Doses from three lots of medicine were distributed to 75 medical facilities across 23 states. The contaminated doses were administered to approximately 14,000 patients between 21 May and 24 September in 2012. This resulted in over 30 deaths and over 500 patients becoming infected with fungal meningitis. The causative agents were a black mould called *Exserohilum rostratum*, found in the majority of these cases, and a filamentous fungus called *Aspergillus fumigatus* [2].

The salutary lesson from the NECC case explains why the pharmaceutical, biopharmaceutical, medical device and biotechnology sectors are subject to rigorous overseeing by regulatory agencies and why they are expected to follow a series of standards and guidelines [3]. This chapter provides an introduction to some of the more important aspects of regulation applicable to the manufacture or development of sterile products.

3.2 A brief history of compliance

Before discussing the regulatory framework of the twenty-first century, it is useful to pause and consider briefly the development of sterile products regulations and consider how and why the current rules of GMP arose.

Although pharmaceutical preparations have been prepared, in a form recognisable today, since the nineteenth century, compliance has only been significantly applied to the manufacture of sterile products since the late 1930s. This was with the first wave of FDA regulations and formation of the Code of Federal Regulations (CFR). In 1938, the Food, Drug and Cosmetic Act was passed. This Act placed a requirement on companies to demonstrate that their product was safe prior to the product being marketed. The Act also allowed the FDA to conduct factory inspections and take companies which were not complying with standards to court, and for the courts to be able to issue penalties [4]. Later, in 1963, the first reference to GMP appeared in the FDA CFRs [5].

Despite the CFRs containing the basis of GMP, it was only following a series of incidents occurring during the 1960s and early 1970s, in relation to sterile medicines, that GMP was instigated.

Arguably the most infamous incident was the 1971/1972 Devonport case in the UK. This incident is described fully in a UK government enquiry, the Clothier Report. A series of untoward reactions (rapid increase in core body temperature, shock, imbalances in body fluids) were observed amongst post-operative patients in the Devonport Section of Plymouth General Hospital. Seven patients showed fever-like reactions and five died between 29 February and 2 March 1971. The common factor between the patients was that each had received intravenous administration of a 5% Dextrose Infusion Fluid. A batch of bottles of this fluid manufactured by a major UK pharmaceutical company was found to be contaminated by the bacterium *Klebsiella aerogenes* along with other Gram-negative coliform bacteria. The concentration of bacteria in the bottles was later shown to have been very high, in excess of 10^6 bacteria per mL [6].

The Clothier Report also covered events linked to Evans Medical (Speke, UK), when on 6 April 1971 deaths occurred due to a 5% Sterile Dextrose Solution (Lot D1192). A similar incident occurred in the US in 1972: the Rocky Mountain Incident. As with the Devonport Incident, the Rocky Mount Incident was caused by contaminated bottles of infusion fluids. At least 378 patients were affected, and 40 died. The clinical features seen in patients who received these contaminated fluids included extreme fever, shaking chills, systemic toxicity, abdominal cramps, nausea, vomiting, diarrhoea, delirium and seizures. The microorganisms associated with the fluids were *Enterobacter agglomerans, Enterobacter cloacae* and other Enterobacter species.

These various events led to the formation of GMP regulations for the UK, which eventually became the basis for GMP regulations for Europe. In the UK, the first 'Guide to Good Pharmaceutical Manufacturing Practice' appeared in 1971, following the 1968 Medicines Act [7].

3.3 Key terminology

Before examining GMP as a set of guidelines, it is important to place it in context. The GMP is part of the 'quality system' and, in turn, is a major part of the wider concept of 'quality assurance'. These terms require understanding and contextualising [8].

3.3.1 Quality

Quality means different things to different people and there are a wide range of contrasting views and opinions concerning what 'quality' means and often terms are ill-defined, used interchangeably and inconsistently [9]. Versions of the old UK GMP 'Orange Guide' provide a useful definition of 'quality' as an organisational wide requirement:

> The essential nature of a thing and the totality of its attributes and properties which bear upon its fitness for its intended purpose. [10]

Similarly, the FDA considers that a focus on quality itself delivers good value:

> Quality and productivity improvement share a common element – reduction in variability through process understanding (e.g. application of knowledge throughout the product lifecycle). Reducing variability provides a win-win opportunity from both public health and industry perspectives. [11]

The principles of quality have been developed through international standards. The key documents for Quality Standards are primarily the International Organization for Standards (ISO) 9001 'Quality Systems – Model for Quality Assurance in Design, Development, Production, Installation, and Servicing'. It is additionally important that quality is at the forefront of sterilisation and sterile products. It also provides the philosophical underpinning of Quality Assurance.

3.3.2 Quality Assurance

Quality Assurance can be defined as an integrated management system that provides an assurance that the contractual and legal obligations of the company, to its customer (ultimately the patient) and the community, are being efficaciously fulfilled. GMP is part of Quality Assurance.

3.3.3 Good Manufacturing Practice

As a subset of Quality Assurance, GMP is one of several 'good practice' guidelines pertaining to drug manufacture and distribution. Other good practice guidelines are outlined below and include Good Laboratory Practice and Good Distribution Practice.

GMP includes Good Control Laboratory Practice (GCLP) for Quality Control laboratories. GMP embraces each manufacturing step, from purchasing raw materials to the finished product [12]. It is open to differing interpretations. The original definition of GMP from the 'Orange Guide' remains a useful one:

> That part of quality assurance aimed at ensuring that products are consistently manufactured to a quality appropriate to their intended use. It is thus concerned with both manufacturing and quality control procedures. [13]

GMP is an agreed system for ensuring that products are consistently produced and controlled according to quality standards. It is designed to minimize the risks involved in any pharmaceutical production and sets the standards for the testing and release of the final product. Importantly, GMPs are *guidelines* and are not prescriptive instructions on how to manufacture products [14].

Importantly, GMP is controlled and proven through documentation. When undertaking processes, there must be detailed, written procedures in place, and for each activity, from production to laboratory testing, each step must be written down.

3.3.4 cGMP (current Good Manufacturing Practice)

Whilst GMP is codified through various published regulatory documents and standards (discussed below), regulatory agencies expect that the philosophy of 'cGMP' be followed. The 'c' standards for 'current' and is placed in front of GMP, to convey that GMPs are not static and instead evolve through technological developments and revised guidelines. The manufacturer is expected to remain up-to-date with cGMP.

Many of the current GMP approaches are based on the identification and assessment of risks. Here manufacturers are expected to use the technology and system available necessary to minimise process risks. Some of the risks to pharmaceutical manufacturing include:

- the contamination of products, both chemical and microbial;
- incorrect packaging or labels on containers, which could mean that patients receive the wrong medicine;
- insufficient or too much active ingredient added to the formulation, resulting in ineffective treatment or adverse effects [15].

3.4 Current regulatory requirements

One of the complexities of regulator standards relating to sterile manufacturing is in undertaking a review of regulatory documentation and in seeking to understand what is required and, consequentially, what a regulator is likely to ask for in relation to a submission or an inspection. This task is made somewhat difficult by the range of different regulatory documents and standards, and due to the fact that these are sometimes contradictory [16].

The standards and guidelines are outlined below and the list below is not exhaustive.

3.5 Federal Drug Administration (FDA)

FDA documentation is divided between US laws, as contained in the CFR and inspectorate guidance documents. The CFR is the codification of the general and permanent rules and regulations published in the Federal Register by the executive departments and agencies of the Federal Government of the United States. The CFRs applicable to sterile manufacturing are those under Title 21 (Food and Drugs). Contained in chapter I of Title 21 are parts 200 and 300, which are regulations pertaining to pharmaceuticals [17]. Of particular importance is:

- Good Manufacturing Practice (cGMP) regulations (CFR sections CFR 210 and 211).

The primary aspects are parts section 211.42, relating to the need for separate and defined grades of cleanrooms; section 211.46 relating to the need for physical aspects of cleanroom design to be in place to prevent contamination; and section 212.42 relating to the material of construction for cleanrooms. Furthermore, these CFRs set out the:

- minimum current methods to be used in and the facilities or controls to be used for the manufacture, processing, packaging and holding of a drug and device;
- a requirement that the drug or device meets the requirements of the Act as to safety;
- the requirement that the drug or device is identifiable and has the required strength, and that it meets the quality and purity characteristics that it purports or is represented to possess.

With the FDA inspection guides, these are non-binding documents designed to provide reference material for investigators and other FDA personnel. They are nonetheless very useful for the manufacturers of sterile products to read, understand and observe, both in terms of following best practice and in order to understand the main concerns of an FDA inspector. However, the reader should note that the guidance documents are not updated very often and may note therefore, reflect cGMP. There are many documents and this chapter cannot list them all. However, the most important document for sterile (aseptic) manufacturing is:

- US Department of Health and Human Services, Food and Drug Administration, 'Guidance for industry: Sterile drug products produced by aseptic processing' – current GMP (2004) [18].

Other inspectorate guidelines of relevance are [19]:

- Guidance for Industry Container and Closure System Integrity Testing in Lieu of Sterility Testing as a Component of the Stability Protocol for Sterile Products;
- High Purity Water Systems;
- Lyophilisation of Parenterals;
- Microbiological Pharmaceutical Quality Control Labs;
- Pharmaceutical Quality Control Labs;
- Validation of Cleaning Processes;
- Dosage Form Drug Manufacturers cGMPs;
- Sterile Drug Substance Manufacturers.

With FDA inspections, there are two FDA drug inspectorates: Center for Biologics Evaluation and Research (CBER) and the other in the Center for Drug Evaluation and Research (CDER). CBER functions to protect and enhance the public's health through the regulation of biologics and related products, including blood and blood products, vaccines, allergenics and emerging technologies such as human cells, tissues, and cellular and gene therapies. CDER is in place to ensure that all prescription and non-prescription drugs marketed in the United States are safe and effective. CDER evaluates all new drugs before they are sold and monitors drugs on the market to ensure that they continue to meet the standards of purity, potency and quality.

3.6 European Good Manufacturing Practices

European GMP relates to European Commission Directive 2003/94/EC, which describes principles and guidelines of GMP in respect to medicinal products for human use and investigational medicinal products for human use. European GMP is set out within:

- *Euradlex*: The Rules Governing Medicinal Products in the European Community, Annex 1, published by the European Commission [20].

In addition, the following document is of relevance to the pre-sterilisation bioburden:

- European Agency for the Evaluation of Medicinal Products Committee for Proprietary Medicinal Products (CPMP) Note for Guidance on Manufacturing of the Finished Dosage Form, CPMP/QWP/486/95.

European GMP is overseen by the European Medicines Agency (EMA) and enforced by national inspection agencies (e.g. in the UK this is the MHRA (Medicines and Healthcare Regulatory Agency)).

3.7 Pharmaceutical Inspection Convention (PIC) and the Pharmaceutical Inspection Co-operation Scheme (PIC Scheme)

International inspectorate bodies are working together more frequently. The primary organisation, which links many global inspectorates together, including the EMA and the FDA, is the PIC/S. The PIC/S scheme exists to provide active and constructive co-operation in the field of GMP. The purpose of the PIC/S is to facilitate the networking between participating authorities and for the exchange of information and experience between GMP inspectors.

The PIC/S publishes a range of documents, and as with FDA inspection guides, are aimed at aiding inspectors so an understanding of these by the manufacturer can be beneficial. Of importance to sterile manufacturers are:

- PIC/S GMP Guide PE 009-9;
- Aide-Memoire Inspection of Utilities PI 009-3;
- Aide-Memoire on Inspection of Quality Control Laboratories PI 023-2;
- Validation of Aseptic Processes PI 007-5;
- Recommendation on Sterility Testing PI 012-3;
- Isolators Used for Aseptic Processing and Sterility Testing PI 014-3;
- Technical Interpretation of Revised Annex 1 To PIC/S GMP Guide PI 032-1.

3.8 World Health Organisation

The World Health Organisation (WHO) is a specialized agency of the United Nations (UN), which acts as a coordinating authority on international public health. WHO enforces similar requirements to the European Union's GMP (EU-GMP).

The primary WHO document is:

- WHO: 'Quality Assurance of Pharmaceuticals: A compendium of guidelines and related materials', vol. 2: Good Manufacturing Practices and Inspection, 2nd edition, Geneva: WHO Library Cataloguing-in-Publication Data [21].

Within the GMP guideline are a number of annexes. These are updated at different intervals and are published on-line. Those relevant to pharmaceutical manufacturing include:

- WHO GMP: main principles for pharmaceutical products. Annex 3, WHO Technical Report Series 961, 2011;
- Active pharmaceutical ingredients (bulk drug substances). Annex 2, WHO Technical Report Series 957, 2010;

- Pharmaceutical excipients. Annex 5, WHO Technical Report Series 885, 1999;

- WHO GMP for sterile pharmaceutical products. Annex 6, WHO Technical Report Series 961, 2011;

- Water for pharmaceutical use. Annex 3, WHO Technical Report Series 929, 2005;

- Application of Hazard Analysis and Critical Control Point (HACCP) Methodology in Pharmaceuticals. Annex 7, WHO Technical Report Series 908, 2003.

3.9 ISO

The International Standard Organisation (ISO) publishes a number of standards of relevance to pharmaceutical manufacturing. Not all of these standards tie in with GMP; an ISO standard only becomes part of GMP if a GMP document specifically refers to it. However, many ISO documents provide general best practice guidance. However, one standard in particular is of great importance. This is the standard for cleanrooms – ISO 14644, for this series of standards is referenced both in EU GMP and the FDA Sterile Drug Products guide [22].

A second important standard is that pertaining to biocontamination control:

- EN ISO 14644-1: Cleanrooms and associated controlled environments; Part 1: Classification of air cleanliness (May 1999) [23];

- ISO 14698-1 and 2, Part 1 – Cleanrooms and associated controlled environments – biocontamination control – General principles and methods; and Part 2 – Evaluation and interpretation of biocontamination data.

There are a host of other ISO standards pertaining to pharmaceutical manufacturer, ranging from HEPA filter standards to irradiation guidance. Some of these ISO standards are referred to in various chapters within this book. The main standards are:

- ISO/DIS 11135.2: Sterilisation of healthcare products – Ethylene oxide – Requirements for the development, validation and routine control of a sterilisation process for medical devices;

- ISO 11135-1:2007: Sterilisation of healthcare products – Ethylene oxide – Part 1: Requirements for development, validation and routine control of a sterilisation process for medical devices;

- ISO/TS 11135-2:2008: Sterilisation of healthcare products – Ethylene oxide – Part 2: Guidance on the application of ISO 11135-1;

- ISO 11137-1:2006: Sterilisation of healthcare products – Radiation – Part 1: Requirements for development, validation and routine control of a sterilisation process for medical devices;

- ISO/FDIS 11137-2: Sterilisation of healthcare products – Radiation – Part 2: Establishing the sterilisation dose;

- ISO 11137-2:2012: Sterilisation of healthcare products – Radiation – Part 2: Establishing the sterilisation dose;

- ISO 11137-3:2006: Sterilisation of healthcare products – Radiation – Part 3: Guidance on dosimetric aspects;

- ISO 11138-1:2006: Sterilisation of healthcare products – Biological indicators – Part 1: General requirements;

- ISO 11138-2:2006: Sterilisation of healthcare products – Biological indicators – Part 2: Biological indicators for ethylene oxide sterilisation processes;

- ISO 11138-3:2006: Sterilisation of healthcare products – Biological indicators – Part 3: Biological indicators for moist heat sterilisation processes;

- ISO 11138-4:2006: Sterilisation of healthcare products – Biological indicators – Part 4: Biological indicators for dry heat sterilisation processes;

- ISO 11138-5:2006: Sterilisation of healthcare products – Biological indicators – Part 5: Biological indicators for low-temperature steam and formaldehyde sterilisation processes;

- ISO/NP 11138-6: Sterilisation of healthcare products – Biological Indicators – Part 6: Biological indicators for hydrogen peroxide vapour sterilisation processes;

- ISO/TS 11139:2006: Sterilisation of healthcare products – Vocabulary;

- ISO 11140-1:2005: Sterilisation of healthcare products – Chemical indicators – Part 1: General requirements;

- ISO/DIS 11140-1: Sterilisation of healthcare products – Chemical indicators – Part 1: General requirements;

- ISO 11140-3:2007: Sterilisation of healthcare products – Chemical indicators – Part 3: Class 2 indicator systems for use in the Bowie and Dick-type steam penetration test;

- ISO 11140-4:2007: Sterilisation of healthcare products – Chemical indicators – Part 4: Class 2 indicators as an alternative to the Bowie and Dick-type test for detection of steam penetration;

- ISO 11140-5:2007: Sterilisation of healthcare products – Chemical indicators – Part 5: Class 2 indicators for Bowie and Dick-type air removal tests;

- ISO/NP 11140-6: Sterilisation of healthcare products – Chemical indicators – Part 6: Class 2 indicators and process challenge devices for use in performance testing of steam sterilisers;

- ISO 11607-1:2006: Packaging for terminally sterilised medical devices – Part 1: Requirements for materials, sterile barrier systems and packaging systems;

- ISO 11607-2:2006: Packaging for terminally sterilised medical devices – Part 2: Validation requirements for forming, sealing and assembly processes, 90.93, 11.080.30;

- ISO 11737-1:2006: Sterilisation of medical devices – Microbiological methods – Part 1: Determination of a population of microorganisms on products;

- ISO 11737-2:2009: Sterilisation of medical devices – Microbiological methods – Part 2: Tests of sterility performed in the definition, validation and maintenance of a sterilisation process;

- ISO/DTS 13004: Sterilisation of healthcare products – Radiation – Substantiation of selected sterilisation doses: Method VDmaxSD;

- ISO 13408-1:2008: Aseptic processing of healthcare products – Part 1: General requirements;

- ISO 13408-2:2003: Aseptic processing of healthcare products – Part 2: Filtration 90.93ISO 13408-3:2006: Aseptic processing of health care products – Part 3: Lyophilisation;

- ISO 13408-4:2005: Aseptic processing of healthcare products – Part 4: Clean-in-place technologies;

- ISO 13408-5:2006: Aseptic processing of healthcare products – Part 5: Sterilisation in place;

- ISO 13408-6:2005: Aseptic processing of healthcare products – Part 6: Isolator systems;

Published by Woodhead Publishing Limited, 2013

- ISO 13408-7:2012: Aseptic processing of healthcare products – Part 7: Alternative processes for medical devices and combination products;

- ISO 14160:2011: Sterilisation of healthcare products – Liquid chemical sterilising agents for single-use medical devices utilising animal tissues and their derivatives – Requirements for characterisation, development, validation and routine control of a sterilisation process for medical devices;

- ISO 14161:2009: Sterilisation of healthcare products – Biological indicators – Guidance for the selection, use and interpretation of results;

- ISO 14937:2009: Sterilisation of healthcare products – General requirements for characterisation of a sterilising agent and the development, validation and routine control of a sterilisation process for medical devices;

- ISO 15882:2008: Sterilisation of healthcare products – Chemical indicators – Guidance for selection, use and interpretation of results;

- ISO 15883-1:2006: Washer-disinfectors – Part 1: General requirements, terms and definitions and tests;

- ISO 15883-2:2006: Washer-disinfectors – Part 2: Requirements and tests for washer-disinfectors employing thermal disinfection for surgical instruments, anaesthetic equipment, bowls, dishes, receivers, utensils, glassware, etc.;

- ISO 15883-3:2006: Washer-disinfectors – Part 3: Requirements and tests for washer-disinfectors employing thermal disinfection for human waste containers;

- ISO 15883-4:2008: Washer-disinfectors – Part 4: Requirements and tests for washer-disinfectors employing chemical disinfection for thermolabile endoscopes;

- ISO/TS 15883-5:2005: Washer-disinfectors – Part 5: Test soils and methods for demonstrating cleaning efficacy;

- ISO 15883-6:2011: Washer-disinfectors – Part 6: Requirements and tests for washer-disinfectors employing thermal disinfection for non-invasive, non-critical medical devices and healthcare equipment;

- ISO/WD 15883-7: Washer-disinfectors – Part 7: Requirements and tests for general purpose washer-disinfectors employing chemical disinfection for bedframes, bedside tables, transport carts, containers, surgical tables, furnishings and surgical clogs;

- ISO/DTS 16775: Packaging for terminally sterilised medical devices – Guidance on the application of ISO 11607-1 and ISO 11607-2;

- ISO/AWI 17210: Test method to demonstrate the suitability of a medical device simulator during steam sterilisation – Medical device simulator testing

- ISO 17664:2004: Sterilisation of medical devices – Information to be provided by the manufacturer for the processing of resterilisable medical devices;

- ISO 17665-1:2006: Sterilisation of healthcare products – Moist heat – Part 1: Requirements for the development, validation and routine control of a sterilisation process for medical ISO/TS 17665-2:2009: Sterilisation of health care products – Moist heat – Part 2: Guidance on the application of ISO 17665-1;

- ISO/DTS 17665-3: Sterilisation of healthcare products – Steam sterilisation – Part 3: Product families;

- ISO/AWI 18362: Processing of cell-based health care products;

- ISO 18472:2006: Sterilisation of healthcare products – Biological and chemical indicators – Test equipment;

- ISO 20857:2010: Sterilisation of healthcare products – Dry heat – Requirements for the development, validation and routine control of a sterilisation process for medical devices;

- ISO 25424:2009: Sterilization of medical devices – Low temperature steam and formaldehyde – Requirements for development, validation and routine control of a sterilisation process for medical devices.

3.10 ICH

The International Conference on Harmonization (ICH) publishes quality and GMP documentation. ICH guidance is applicable to those countries and trade groupings that are signatories to ICH (including the EU, Japan and the USA). The ICH has produced a number of guidelines relating to the quality of medicines. These include:

- Q7 'GMP for active pharmaceutical ingredients';

- Q11 'Development and manufacture of drug substances (chemical entities and biotechnological/biological entities), Step 3'.

Some important ICH documents have been 'adopted' by regulatory agencies as part of their formal GMP systems. For example [24]:

- Q8: 'Pharmaceutical Development';
- Q9: 'Quality Risk Management', which was adopted as part of EU GMP in 2008 and by the FDA in 2010;
- Q10: 'Note for Guidance on Pharmaceutical Quality System'.

These are established as part of EU GMP, and form a tripartite approach to total quality management system for the pharmaceutical industry. The process outlined is intuitive and based around answering three basic risk-centric questions [25]:

1. What could happen?
2. How likely is it to occur?
3. What is the impact?

3.11 Pharmacopoeias

Of the three main international pharmacopoeias – United States, Europe and Japan – it is the US pharmacopoeia which contains the greatest number of chapters of relevance to sterile manufacturing, covering the spectrum from laboratory tests to pharmaceutical manufacturing instructions.

The USP includes two distinct types of chapters: standards (chapter numbered below 1000) and informational documents (chapters numbered above 1000). Amongst the chapters, those of direct relevance to sterile manufacturing are [26]:

- Biological Indicators – Resistance Performance Tests: Total Viable Spore Count;
- Microbial Examination of non-sterile Products: Microbial Enumeration Tests;
- Microbial Examination of non-sterile Products: Tests for Specified Microorganisms;
- Mycoplasma Tests;
- Sterility Testing;
- Bacterial Endotoxins Tests;
- Alternative Microbiological Sampling Methods for non-sterile Inhaled and Nasal Products;
- Disinfectants and Antiseptics;

- Microbiological examination of non-sterile products: Acceptance criteria for Pharmaceutical preparations and substances for Pharmaceutical use;
- Application of Water Activity Determinations to non-sterile Pharmaceutical Products;
- Microbial Characterisation, Identification, and Strain Typing;
- Microbial Control and Monitoring Environments Used for the Manufacture of Healthcare Products;
- Microbiological Best Laboratory Practices;
- Sterility Testing – Validation of Isolator Systems;
- Sterilisation and Sterility Assurance of Compendial Articles;
- Terminally Sterilised Pharmaceutical Products-Parametric Release;
- Validation of Alternative Microbiological Methods;
- Validation of Microbial Recovery from Pharmacopoeial Articles.

There are some equivalent chapters within the European and Japanese pharmacopoeias in relation to sterility testing, testing of non-sterile products and endotoxin testing. In general, these pharmacopoeias do not cover processing or manufacturing in any great detail, instead focusing on laboratory test methods.

3.12 National standards

Within the EU, GMP inspections are performed by National Regulatory Agencies. Sometimes these agencies publish additional advice and guidance. Elsewhere, many other countries have similar GMPs to the EU and FDA GMP standards, such as Australia, Canada, Japan and Singapore; whereas many other regions adopt WHO GMP, which is strongly influenced by European GMP.

In addition to the documents described above, inspectors anticipate that sterile manufacturers will be aware of and keep up-to-date with 'current good manufacturing practices' (cGMP) [27]. This is a term to describe the evolvement of GMPs in between the update of regulatory guidelines. Recent examples include the need for manufacturers to show evidence of a risk-based approach to pharmaceutical processing, together with the use of Process Analytical Technology (PAT), which allows for 'real time' process data to be collected.

3.13 Other sources of guidance

Various professional and trade associations also issue guidance documents. These bodies include the PDA (Parenteral Drug Association), AAMI (Association for the Advancement of Medical Instrumentation), ASTM (American Society for Testing and Materials), Pharmig (Pharmaceutical Microbiology Interest Group), PHSS (Pharmaceutical and Healthcare Sciences and Society) and IPSE (International Society for Pharmaceutical Engineering).

3.14 Regulatory inspections

Any manufacturer of a sterile medicinal product or who operates a sterilisation process that links into the production of a sterile product will be subject to a regulatory inspection from their national agency and from overseas agencies, if the product is intended for distribution into territories that fall under the auspices of a particular agency. The way by which a regulatory agency will perform a regulatory inspection varies according to that agency. Some agencies place a greater emphasis upon walking the plant and looking for non-compliant activities, while others are more concerned with verifying documentation to ensure that what is written in a manufacturing licence or product specification matches what is contained within the batch record. Other inspections are balanced between these two poles.

More commonly, regulators, since the start of the twenty-first century, have adopted a risk-based approach to regulations, guidelines and inspections. Consequently, risk assessment should be firmly built into the pharmaceutical organisation's quality system. This direction was captured by the FDA when they issued a document entitled 'Pharmaceutical cGMPS for the 21st Century – A Risk-Based Approach' [28] (originally in 2003 and since subject to several updates). The methodology outlined was to use risk-based and science-based approaches for regulatory decision-making throughout the entire life-cycle of a product.

The use of risk management for sterile manufacturing is linked to a wider process called 'Quality Risk Management' [29]. Quality risk management is a systematic process for the assessment, control, communication and review of risks to the quality of the medicinal product. It can be applied both proactively and retrospectively.

Risk management has always been an intrinsic part of the world of pharmaceuticals and healthcare, in terms of drug and patient safety, but it has not always been systematic in application or documented [30]. Two important points to remember for any risk assessment are that first there is no such thing as 'zero risk' and therefore a decision is required as to what is 'acceptable risk'. Second, risk assessment is not an exact science – different people will have a different perspective on the same hazard. A significant change happened when the ICH (International Conference on Harmonisation) published a document called ICH Q9, which was later 'adopted' by the FDA and as Annex 20 of the EU GMP Guide. The ICH document is outlined above.

Risk management is fundamentally about understanding what is most important for the control of product quality and then focusing resources on managing and controlling these to ensure that risks are reduced and contained. Before risks can be managed or controlled, they need to be assessed [31].

3.15 Conclusion

Ensuring that sterilisation processes are safe and effective, and that devices and products are free from contamination, is of paramount importance [32]. Therefore, various standards (binding and non-binding) are in place, supported by a regulatory framework and inspection system.

The objective of this chapter was to provide an introduction to the standards and regulations that are of relevance to the development and manufacture of sterile products, or which are applicable to sterilisation processes in general. By way of introduction, the chapter described some of the historic events that led to the codification of GMP.

3.16 References

1. Rutala, W.A. (1995), 'Antisepsis, disinfection and sterilization in the hospital and related institutions', in: Balows, A. (ed.), *Manual of Clinical Microbiology*, Washington, DC: ASM, 227–45.
2. Outterson, K. (2012), 'Perspective: Regulating compounding pharmacies after NECC', *New England Journal of Medicine*, 367(21): 1969–72.
3. Sandle, T. and Saghee, M.R. (2012), 'Compliance aspects of sterile manufacturing', in: Saghee, M.R. (ed.), *Achieving Quality and Compliance Excellence in Pharmaceuticals: A Master Class GMP Guide*, New Delhi: Business Horizons, pp. 517–60.

4. Center for Drug Evaluation and Research, Time Line: Chronology of Drug Regulation in the United States, Rockville, MD, US Food and Drug Administration. Available from: *www.fda.gov/cder/about/history/time1.htm*
5. Federal Register (1963), 'Drugs: Current Good Manufacturing Practice in Manufacture, Processing, Packing or Holding', Part 133, 28 FR 6385, 20 June.
6. Beaney, A.M. (2006), *Quality Assurance of Aseptic Preparation Services*, 4th edition, London: Pharmaceutical Press.
7. Anon. (1968), *The Medicines Act*, London: HM Stationery Office.
8. Sandle, T. and Saghee, M.R. (2013), 'Basic concepts of global GMP requirements', in: Saghee, M.R. (ed.), *Pharmaceutical Regulatory Inspections – A Practical Guide*, Passfield, UK: Euromed Communications.
9. Johnson, B. (1998), *Managing Operations*, Oxford: Blackwell.
10. Anon. (1983), *Guide to Good Manufacturing Practice*, 3rd edition, London: HM Stationery Office.
11. FDA (2004), 'Pharmaceutical cGMPs for the 21st century – A risk-based approach – Final report', Department of Health and Human Services, Rockville, MD: US Food and Drug Administration. Available from: *http://www.fda.gov/cder/gmp/gmp2004/GMP_finalreport2004.htm*
12. Brooker, C. (2010), *Mosby's Dictionary of Medicine*, Edinburgh: Nursing and Health Professions, Elsevier.
13. Anon. (1977), *Guide to Good Pharmaceutical Manufacturing Practice*, 2nd edition, London: HM Stationery Office.
14. Finke, M., Schulz, H. and Aktuelles, Z.U. (2003), 'GMP-Regularien (GMP regulatory documents: current issues)', *Pharmazeutische Industrie*, 65(10), 1065–9.
15. Todd, J.I. (2007), Performing your original search, good manufacturing practice', *Revue scientifique et technique*, 26(1):135–45.
16. Sandle, T. (2013), 'Preparing for regulatory inspections of sterile facilities: the focal points', in: Saghee, M.R. (ed.), *Pharmaceutical Regulatory Inspections – A Practical Guide*, Passfield, UK: Euromed Communications.
17. 21 CFR 211: Current Good Manufacturing Practice for finished pharmaceuticals. *Code of Federal Regulations, Food and Drugs*, Washington, DC: US Government Printing Office.
18. FDA (2004), 'Guidance for Industry. Sterile Drug Products Produced by Aseptic Processing – Current Good Manufacturing Practice', Rockville, MD: US Food and Drug Administration.
19. FDA Inspection Guides, US FDA. Available from: *www.fda.gov/ICECI/Inspections/Inspection Guides/default.htm* (Accessed 28 May 2012).
20. Euradlex (2009), *The Rules Governing Medicinal Products in the European Community*, Annex 1, Brussels: European Commission.
21. WHO (1992), 'Good manufacturing practices for pharmaceutical products', in: *WHO Expert Committee on Specifications for Pharmaceutical Preparations*, 32nd report. Geneva: World Health Organization (WHO), Technical Report Series, No. 823, Annex 1.
22. Schicht, H.H. (2003), 'The ISO contamination control standards – A tool for implementing regulatory requirements', *European Journal of Parenteral and Pharmaceutical Sciences*, 8(2): 37–42.

23. ISO 14644-1 (1999), 'Cleanrooms and Associated Controlled Environments – Part 1: Classification of Air Cleanliness', Geneva: International Standards Organisation.

24. International Conference on Harmonisation of Technical Requirements for Registration of Pharmaceuticals for Human Use (2008), *ICH Harmonised Tripartite Guideline, Q10*: Pharmaceutical Quality System.

25. Jackson, S. (2001), 'Successfully implementing total quality management tools within healthcare: What are the key actions?' *International Journal of Health Care Quality Assurance*, 14(4): 157–63.

26. Sutton, S. and Tirumalai, R. (2011), 'Activities of the USP Microbiology and Sterility Assurance Expert Committee during the 2005–2010 revision cycle', *American Pharmaceutical Review*, July/August, 12–30.

27. US Food and Drug Administration (2002), 'Pharmaceutical cGMPs for the 21st century – A risk based approach', Rockville, MD: US Food and Drug Administration.

28. US Food and Drug Administration (2003), 'Pharmaceutical cGMPs for the 21st century: A risk-based approach', Rockville, MD: US Food and Drug Administration.

29. World Health Organisation (1999), 'Quality assurance of pharmaceuticals: A compendium of guidelines and related materials', vol. 2, *Good Manufacturing Practices and Inspection*, Geneva: World Health Organisation.

30. Winckles, H.W. and Dorpem, J.W. (1994), 'Risk assessment and the basis for the definition of sterility', *Medical Device Technology*, 5, 38–43.

31. Sandle, T. (2011), 'Risk management in pharmaceutical microbiology', in: Saghee, M.R., Sandle, T. and Tidswell, E.C. (eds), *Microbiology and Sterility Assurance in Pharmaceuticals and Medical Devices*, New Delhi: Business Horizons, pp. 553–88.

32. Rutala, W.A. and Weber, D.J. (2010), 'Disinfection and sterilization in healthcare facilities', in: Lautenbach, E, Woeltje, K and Malani, P.N. (eds), *Practical Handbook for Healthcare Epidemiologists*, New York: Slack, Inc, pp. 61–80.

Published by Woodhead Publishing Limited, 2013

4

Gamma radiation

DOI: 10.1533/9781908818638.55

Abstract: Gamma radiation is an established sterilisation method for medical devices and one which is particularly suited to plastics. A more recent application has been in the sterilisation of single-use disposable components. The technology has an advantage over other types of sterilisation in that it is capable of deep penetration, although for surface level sterilisation, alternative processes such as electron beams are faster. This chapter examines the ways in which gamma radiation works, its applications, and outlines the key validation requirements.

Key words: gamma radiation, electromagnetic, gamma rays, sterilisation, sterility assurance level, medical devices, plastic disposables, pharmaceuticals, microorganisms, biological indicators.

4.1 Introduction

Gamma rays are a form of electromagnetic radiation, whereby gamma radiation kills microorganisms by destroying cellular nucleic acid [1]. The use of gamma irradiation is relatively widespread and was first described in the *British Pharmacopeia* in 1963 and in the *United States Pharmacopeia* in 1965 (17th edition). The use of gamma radiation became more widespread in the 1980s, following concerns with the ecological and toxicological risks associated with ethylene oxide. However, it is only in recent years that the use of gamma irradiation has increased within the healthcare sector and the pharmaceutical industry. This arises from the use of gamma radiation to sterilise consumables and single-use technologies used for aseptic operations. The use of single-use disposable technologies has advanced, because organisations have moved away from equipment that needs to be sterilised or consumables that are recycled. This has established gamma radiation as the most widely-used method for sterilisation [2].

Whilst gamma radiation is very suitable for plastic materials, it cannot be used for aqueous drug products and pharmaceuticals with a proteinaceous component, because the process can degrade such products. This chapter outlines the application of gamma radiation, discusses the way in which it works, and describes the important aspects of validation.

4.2 Application of gamma radiation

The primary application of gamma radiation is for medical devices, ranging from sterile dressings, tubes, catheters, syringes, infusions assemblies and implants; and single-use disposable technologies, such as bags for holding products or devices for making aseptic connections. It is in this latter application that gamma radiation processing has seen the largest growth. Single-use technologies have reduced the need for pharmaceutical and biopharmaceutical companies to invest as much time and money into cleaning; eliminates the need for the organisation to perform in-house sterilisation, reduces the use of chemicals, reduces storage requirements, reduces process downtime, increases process flexibility and avoids cross-contamination. Single-use plastic items cannot be sterilised using heat (styrene and other plastics are temperature-sensitive); instead such materials are typically sterilised using gamma rays (electromagnetic radiation) [3]. Gamma radiation is also used in the food industry to dry or to dehydrate fruit vegetables, herbs and meat.

The main reason why gamma radiation is selected as a sterilisation method is due to its relatively high penetrability and as there is only a small temperature rise (typically <5°C) associated with its use. This means that the technology is suitable for sterilising heat-liable and heat-sensitive products, which could not be processed by steam sterilisation. Another reason for the wide use of the method is because the technology allows for high volume processing.

4.3 Sterilisation method

Gamma radiation is one of the three types of natural radioactivity, the other two being alpha and beta radiation. Gamma radiation is in the form of electromagnetic rays, like X-rays or ultra-violet light, of a short (less than one-tenth of a nanometre), and thus energetic, wavelength. Gamma radiation is a physical means of sterilisation or decontamination, as the rays pass through the product being sterilised (or 'irradiated'). In doing so, gamma radiation kills bacteria, where there is sufficient energy, at the molecular level by breaking down bacterial DNA and inhibiting bacterial division [4].

The most common source of gamma rays for radiation processing comes from the radioactive isotope Cobalt 60, although other radionuclides can be used such as Cesium 137 (a fission product of uranium). Each element decays at a specific rate and gives off energy in the form of gamma rays and other particles. Cobalt 60 is manufactured specifically for the gamma radiation process from non-radioactive Cobalt 59 (through neutron bombardment of the inactive Cobalt 59). The radioactive Cobalt 60 functions as the isotope source. High-energy photons are emitted from the Cobalt 60 to produce ionisation (electron disruptions) throughout a product [5]. The gamma process does not create residuals or impart radioactivity in processed products [6].

Five facts about Cobalt–60:

1. Cobalt–60 is a synthetic radioisotope of cobalt, made by the nuclear industry.

2. Cobalt–60 has a half-life of 5.27 years, after which it becomes stable isotope nickel–60.

3. Cobalt–60 sterilises but the energies given out are insufficient to induce radioactivity, thus rendering the product sterile and safe.

4. Cobalt–60 emits two different types of gamma rays of different wavelengths.

5. When Cobalt–60 is placed in water, it creates a blue glow caused by light emission from atomic particles passing through water.

Unlike other forms of radiation, the isotope cannot be turned off and is thus continually radioactive. Cobalt–60 is normally derived as pellets, which are placed into stainless steel tubes called 'pencils'. The pencils are, in turn, housed in a reinforced concrete structure called a cell (usually 2 m thick), since shielding from gamma rays requires large amounts of mass. The Cobalt–60 pencils within the cell are held within a source rack. The rack will have two operating positions. These are either the storage position, where the rack is either immersed in water or sometimes deep within concrete; or the operational position, whereby the rack is raised and the device to be sterilised is exposed to the radiation source and, over time, sterilised [7].

Gamma radiation is often referred to as a 'cold process', for the temperature of the processed material does not significantly increase. The sterilisation process is not dependant on humidity, temperature, vacuum or pressure, which means that the process is suitable for materials that cannot be subjected to high temperature sterilisation. Thus there are fewer variables to be controlled compared with methods such as ethylene oxide. The important variables for gamma radiation are the strength of the radiation dose and the exposure time. The measurement of radiation is expressed in units called kiloGrays (kGy). One Gray is the absorption of one joule of radiation energy by one kilogram of matter [8]. In the past, the term 'rads' (Radiation Absorbed Dose) was used. The 'Gray' is the accepted SI unit, with 1 Gray being equivalent to 100 rads.

4.4 Process requirements

The gamma sterilisation process involves the product being placed into special containers called totes, normally constructed from aluminium. The amount of product that can go into a tote is established during validation. Simply, the tote is then exposed to the sterilisation source for a period of time. Arguably, gamma radiation is the simplest of all sterilisation technologies, because there are very few variables to be controlled.

When undertaking sterilisation by gamma rays, there are a number of considerations to be made. These are examined below.

4.4.1 Packaging and dose determination

Although gamma radiation is commonly used to sterilise plastics, not all types of plastics can be treated at a sufficient dose to achieve sterilisation without degrading the plastic. This is because the imparted energy from the gamma rays can react with certain materials in the same way that they react with microorganisms. Ionising radiation generates free radicals in plastic polymers, leading to degradation from chain scission (changes in molecular weight) or alterations to cross-linking. Potential radiation effects on some materials include embrittlement (change to material hardness), discolouration (often yellowing caused by surface oxidation), unpleasant odour (from volatile material formed by reactions from within the polymers), or lack of functionality due to a compromised physical trait, such as tensile strength.

Therefore the assessment of degradation is required beforehand and must continue to be made throughout the shelf-life of the material. The plastic material to be irradiated is normally referred to as the product. Different products tend to be placed into an outer packaging in order to protect the irradiated product and to keep it sterile post-sterilisation. Once sterilised, the product remains sterile provided that the outer packaging remains intact. A common dose used for plastics is in the range 15–25 kGy. In general, a dose of 25 kGy is the most commonly applied dose, which relates back to pioneering studies involving the inactivation of spores of the bacterium *Bacillus pumilus*.

Given the range of different types of products and packaging configurations, the required gamma radiation dose to achieve sterilisation or to protect the product from degradation will vary considerably. For example, a relatively low dose of radiation is required to sterilise a plastic such as polypropylene compared with a different plastic such as polystyrene. Furthermore, the assessment of the dose is more straightforward for small items and more complex for single-use systems. This is because single-use systems have multi-variables which affect sterilisation, including tubing length, different numbers and types of filters, and differences in the design of containers, bags and valves.

In addition to the material, a second factor is the packaging of the material into the tote. A tote has fixed internal dimensions and is designed to transport the product through the radiation process. The weight and dimensions of the tote must be accounted for when establishing the radiation dose.

The dose determination is the key validation step when using gamma radiation. The dose is the amount of gamma radiation absorbed by an item undergoing sterilisation. This is normally expressed as a range, where a minimum and maximum dose is stated for a specific time period (dose and time combined is termed the 'dose rate'). The dose range and time are established through validation. In general, the higher the dose rate, the lower the adverse effects upon polymer products. This is mainly due to the diffusion of oxygen during the irradiation process. The dose rate at any point is dependent upon the proximity and orientation of the product, the density of the product, and in relation to any shielding of the product (i.e. packaging materials).

4.4.2 Validation steps

In order to validate a load, there are three aspects to consider. These are the dose range, measuring the effectiveness of the sterilisation and dose mapping. These aspects are examined in turn:

a) *Irradiation validation* – this is designed to set the dose range. The primary focus is to determine if the irradiation process damages the packaging material or the product to be sterilised. This is assessed by calculating the maximum dose. This assessment is examined through stability trials, whereby samples are held under defined storage conditions (temperature and relative humidity) and examined at periodic intervals for discolouration, brittleness and other damage [9].

b) *Sterilisation validation* – The aim of this validation step is to determine the dose required to achieve a sterility assurance of 1×10^{-6}.

The international standard for radiation sterilisation is ISO 11137 (14). According to the standard, to ensure consistent sterility assurance, lot-to-lot variability of bioburden must be known and controlled. Data should be collected and analysed for each batch of raw material, intermediate or product to ensure process control. Post-sterilisation, a sterility test is required.

This assessment involves four steps:

1. Determination of the bioburden of the product. This is normally undertaken using 10 units per batch and from 3 different batches of product. In doing so, it is important to ensure that the product used is representative of the product normally manufactured. The bioburden determination is normally carried out by the manufacturer of the product, unlike the Sterility Test, described below, which is normally carried out by the gamma radiation plant. It is important to ensure that the bioburden recovery method is accurate, for insufficient recovery of microorganisms during bioburden tests would result in an underestimation of the true bioburden of the product and lead to an inadequate sterilisation dose being applied to the product [10].

The bioburden of the product is dependent upon several factors. These include the nature and source of the raw material, the components used in manufacturing, the product design and size, the manufacturing process, the manufacturing equipment and the manufacturing environment (i.e. the type of cleanroom used).

For products manufactured using approved suppliers and assembled within cleanrooms certified as ISO 14644 Class 7 under localized unidirectional airflow protection, the expected bioburden would be relatively low (i.e. not more than 10 microorganisms per device). Additional data relating to the risk from the manufacturing environment can be provided through microbiological environmental monitoring (Chapter 13).

There are different methods for bioburden determination. One of the most common methods is the Repetitive (Exhaustive) Recovery Method. This method involves washing the sample product repeatedly with sterile diluent, until it is estimated that no further microorganisms will be recovered. The washing process can include the addition of sterile glass beads or ultrasonication to facilitate microbial recovery. The eluent from the washing should be tested using an appropriate total viable count (TVC) test method, where membrane filtration is the method of choice, followed by the pour plate technique.

The microbial counts from all washes are compared in order to assess the total bioburden. Such extraction methods require validating. Method validation involves inoculating a sterile disposable item with a known number of microorganisms and then assessing the number recovered from the washing steps to the theoretical inoculum challenge. A valid method will achieve a recovery of ≥70%. The variation with the validation method is the process of drying the microbial challenge organism onto the plastic item prior to washing.

2. The calculation of the appropriate dose is based on the resistance of an identified microbial population, which is based on the total number of bacteria and fungi and the types of species recovered, as characterised using microbiological identification techniques. The species recovered should be compared with species known to have some resistance to radiation. Some bacteria are relatively more resistant that others to gamma radiation, most notably *Streptococcus faecium* and *Micrococcus radiodurans* [11].

3. From this, an appropriate radiation dose is assigned using a table of standard resistance, as indicated in the ISO 1137 standard.

4. The calculated dose is verified using an appropriate sample size (normally 100 units of the product) to determine if the dose is efficacious. This is often called the 'sterility test', although it bears no relation to the Sterility Test described in the pharmacopoeia (Chapter 18).

    The test is undertaken by placing individual units of product into sterile bottles containing microbiological culture media (i.e. soyabean casein digest medium) and incubating for 14 days. This is the 'sterility test'; although it bears some similarities, the direct inoculation sterility test described in the United States or European pharmacopoeias it is not equivalent. Any bottle of media that exhibits microbial growth (turbidity) is indicative of the product not being sterile and that the sterilisation cycle is inappropriate for the product.

    As with the bioburden determination method, the test for sterility requires validation. The object of the validation is to show that the product material does not inhibit the growth of microorganisms (a bacteriostasis and fungistasis test). Inhibition of microorganisms would lead to the risk of a false negative result occurring. The method validation involves using the same type and volume of culture media used for the sterility test. The product is inoculated with known numbers of a bacteria culture and a fungal culture. The inoculated product is then incubated. Any product that shows no growth or slowed growth is considered bacteriostatic or fungiostatic and the method declared unsuitable. Within the medical device industry, an acceptance criterion of a sterility assurance level of 10^{-2} has been used, which means that two units could fail the sterility test and results could be deemed as acceptable. This level of assurance is unacceptable for single-use technologies used in conjunction with aseptically manufactured products, which require a minimum sterility assurance level of 1×10^{-6}. In such cases, further modification of the method is required, such as increasing the volume of culture media or using culture media will an added neutraliser [12].

When assessing the data to determine the final sterilisation dose for routine batches of product, it is typical to use a high dose, normally referred to as the Dmax. This is established in the validation in order to set a level of over kill. This provides additional assurance that should the product bioburden increase or should more resistant strains appear, the dose rate will probably remain effective.

A further important consideration is, given that the bioburden test and sterility test are carried out by the product manufacturer and gamma irradiation plant respectively, then similar methods, culture media and incubation parameters must be employed. If this is not done, the failure to recover a certain microorganism with the sterility test, where such an organism was present for the bioburden test, may be due to the inability of the organism to grow under the test conditions as much as an indication that the organism has been destroyed.

Variations to the bioburden method are permitted within the ISO 11137 standard, such as the VDmax25, which permits fewer units of product to be tested and for similar items to be grouped together for the validation (a matrix approach). This variation can only be used where it has been established that the bioburden level is relatively low (<1000 cfu). When considering whether different products can be grouped together, account must be made of the materials, construction processes, surface area and handling.

c) A further important aspect of the validation is dose mapping. For this, the product, in its final packaging configuration, is profiled in order to identify the high and low zones of absorbed dose in the product load in relation to the energy field it travels through. The mapping process also establishes the sterilisation cycle time.

The object of the validation is to set processing parameters and the product release specification. The validation parameters are established through a performance qualification (dose mappings), which is typically run three times using the maximum packaging size. The main steps for undertaking a performance qualification, for each product, are:

i) evaluate product and process suitability;
ii) decide on the container presentation;
iii) undertake dose mapping;
iv) evaluate results;
v) establish release specification;
vi) establish parameters for routine product sterilisation.

The level of radiation is assessed using dosimeters. It is important to assess the number of dosimeters required to assess the radiation dose. With a standard tote, it is typical to use 1520 dosimeters [13]. This number is necessary to achieve an accurate assessment, because the radiation dose applied to the product packaged at the outer edge of the tote is often higher than the dose received by the material in the inner centre of the tote; for example, the material packed into the centre of the tote receives the lowest dose of gamma radiation and the material at the outer edge of the tote receives the highest dose.

The key parameters for the assessment are product weight and volume, dimensions of packaging components and density, and the configuration of the packaging components. With the dimensions, it is important that the product is evenly distributed, because the radiation dose is applied at the same level from both sides. With the issue of load configuration, this point is sometimes overlooked. It is nonetheless important that the components packaged during validation must be replicated for all successive radiation runs, because if the orientation alters, then this can cause changes to the density mix and thus the effectiveness of the irradiation. Once the validation parameters are established, they are to be used for routine processing, with no parameter permitted to vary by more than 10% of the established parameter.

Once established, it is necessary that any future changes in product, its package, or the presentation of product for sterilisation, shall be assessed for their effect on the appropriateness of the sterilisation process. It is prudent to re-assess the validation parameters at least on an annual basis and to assess the bioburden of the product quarterly, in order to determine that the gamma radiation process remains effective. This assessment may include fractional studies. Here the product is irradiated and tested at sublethal doses, that is at levels of gamma radiation at the minimum established in the validation study, to check for continued dose efficacy, and confirmed by sterility testing.

4.4.3 Gamma radiation process

On completion of the validation, and assuming the completion of appropriate documentation, the product can be subject to routine sterilisation. The sterilisation process is based on the establishment of validation parameters and each of the following steps must be in place:

- product and packaging description;
- various loading configurations;
- minimum allowable dose (for sterilisation);
- maximum allowable dose (for material compatibility);
- dosimeter placement for routine monitoring of the minimum and maximum dose (as identified during the dose mapping);
- any special handling requirements (i.e. temperature or humidity).

There are two different methods of gamma radiation: continuous or batch. With the continuous method, an automated conveyance system functions to move the product past a gamma source and back out on a continuous basis until the end of the cycle is achieved. With the batch method, a set number of totes are used. The totes are positioned in the irradiation chamber. The radioisotope is then moved into an exposure position, and the product is irradiated for a specified period of time. The method selected is dependent upon the method used during the validation, which would reflect the type of radiation plant. When undertaking irradiation, it is important that the distribution of gamma radiation applied to the product is even.

With both methods, the process of gamma irradiation involves packing the items to be sterilised into a tote. Special indicator labels should be fixed to each item to indicate if irradiation has been successful. Labels, post-irradiation, should be checked as part of batch release.

4.5 Regulatory aspects

The regulatory requirements for gamma radiation are less defined than for sterilisation by filtration, moist or dry heat, or by ethylene oxide. These methods of sterilisation normally involve a direct biological challenge, as with biological indicators for steam sterilisation or a high population microbial challenge for filter validation. In contrast with gamma radiation, the biological assessment is normally derived from the assessment of the product bioburden; in the past, *Bacillus pumilus* was used as a biological indicator to measure gamma irradiation. Furthermore, with the 2012 revision to the biological indicator monograph to the *European Pharmacopeia* (monograph 5.1.2), the practice of using biological indicators for radiation sterilisation cycles is no longer recommended. This is because the assessment of the product bioburden during validation is deemed to be a more accurate means of assessing potential resistance to the gamma radiation process.

For gamma radiation, the applicable standard is ISO 11137 'Sterilisation of healthcare products – Radiation' [14]. This standard is also applicable to electron beam radiation (Chapter 5). The standard was developed in association with the Association for the Advancement of Medical Instrumentation (AAMI).

The ISO 11137 standard is divided into three parts. The first part deals with validation and routine control methods, the second part with the establishment of radiation doses for items to be sterilised, and the third part relates to dosiometry. The standards function to determine how much radiation is permitted in order to achieve the desired level of sterilisation when measured in terms of sterility assurance. The sterility assurance level is normally 10^{-6}, that is, a theoretical concept where it is assumed that no more than one bacterium is one million would have a chance of surviving the sterilisation process.

The official scope of the ISO 11137 standards is limited to medical devices. However, in the absence of any other applicable standards, the scope is often extended to all products and equipment sterilised by gamma radiation.

For pharmaceutical operations, as with any sterilisation process, gamma radiation should be subject to quality auditing using Good Manufacturing Practice (GMP) guidelines as well as to the ISO standard [15]. When conducting an audit of gamma irradiation processes, the following areas should be considered when developing the audit checklist [16]:

a) Is the product suitable for sterilisation? This requires a review of any physical changes to the material from the radiation process. This should include an assessment of extractables and leechables, both before and after the sterilisation process [17].

b) The temperature sensitivity of the product, whilst undergoing gamma radiation, should be accounted for.

c) Ensuring that the packaging used for the product was suitable, does the package allow the radiation dose to be absorbed by the product as defined in the validation and does the package remain intact post irradiation?

d) Determining if the validation parameters are consistent, such as the volume and density of the product in packaging and the configuration of the load placed into the tote.

e) The dose required should be checked. This should include assessment of the lower and upper range and the measures in place, to ensure that each item of product within the tote has received the minimum dose required.

f) The dose mapping validation data should be checked against the routine radiation cycles to determine if the parameters match.

g) Determine evidence of sterility. This will include an assessment of radiation parameters and radiation indicators.

h) Decontamination procedures.

i) In addition to the above, the plant should be checked to determine if it is compliant with appropriate regulations for nuclear facilities and that appropriate segregation and labelling of components is in place.

These points should be assessed in order to establish confidence that the plant undertaking the gamma radiation process does so in a consistent and effective way.

4.6 Conclusion

Gamma radiation, as a sterilisation method, confers the advantage of being relatively low cost, effective (in having excellent penetration) and avoids leaving toxic residues. However, the radiation process may degrade some polymers, rendering it unsuitable from some materials. In addition, the process parameters must be correctly defined in order for the sterilisation process to be effective.

This chapter sets out to provide an aid for those tasked with establishing sterilisation cycles and those who are required to audit such processes. In doing so, the article has examined some of the key parameters required for sterilisation by gamma radiation. The sterilisation technique remains one of the less defined by regulatory agencies and yet it is seemingly the fastest growing technique used within the pharmaceutical industry, as the trend towards sterile, plastic disposable consumables increases. Therefore, care is required to ensure that a process is developed for a specific product.

4.7 References

1. Gaughran, E.R.L. and Morrissey, R.F. (1980), *Sterilisation of Medical Products*, vol. 2, New York: Multiscience, pp. 35–9.
2. Samavedam, R., Goldstein, A. and Schieche, D. (2006), 'Implementation of disposables: Validation and other considerations', *American Pharmaceutical Review*, 9: 46–51.
3. Sandle, T. and Saghee, M.R. (2011), 'Some considerations for the implementation of disposable technology and single-use systems in biopharmaceuticals', *Journal of Commercial Biotechnology*, 17(4): 319–29.
4. Booth, A. (1998), *Sterilisation of Medical Devices*, USA: Interpharm Press.
5. L'Annunziata, M.F. (2007), *Radioactivity: Introduction and History*. Amsterdam: Elsevier BV, pp. 55–8.

6. Dendy, P.P. and Heaton, B. (1999), *Physics for Diagnostic Radiology*, Boca Raton, FL: CRC Press.

7. Audi, G., Wapstra, A.H., Thibault, C., Blachot, J. and Bersillon, O. (2003), 'The NUBASE evaluation of nuclear and decay properties', *Nuclear Physics*, A729: 3–128.

8. Vértes, A., Nagy, S. and Klencsár, Z. (2003), *Handbook of Nuclear Chemistry*, vol. 3, Amsterdam: Kluwer Academic Publishers.

9. Majewski, S., Bowen, M., Zorn, C., Johnson, K., Hagopian, V., *et al.* (1989), 'Radiation damage studies in plastic scintillators with a 2.5-MeV electron beam', *Nuclear Instruments and Methods in Physics Research*, 281(3), 500–7.

10. Anellis, A., Berkowitz, D. and Kemper, D. (1973), 'Comparative resistance of nonsporogenic bacteria to low-temperature gamma irradiation', *Applied Microbiology*, 25(4), 517–23.

11. Anellis, A., Berkowitz, D. and Kemper, D. (1973), 'Comparative resistance of nonsporogenic bacteria to low-temperature gamma irradiation', *Applied Microbiology*, 25(4): 517–23.

12. Sandle, T. (2011), 'Practical approaches to sterility testing', in: Saghee, M.R., Sandle, T. and Tidswell, E.C. (eds), *Microbiology and Sterility Assurance in Pharmaceuticals and Medical Devices*, New Delhi: Business Horizons, pp. 173–92.

13. Pattison, J.E., Bachmann, D.J. and Beddoe, A.H. (1996), 'Gamma dosimetry at surfaces of cylindrical containers', *Journal of Radiological Protection*, 16(4): 249–61.

14. ANSI/AAMI/ISO 11137–1 (2006), Sterilisation of healthcare products – Radiation – Part 1: Requirements for development, validation, and routine control of a sterilisation process for medical devices.

15. Genova, T.F., Hollis, R.A., Crowell, C.A. and Schady, K.M. (1987), 'A procedure for validating the sterility of an individual gamma radiation sterilised production batch,' *Journal of Parenteral Science and Technology*, 41(1), 33–6.

16. Beck, J.A. (1990), 'Auditing radiation sterilisation facilities', *International Journal of Radiation Applications and Instrumentation, Part C: Radiation Physics and Chemistry*, 35(4–6): 811–15.

17. Pora, H. and Rawlings, B. (2009), 'A user's checklist for introducing single-use components into process systems', *BioProcess International*, 7(14): 9–16.

5

Electron beam processing

DOI: 10.1533/9781908818638.69

Abstract: One of the emerging sterilisation methods for medical devices and plastic disposable items is electron beam (e-beam) processing. The system has an advantage over ethylene oxide (the most widely used sterilisation method) in terms of having a lesser impact upon the structure of plastics and it is a faster process than gamma radiation. In terms of disadvantages, the e-beam does not have the level of surface penetration afforded to gamma radiation. This chapter examines the way in which e-beam radiation works, its applications, and explores the relative advantages and disadvantages of the technology.

Key words: electron beam, sterilisation, gamma radiation; sterility assurance level; medical devices; plastic disposables; pharmaceuticals; ethylene oxide; microorganisms; biological indicators.

5.1 Introduction

Electron beam processing (commonly referred to as e-beam) is a sterilisation method which uses high energy electrons to sterilise an object. In terms of sterilisation technology, it is a method of irradiation and is sometimes described as electron irradiation, the act of applying radiation (or radiant energy) to a material. Therefore, e-beam is similar to X-rays and gamma radiation in that each form of radiation ionises the material it strikes by stripping electrons from the atoms of the exposed surface [1]. This ionised environment is very damaging to the microorganisms. The key difference, in terms of application, is that e-beam has the shortest process cycle times of any currently recognised sterilisation method.

The e-beam method is generally applied to medical devices and to consumables used in sterile processes. Devices sterilised by e-beam include surgical dressings, wound care products, electrocautery devices (apparatus for surgical dissection), intravenous administration kits, dialysers, endoscopy loops, cardiac catheters and stents are routinely and terminally sterilised by electrons. The method is also used by the food industry.

E-beam is used for applications other than sterilisation. An example is to create the cross-linking of polymers for plastics manufacture, where the e-beam dose affects a change in the properties of a polymer to alter either its mechanical, thermal or chemical properties [2].

The first trials with ionising irradiation were undertaken in 1895 and patented in 1921, although the method was not widely used for several decades due to technological limitations. Early applications related primarily to gamma radiation. In 1965, in the USA, the Surgeon General stated that the e-beam process was safe to use on medical device packaging. Throughout the 1970s and 1980s, technological changes enabled the energy level within the electron beam to be better controlled, which allowed the technology to be applied to a greater range of medical devices. These developments have, coupled with additional evidence that e-beam causes less damage to many materials when compared with gamma radiation or ethylene oxide [3], has furthered the popularity of the technology. Nevertheless, the use of e-beam remains less frequently used than either gaseous sterilisation (i.e. ethylene oxide) or sterilisation using gamma rays.

E-beam is a specialist process and, like gamma radiation, is normally contracted out to a specialist contractor to perform. As such, the manufacturer must be satisfied that the contract facility is suitable, that appropriate validation has been performed, and that audits to the appropriate standards are undertaken to verity the suitability of the contract facility.

This chapter presents an overview of e-beam sterilisation, including the application of the technology, the mechanism of sterilisation and the key advantages and disadvantages. Given that there are many similarities with the e-beam sterilisation process and that of gamma radiation, this chapter does not overly repeat these and the reader is advised to review the principles pertaining to gamma sterilisation in addition to reading this chapter.

5.2 Application of e-beam radiation

Within the pharmaceutical and medical device sectors, e-beam processing is used for the sterilisation of medical products and aseptic packaging materials. The process is also used within the food industry to render certain foods suitable for human consumption, such as for the elimination of any live insects that might be residing within the food stuff [4]. In terms of scientific principles, there are similarities with the e-beam used for sterilisation and the electron beams used for radiation therapy, such as for treating skin lesions such as basal cell carcinomas [5].

With the sterilisation of medical devices, e-beam has proved to be particularly effective for so-called combination products, which incorporate biologics, drugs and sometimes nanoparticles, into a single medical device. Examples include simple adhesive bandages that carry antibiotics, complex antimicrobial hydrogels (a binding, thickening and stabilising agent) in wound dressings, prefilled syringes and drug-eluting stents. Moreover, in relation to sterile disposable technologies, these normally consist of many different plastic materials, such as housings, tubing, connectors, valves and seals. Combination products, by their nature, bring greater compatibility issues to any sterilisation task. Nonetheless, due to the fact that greater control of the sterilisation doses can be achieved, e-beam is often more suitable than gamma radiation for such products.

5.3 Sterilisation method

The electron beam is typically created using a high-energy electron beam accelerator, called a linear accelerator, sometimes abbreviated to linac. A linear particle accelerator functions to increase the velocity of charged subatomic particles or ions, by subjecting the charged particles to a series of oscillating electric potentials along a linear beamline. Advanced electronics are used to precisely control the rate of electron emission. This takes the form of a 'shower' of accelerated electrons, which are passed through a high voltage emitter and directed towards a target. An electron is a subatomic particle with a negative elementary electric charge.

The electrons are generated from a tungsten or tantalum filament and directed by a high voltage source inside a vacuum chamber. The energetic electrons pass through a metallic foil that is thin enough to allow electron transmission but strong enough to maintain a powerful vacuum. Unlike gamma radiation, where the radiation source is permanently active, an electron beam accelerator can be switched on and off.

The Electron-Beam Linear Accelerator works in a similar way to a cathode-ray tube, as commonly used in television sets in the twentieth century. Instead of electrons being widely dispersed and hitting a phosphorescent screen at low energy levels, as with the cathode-ray tube, the electrons are concentrated and accelerated close to the speed of light. This produces very fast reactions on the molecules contained within the product subjected to the sterilisation process.

An alternative to the linear electron accelerator is the direct current machine, which produces electrons at a lower energy level. With these devices, electrons of high energy are generated by accelerating them across a large drop in potential. These devices are less common.

All electron accelerators include a source (of electrons), an evacuated accelerating chamber, and a system for extraction from the vacuum and distribution over the product surface. Most accelerators obtain their electrons from a heated filament source called an electron gun. The energy of these electrons is then increased in one or more stages as they pass through a vacuum with an applied electric field. The electric field is usually created by direct current (DC) accelerators, which generate and maintain the full accelerating voltage between two electrodes. As the voltage is raised to millions of volts, electrical insulation becomes a major engineering problem.

A second generation of particle accelerators are based on radio frequency (rf) power technology. These high frequency waves generate very intense electrical and magnetic fields in suitably shaped conducting cavities. By matching the field oscillations with the injection of charged particles, the rf fields drive the particles to high energies without having to create the full final potential at any one instant. They do not therefore require the large-scale insulation of DC units and are also more compact devices [6].

As the energetic electrons enter the atmosphere, they collide with air molecules and scatter, creating atmospheric plasma that acts as an electronic 'brush', delivering energy directly to surfaces as well as around product contours, such as bottle cap threads. To facilitate the process, e-beam sterilisation sometimes takes place under elevated temperatures and in a nitrogen-rich atmosphere. However, the use of an increased temperature is uncommon and e-beam is generally regarded as a cold sterilisation process.

In addition, electron beams will penetrate through thin packaging materials, and each collision creates secondary electrons under the surface. These continue to create more electrons in a shower effect. Radiation is scattered forward and the peak dose actually lies a short distance below the surface.

As surfaces are exposed to electron beams, energy is absorbed according to the intensity of the beam and the speed at which the product moves through the treatment zone. To ensure that the correct dose is applied to the product to be sterilised, a conveyer or cart system moves the product under the e-beam at a predetermined speed in order to obtain the desired electron dosage. Products move in and out of the irradiation area continuously. The density and electron energy applied depends upon the thickness of the product, placing an importance upon assessing the weight and dimensions of the product.

Thus the effectiveness of e-beam sterilisation varies according to the electron energies created and then subsequently applied to the product to be sterilised. The energy level typically falls between 3 MeV and 12 MeV (million electron volts), with accelerators usually operating at a single energy level. Energy levels of less than 3 MeV are usually reserved for surface treatment or thin film irradiation. Systems with 5 to 10 MeV output energy can process thicker products such as pre-packaged products in corrugate shipper cartons. Electrons from electron accelerators have a usable penetration of about 3 mm in water for each million volts of accelerating potential. A 10 MeV beam will therefore penetrate about 3–5 cm of material. In lower density materials, the penetration will be correspondingly higher.

The beam energy for medical device sterilisation is normally limited to 10 MeV, as levels greater than this can cause the creation and activation of short half-life radionucleides, especially within certain metals, which damages the product [7]. This means that e-beam is best suited to materials of no more than 3 cm in thickness.

As with gamma irradiation, the irradiation dose (amount of absorbed electron energy) is typically measured in Kilograys (kGy). A dose of 1 Gy means 1 joule of radiation energy has been deposited in each kilogram of material. To achieve a specific radiation effect it is necessary to apply a specific dose. For example, to sterilise medical devices, doses of the order of 25 kGy are required. The dose delivered to any surface point can be measured using a radiochromic film, which changes colour in precise proportion to the amount of electron beam energy absorbed.

There are some safety and environmental issues associated with e-beam. In relation to the environment, during the e-beam process, small amounts of ozone are released and exhausted into the air and, if not controlled, can cause atmospheric pollution. In terms of safety, the primary risk is with a person coming into contact with the beam. To safeguard against this, workers in the area need to wear protective vests and ensure access control is strictly enforced.

5.4 Microbial destruction

The relationship between microbial kill rate and absorbed energy dose is well characterised and the kill methods for e-beam radiation are essentially the same as that caused by gamma radiation [8]. E-beam sterilisation primarily kills microorganisms by penetrating the microbial cells and breaking down chains of DNA (chain cleavage), which leads to microbial cell death [9]. A secondary kill method is from an indirect chemical reaction as a result of disruption of cell mechanisms [10]. This generates unpaired and highly reactive compounds or atoms, which further react with the microorganisms [11]. Radiation effects on cells and microorganisms are dependent on the effects of wavelength, dose rate and exposure time.

Where a biological indicator is required to measure the effectiveness of e-beam sterilisation, *Bacillus pumilus* (strain E601) is the most common challenge microorganism in the endospore state. This is due to the relatively high resistance of these microorganisms to radiation.

5.5 Process requirements

When undertaking sterilisation by e-beam, there are a number of considerations to be made. These are outlined below.

5.5.1 Material compatibility

Prior to using e-beam radiation for the sterilisation of healthcare products, it is important to determine the effect that the radiation will have on the materials used in the product, its components and packaging [12]. Because each polymer reacts differently to ionizing radiation, it is necessary to verify that the maximum dose likely to be administered during the sterilisation process will not adversely affect the quality, safety or performance of the product throughout its shelf life [13]. For this, experimental samples of the product should be irradiated to a point just past the highest dose to be administered during routine processing. For example, a product that is to receive a sterilizing dosage of 25 to 40 kGy should be tested by irradiating samples to at least 40 kGy. In order to make an assessment, it is advisable to irradiate samples at twice the anticipated maximum dose.

A second consideration is that products are not necessarily manufactured in a uniform manner. The ISO 11137 guidance document [14] recommends that the development of a test programme should address 'variations in the manufacturing processes, tolerances, radiation doses, radiation source, raw materials and storage conditions'. Thus the initial assessment should use at least three different batches of product, so that variations with the manufacturing process are captured.

Evaluation and test results should be maintained in the product's device history file. This provides physical confirmation that all product claims and specifications have been met. If product testing indicates a potentially adverse effect from high levels of radiation, a maximum permissible dose should be established by the manufacturer and emphasised in the processing instructions provided to the contract company undertaking the sterilisation [15].

5.5.2 Sterilisation dose selection

Whereas the object of the material compatibility test is to assess the effect that the maximum dose has upon the material, the process of selecting a sterilisation dose is intended to establish the minimum permissible dose necessary to provide the required or desired sterility assurance level (SAL), meaning the 'probability of a viable microorganism being present on a product unit after sterilisation'. This requirement is dependent upon the intended use of the product. For example, a product that is to be used in the body's fluid path, is considered a Class III device. Under this classification, the product must receive a sterilisation dose high enough to ensure that the probability of an organism surviving the dosage is no greater than one in one million units tested (1×10^{-6}).

Whilst the probability of one microorganism surviving after irradiation decreases logarithmically with increasing dosages, it is additionally important to consider the microbial population characteristics that define a product's pre-sterilisation bioburden (the population of viable microorganisms on a product) and the types of microorganisms present (the microflora). Relevant characteristics include the magnitude of the population and the resistance of the population to radiation (radiosensitivity) [16]. One of the most important issues in e-beam sterilisation is the D-value that is required for the reduction of the survival fraction to one-tenth and the D-value is a specific value for each microorganism. The required absorbed dose increases, depending on the target reduction level.

Once the minimum sterilisation dose has been established, the actual dose applied during processing is set somewhere above this, so that total kill is achieved, although the level must be below the maximum permitted dose in order to safeguard the material.

5.5.3 Product dose mapping

A further consideration is that the dose applied may be different for one item of product compared with many items, and in relation to the product itself and its primary and secondary packaging. A dose mapping study should be performed in order to identify minimum and maximum dose zones within the product load using a predetermined loading pattern. This verifies that the minimum sterilisation dose is achieved while material integrity is maintained by staying within the maximum allowable dosage. In addition, the dose mapping study establishes the reproducibility of the sterilisation process and is used in the selection of the dose monitoring locations for routine processing.

A further consideration is the rate at which irradiation takes place. The power of the radiation source determines the rate at which product can be processed and hence the maximum total capacity of the plant. It is important to ensure all areas of the product are adequately exposed. A processing efficiency factor is used to assess the requirements for dose and power in relation to process speed (or throughput). This can be expressed thus:

Throughput (T) = Power (W)/Dose (D). Energy absorption
efficiency (a)   [5.1]

where throughput is in kg/sec, power is in watts, efficiency of absorption (a) is expressed as a percentage and the dose is in kGrays.

Once the beam power needed to treat the plant capacity has been determined, the line speed can be calculated from the dimensions and unit weight of the product, thus:

Line Speed (L) = W.a./(D.d.s)   [5.2]

where d = density and s is the cross-sectional area of the product irradiated in the direction of travel of the conveyor.

Published by Woodhead Publishing Limited, 2013

With most processes, a time of around 15 minutes is generally sufficient for the sterilisation of medical devices.

5.5.4 Sterilisation process

When medical devices are sterilised by e-beam, the product is held within product carriers (a tote). A process conveyor moves the carrier through the beam. The speed range of the conveyor is adjusted so as to deliver the precise dose to the product. The conveyor functions to move the carriers into and out of the radiation shield, from the load station to the unload station. The speed is monitored and controlled by a programmable logic controller [17].

5.5.5 Certification

Information that is gathered or produced during the validation process should be documented and reviewed for acceptability by a designated individual or group and maintained in the product's device history file. The manufacturer of the device should expect a certificate of conformance with each e-beam processing session.

5.5.6 Sterilisation dose audit

In accordance with the international standard ISO 11137, an audit must be performed to determine the continued validity of the sterilisation dose any time there is a change in the manufacturing process that could significantly affect the level or nature of the bioburden. Here, there is a requirement for the manufacture of the device to be sterilised to inform the contract sterilisation facility. In the absence of any change, a sterilisation dose audit is to be performed every three months. This activity should be undertaken by the manufacturer in conjunction with the contract facility.

5.6 Advantages of e-beam radiation

The advantages of e-beam sterilisation include the fact that the sterilisation process is relatively fast, when compared with both gamma radiation and ethylene oxide processes. This is because low voltage electron beams have the advantage of depositing energy at or near the surface, resulting in an extremely high rate of dose delivery. The fast dose also serves to protect the product being sterilised. The process is also operationally cost effective, although the construction of the e-beam sterilisation institution and the linear accelerators are relatively expensive.

In relation to gamma radiation, e-beam is a considerably faster process. Gamma radiation delivers a certain dose that can take a period of time from minutes to hours, depending on the thickness and the volume of the product. E-beam irradiation can give the same dose in a few seconds.

A further advantage is that the process has a high level of consistency in achieving sterilisation. Furthermore, e-beam is compatible with most types of materials, especially plastics. For certain types of materials, such as those sensitive to oxidative effects, e-beam is more suitable than gamma radiation due to the shorter exposure times required for e-beam dosing. Depending upon the material type, e-beam may also cause less material degradation than gamma radiation.

With medical devices, e-beam has a further advantage over the most common form of sterilisation: ethylene oxide [18]. This is in relation to the seal integrity on medical packaging pouches. A two-polymer bond is typically used to create the seal. When certain seals are subjected to ethylene oxide, sometimes these bonds are weakened or broken down, which can create an open environment and thus create a contamination risk. This is not the case with e-beam sterilisation.

A further advantage is that the material, post-sterilisation, is safe to handle and does not require any quarantine.

5.7 Disadvantages of e-beam radiation

The disadvantages of the e-beam process are similar to those associated with gamma radiation. Radiation can cause the breakdown of packaging materials at high energy levels. Here, the carbon–carbon bonds that connect atoms can become detached and possibly destroyed. This issue can lead to decreased tensile strength within a polymer [19]. A further problem with this breakdown is the creation of free radicals (chain scissioning) from polymers [20]. This can lead to the material becoming part of the product [21].

However, this risk is generally offset by the dose level required to decontaminate a product, through its medical packaging, being relatively low. Furthermore, e-beam may be less damaging than gamma radiation, for when a dose is delivered rapidly by e-beam this reduces the polymer's degradation and embrittlement.

There are further ways to safeguard against radiation-related degradation. These include using specialised chemistry that incorporates free-radical scavengers or antioxidants, freezing or lowering the sterilisation temperature, removing water from the device and package, and defining a narrow dose range [22].

A further disadvantage may arise if the product is affected by excessive rises in temperature. The energy deposited in the product by irradiation (the dose) will cause the temperature of the product to rise. Temperature rise is about 0.3°C for each KGy of dose when irradiating medical products. This rise is far lower than with heat sterilisation methods.

5.8 Conclusion

This chapter has provided an overview of e-beam sterilisation. In doing so, it has demonstrated the relative similarities between e-beam and gamma radiation in terms of their effect on the microbial cell and their application to many types of medical devices. The advantage and disadvantage of e-beam compared with gamma relates to its more limited penetration [23]. As different forms of radiation penetrate items to different degrees, e-beam is more suited for thinner materials, for electrons are much less penetrating than X-rays and gamma rays. However, where thinner materials require sterilisation, the e-beam is the faster process.

5.9 References

1. Scholla, M.H. and Wells, M.E. (1997), 'Tracking trends in industrial sterilisation', *Medical Device and Diagnostic Industry*, September: 92–5.
2. Cheng, Z.Y., Bharti, V., Mai, T., Xu, T-B., Zhang, Q.M., *et al.* (2000), 'Effect of high energy electron irradiation on the electromechanical properties of Poly(vinylidene Fluoride-Trifluoroethylene) 50/50 and 65/35 copolymers', *IEEE Trans. on Ultrasonics, Ferroelectrics and Frequency Control*, 47(6): 1296–307.
3. Allen, D. (1998), 'Sterilisation and medical packaging', *Pharmaceutical and Medical Packaging News*, April: 1–4.
4. Higgins, K.T. (2002), Radical issues in irradiation packaging. *Food Engineering Magazine*, 1–4. Available from: *http://www.foodengineeringmag.com/articles/engineering-r-d-radical-issues-in-irradiation-packaging* (Accessed 1 July 2012).

5. Beddar, A.S. (2001), 'Mobile linear accelerators for intra-operative radiation therapy', *American Association of Operating Room Nurses Journal*, 74 (5): 700.

6. Cleland, M.R., O'Neill, M.T. and Thompson, C.C. (1993), 'Sterilisation with accelerated electrons', in: Morrissey, R.F. (ed.), *Sterilisation Technology: A Practical Guide for Manufacturers and Users of Health Care Products*, New York: Van Nostrand Reinhold.

7. Cleghorn, D.A., Dunn, J. and Nablo, S.V. (2002), 'Sterilisation of plastic containers using electron beam irradiation directed through the opening', *Journal of Applied Microbiology*, 93: 937–43.

8. Borick, P.M. and Fogarty, M.G. (1967), 'Effects of continuous and interrupted radiation on microorganisms', *Applied Microbiology*, 15: 785–9.

9. Bly, J.H. (1988), *Electron Beam Processing*, Yardley, PA: International Information Associates.

10. Alexander, P. and Bacq, Z.M. (1961), 'The nature of the initial radiation damage at the sub-cellular level', in: R.J.C. Harris (ed.), *The Initial Effects of Ionizing Radiation on Cells*, New York: Academic Press, Inc, p. 3–19.

11. Anderson, A.W., Hordan, H.D., Cain, R.F., Parrish, G. and Duggan, D. (1956), 'Studies on a radio-resistant micrococcus. Part I: Isolation, morphology, cultural characteristics and resistance to gamma radiation', *Food Technology*, 10: 575–8.

12. Genova, T.F., Hollis, R.A., Crowell, C.A. and Schady, K.M. (1987), 'A procedure for validating the sterility of an individual gamma radiation sterilised production batch', *Journal of Parenteral Science and Technology*, 41(1): 33–6.

13. English, L.K. (1986). 'How high-energy radiation affects polymers', *Materials Engineering*, May: 41–4.

14. American National Standard (1994), ANSI/AAMI/ISO 11137-1994, Sterilisation of health care products – Requirements for validation and routine control – Radiation sterilisation.

15. Ishigaki, I. and Yoshii, F. (1992), 'Radiation effects on polymer materials in radiation sterilisation of medical supplies', *Radiation Physics and Chemistry*, 39(6): 527–33.

16. Gaughran, E.R.L. and Morrissey, R.F. (1980), *Sterilisation of Medical Products*, vol. 2, Montréal, Québec: Multiscience, pp. 35–9.

17. Allen, J.T., Calhoun, L.R., Helm, J., Kruger, S., Lee, C., *et al.* (1995), 'A fully integrated 10-MeV electron beam sterilisation system', *Radiation Physics and Chemistry*, 46(4–6): 457–60.

18. Baker, J. (1995), 'Ethylene oxide sterilisation update', *Medical Device Technology*, 6: 23–24.

19. Greenburg, E.F. (2000), 'Irradiation a material issue', *Packaging Digest*, 1–4, 37(12): 30.

20. Donohue, J. and Apostolou, S.F. (1990), 'Free-radical degradation and protection in irradiated plastic', *Medical Device and Diagnostic Industry*, April: 124–9.

21. Shaw, J.H. (1997), 'The effect of gamma irradiation on ultra-high molecular weight polyethylene', *Medical Devices Agency*, 1–30.

22. Gopal, N.G.S. (1988), 'Guidelines for radiation sterilisation of pharmaceuticals and decontamination of raw materials', *Radiation Physics and Chemistry*, 32: 619–22.
23. Silindir, M. and Ozer, Y. (2012). 'The effect of radiation on a variety of pharmaceuticals and materials containing polymers', *PDA Journal of Pharmaceutical Science and Technology*, 1, 66(2):184–99.

6

Dry heat sterilisation

DOI: 10.1533/9781908818638.83

Abstract: Dry heat sterilisation is a method by which super-heat is applied to a device in order to sterilise it. Through this mechanism, the application of the sterilisation technology is only applicable to devices which can withstand temperature above 170°C. At higher temperatures, dry heat can additionally be used for depyrogenation, the inactivation of endotoxin. This chapter focuses on sterilisation, with Chapter 12 covering the depyrogenation aspects more fully. This chapter examines the way by which dry heat destroys microorganisms and describes the additional mechanism for endotoxin inactivation. It then proceeds to describe the science behind dry heat, in terms of heat transfer, before discussing the main devices used for dry heat sterilisation. It chapter closes with an overview of the validation requirements.

Key words: dry heat, sterilisation, heat transfer, convection, *Bacillus subtilis var niger*, depyrogenation, endotoxin, aseptic filling.

6.1 Introduction

Dry heat sterilisation is sterilisation by thermal (heat) conduction. The dry heat sterilisation process is accomplished by conduction, which is where heat is absorbed by the exterior surface of an item and then passed inwards to the next layer. Eventually, the entire item reaches the peak temperature needed to achieve sterilisation. The proper time and temperature for dry heat sterilisation, at which microbial kill theoretically becomes effective, is 160°C for 2 hours or 170°C for 1 hour. Dry heat destroys microorganisms by causing coagulation of proteins [1].

Within the biopharmaceutical sector, dry heat sterilisation is a process that is more commonly deployed as a depyrogenation step, which results in the inactivation of bacterial endotoxin as well as the destruction of microorganisms [2]. Whilst depyrogenation aspects are covered in Chapter 12, this chapter looks at the use of dry heat for routine sterilisation procedures.

The temperatures and times required for dry heat sterilisation are far higher than autoclave temperatures (as described in Chapter 7, which examines steam sterilisation). This is because the mechanisms of microbiological inactivation as a result of exposure to dry heat are quite different and much slower than those applying to saturated steam. This results in dry heat being less suitable for the sterilisation of components.

There are three forms of heat transfer, convection, conduction and radiation. With dry heat ovens, convection is the primary means of heat transfer [3]. Convective heat transfer is the transfer of heat from one place to another by the movement of fluids and involves the combined processes of conduction (heat diffusion) and heat transfer by bulk fluid flow (sometimes called heat advection). The convection heat transfer mode comprises two mechanisms. In addition to energy transfer due to random molecular motion (diffusion), energy is also transferred by bulk, or macroscopic, motion of the fluid [4]. This motion is associated with the fact that, at any instant, large numbers of molecules are moving collectively or as aggregates. Such motion, in the presence of a temperature gradient, contributes to heat transfer [5]. With ovens, convection is forced convection. In this case the fluid is forced to flow by use of a pump, fan or other mechanical means [6].

6.2 Microbial kill and endotoxin inactivation

6.2.1 Microbial destruction

Given sufficient heat applied to an article for a prolonged period of time, dry heat can effectively destroy a given microbial population. The mechanism of destruction is the same as that applied through steam sterilisation (Chapter 7). Dry heat coagulates the proteins in any organism, causing oxidative free radical damage, the drying of cells and

Published by Woodhead Publishing Limited, 2013

can even, depending upon the time-temperature combination, incinerate the microbial cell. For dry heat to be effective, the items to be sterilised should be free from soiling substances and be dry, since water droplets can interfere with the process, particularly in relation to short sterilisation run times.

The typical response of microbial populations to dry heat is exponential. The slow reaction rates seen in dry heat sterilisation indicate that the mechanisms of microbial inactivation are most likely the results of intracellular oxidative reactions. Because the biochemistry of inactivation differs, microorganisms which have resistance to thermal sterilisation by saturated steam are not necessarily also resistant to dry heat. Spores of *Geobacillus stearothermophilus*, used to evaluate steam sterilisation, are not as resistant to dry heat as spores of *Bacillus subtilis var niger* [7]. This intrinsic difference affects the type of biological indicator used for the validation of a heat sterilisation device (validation aspects are discussed below).

6.2.2 Endotoxin inactivation

As indicated above, dry heat is not only capable of sterilising, but also capable of depyrogenation, that is the destruction or inactivation of bacterial endotoxin, a component of the microbial cell wall (Chapter 2). Thermal inactivation of endotoxin is not as well understood as thermal inactivation of microorganisms. Interpretation of experimental data has been complicated by problems relating to analytical techniques, different microbiological sources of endotoxin, the chemical purity of endotoxin, the 'carrier' used in studies, and perceived differences in reaction rates between convectional and radiant heat transfer [8].

The general form of endotoxin inactivation appears to follow Second-Order kinetics. At any particular temperature, there is an initially rapid rate of reaction. This is followed by a slower, flatter 'tail'. This means that at any particular temperature, there is an upper boundary limit to the proportion of endotoxin that can be inactivated [9]. At temperatures of around 100°C, there is practically no evidence of endotoxin inactivation; at temperatures around 170°C, the upper boundary limit of inactivation of endotoxin appears to be around 2-$\log_{10}$ reductions, requiring more than 24 hours exposure to reduce a challenge of 1000 EU (endotoxin units) to no more than 10 EU. The FDA validation requirement for depyrogenating processes of 3-$\log_{10}$ reductions is only possible at temperatures above 170°C. In practical time scales, temperatures of greater than 210°C are necessary to achieve 3-$\log_{10}$ reductions. At 250°C, 5- or 6-$\log_{10}$ reductions are possible. The application of dry heat for depyrogenation is fully discussed in Chapter 12.

6.3 Application of dry heat sterilisation

Dry heat sterilisation requires a higher temperature than moist heat and a longer exposure time. The method is, therefore, more convenient for heat-stable, non-aqueous materials that cannot be sterilised by steam because of its deleterious effects or failure to penetrate, such as glass or metal objects [10]. Such materials include glassware, powders, oils and some oil-based injectable pharmaceuticals.

The principle application of dry heat in pharmaceutical manufacture is in the sterilisation and depyrogenation of glassware (ampoules and vials) prior to aseptic filling. There are three types of dry heat sterilisation/ depyrogenation technology, ovens, unidirectional airflow (UDAF) tunnels and radiant heat tunnels. The latter are continuous or semi-continuous in their operation and amenable to large-scale fast throughput aseptic operations.

Preparations to be sterilised by dry heat are filled in units that are either sealed or temporarily closed for sterilisation. The entire content of each container is maintained in the oven for a given time and at the temperature combination. Other conditions may be necessary for different preparations to ensure the effective elimination of all undesirable microorganisms.

The oven should normally be equipped with a forced air system to ensure even distribution of heat throughout all the materials processed. This should be controlled by monitoring the temperature, and verified, across different zones, using thermocouples at the time of validation. Containers that have been temporarily closed during the sterilisation procedure are sealed after sterilisation using aseptic techniques to prevent microbial recontamination.

6.3.1 Ovens

The simplest form of dry heat sterilisation uses ovens. The typical form of commercial batch dry heat sterilisation processing is the forced convection hot air oven, with horizontal or vertical air supply. For these devices, the heating elements are electrical. Air is drawn into the oven through HEPA (High Efficiency Particulate Air) filters, heated by passage over the heating elements and forced through the oven and over its contents. The steriliser exhaust may or may not be protected by HEPA filters, depending upon the type of environment that the oven is housed in.

In the interests of energy efficiency, the greater part of the heated air is recirculated through the oven and past the heating elements again. A balance between recirculated air and 'fresh' air is usually achieved through a system of electrically operated baffles and dampers. During the initial phase, where the temperature is increased, the greater part of the air is re-circulated, whereas to maintain constant temperature during the sterilisation hold, this is affected by introduction of external air. The system may also be designed to allow some control over the rate at which oven temperature can be increased and cooled down, because the rate of temperature change may be of significance to the physical properties of some products. It may also affect the performance of HEPA filters; excessive particle shedding from HEPA filters may occur if the temperature change is much greater than about 1.5°C per minute. To guard against this, sterilising ovens are microprocessor controlled.

Sterilising ovens may be single- or double-ended. When a double-ended oven bridges non-sterile and aseptic cleanrooms, it is typical to find a pressure differential positive to the external environment being maintained in sterilising ovens. As with autoclaves, ovens used in these situations are equipped with door interlocks to prevent both doors being opened at the same time.

6.3.2 UDAF sterilising tunnels

The principal continuous process application of forced air convection is the UDAF tunnel. These are used in aseptic pharmaceutical manufacture, specifically to bridge between vial washing areas and aseptic filling cleanrooms. The UDAF tunnel is little more than a forced convection vertical flow hot air sterilising oven modified to allow for continuous throughput of the material to be sterilised. In the sterilising zone, controlled proportions of recirculated and external air are passed over heating elements and on through HEPA filters. The heated air is forced vertically down over a horizontally moving perforated belt, which carries the material through the tunnel.

UDAF tunnels have four distinct HEPA filter-protected zones. The first of these is the in-feed protection zone, the second is the sterilising zone, the third is the cooling zone and the fourth serves to protect the region between the cooling zone and the aseptic filling cleanroom.

The first HEPA filter-protected zone is an air curtain, which sweeps over the in-feed zone to the tunnel upstream of the sterilising zone. UDAF tunnels are most often linked directly to continuous washers. The purpose of this protection is to prevent microorganisms, contaminated air and aerosols from the washer intruding into the sterilising zone of the tunnel. It is also the primary source of the positive pressure differential, which serves to protect the entire sterilising and bridging system.

The second zone is the sterilising zone. Design temperatures in this zone may be as high as 400°C. The particulate quality required in this zone for pharmaceutical applications is for fewer than 3500 particle of 0.5 μm or greater in diameter per cubic metre of air (class 5 of the cleanroom standard ISO 14644-1).

The third HEPA filter-protected zone is for cooling. HEPA filtered environmental air or HEPA filtered chilled air is used to cool the sterile material to temperatures suitable for filling or other subsequent purpose. Cooling zones are usually designed to reduce the degree of stress occurring in glassware as a result of thermal shock. The temperature reduction in UDAF sterilised glassware tends to follow an exponential relationship, with 200°C drops in the first minute of cooling being typical. Tunnels are designed to run with initial cooling rates (linearised cooling), in order to reduce the incidence of breakage in glassware post-sterilisation.

Sterilisation of the interior of the cooling zone is achieved by thorough cleaning, disinfection and/or fumigation with formaldehyde. Some recent tunnel developments allow for sterilisation of the cooling zone by diversion of hot air through the cooling zone HEPA filters. The out-feed zone from UDAF tunnels must, like the in-feed zone, be designed to protect the aseptic filling cleanroom from the external environment and to protect the uniformity of heating conditions in the sterilising zone. Different levels of control in this region may be required to maintain the same pressure differentials according to the dimensions of the materials passing through the tunnel, and indeed between the tunnel being in use or out of use. It is usual to find the flow of filtered air being maintained at a constant velocity, with differential pressures being controlled through a baffle or pressure plate system operated to minimise the cross-sectional area of the open end of the tunnel.

6.3.3 Radiant heat tunnels

Radiant heat tunnels are designed to be larger, longer and slower than UDAF tunnels, to achieve somewhat lower (~300°C) sterilising temperatures [11]. These devices are an older technology, and simpler and easier to operate and maintain than UDAF tunnels. However, such devices may present a risk of heating elements breaking down and shedding particulates.

Like UDAF tunnels, they have four distinct zones, but only three are HEPA filter protected. The in-feed zone is vertical laminar flow HEPA filter-protected in the same way as in UDAF tunnels. These tunnels are also commonly connected permanently to continuous washers.

The sterilising zone has heating elements above and below a perforated moving belt, which carries the product through the tunnel and on into the aseptic filling cleanroom. Quartz glass, (glass containing high-purity silica in amorphous (non-crystalline) form), is the material of choice for heating elements. The sterilising zone is maintained at a positive pressure differential to the in-feed zone by 'spill-over' air from the downstream cooling zone. Cooling in radiant heat tunnels follows exactly the same principles as cooling in UDAF tunnels; specifically passage of vertical flow HEPA filtered laminar air over the sterilised material. Out-feed protection is also achieved by provision of HEPA filtered air.

6.4 Validation of dry heat devices

In order to verify that dry heat devices can sterilise components, both thermometric and microbial validation are required; the demonstration of endotoxin inactivation is required for devices intended to depyrogenate (Chapter 12).

For sterilisation, the purpose of dry heat process development is to determine time and temperature combinations that will achieve a 10^{-6} Sterility Assurance Level or better, or to develop an 'overkill' cycle that will deliver 12-$\log_{10}$ reductions relative to spores of a biological indicator. The bioindicator strain proposed for validation of the sterilisation process is spores of *Bacillus subtilis var niger* (ATCC 9372 or CIP 77.18), for which the D-value is 5–10 minutes at 16°C using about 10^6 spores per indicator. If depyrogenation as well as sterilisation is required, the purpose of dry heat process development is, for pharmaceutical product-contact components, to determine time and temperature combinations that will effect a standard 3- $\log_{10}$ reduction of bacterial endotoxin.

In terms of typical cycles used for validation, the USP refers to temperatures 'in excess of 250°C' for depyrogenation and the *European Pharmacopeia* lists 250°C for 30 minutes or 200°C for 60 minutes as suitable combinations of time and temperature to depyrogenate glassware suitable for use in pyrogen testing.

Validation and routine control of dry heat processes is similar to validation and control of steam sterilisation. Engineering qualifications should focus on the heating and air circulatory systems, which are central to dry heat sterilisers. Most heating elements in dry heat sterilisers are electrically powered. They should always be equipped with current monitoring devices linked to alarm systems to allow immediate detection of burn-out. Heat transfer in ovens and UDAF tunnels is dependent upon the continued effectiveness of the re-circulatory fans. The quality and condition of the drive belts can be of significance.

The integrity of HEPA filters must be verified as installed by a particulate challenge test (DOP testing). In view of the potential damage to measuring equipment through exposure to air streams that may be hotter than 300°C, it is acceptable to perform particulate challenge testing with heating elements switched off, or preferably with the downstream air samples cooled.

Performance Qualification (PQ) relates to the actual effectiveness of the oven or tunnel in relation to sterilisation as distinct from its effectiveness as a piece of engineering equipment. This involves producing and evaluating thermal data and biological data. Where a dry heat device is used for depyrogenation, the use of biological indicators is less common and instead biological studies with bacterial endotoxin are performed, the inference being that if the device inactivates endotoxin it will also be capable of destroying bacterial spores. Challenged product items are prepared with endotoxin air-dried on to them (Chapter 12).

Where dry heat devices are used as sterilisers, the biological challenge is with endospores as biological indicators. With biological indicators, the key relationship is expressed as the D-value (decimal value). This is defined as the time taken to reduce a population by 10% of its initial number at a particular and constant temperature (T). For example, the D-value of spores of *B. subtilis var. niger* at 170°C (D_{170}) could typically be 1.5 minutes. A further factor is the Z-value, which refers to the change in temperature required to produce a 10-fold change in the D-value. Z values are often around 20°C.

6.5 Advantages and disadvantages of dry heat sterilisation

As with other forms of sterilisation, dry heat has advantages and disadvantages with its application. The advantages relate to the process being an effective method, as dry heat by conduction reaches all surfaces of instruments, even for instruments that cannot be disassembled. With certain articles, such as protection of sharps or instruments with a cutting edge, fewer problems with dulling of cutting edges are encountered compared with steam sterilisation. Dry heat avoids the 'wet pack' problems associated with autoclaves in humid climates [12]. A further advantage of steam is that dry heat in relation to other processes, leaves no chemical residue.

The disadvantages relate to the limitations in applicability for plastic and rubber items that cannot be dry-heat sterilised, because the temperatures used are too high for these materials without the risk of degradation. With items that can be dry heat sterilised, there can be problems with the method of heat transfer, because dry heat can penetrate materials slowly and unevenly. A further disadvantage, operationally, is the cost of the electricity required to produce high levels of heat for a sustained period of time.

6.6 Conclusion

This chapter has examined dry heat sterilisation. Dry heat is used either to sterilise components or to sterilise and depyrogenate components. This chapter has focused on sterilisation, with depyrogenation issues discussed in Chapter 12.

For dry heat sterilisation, higher temperatures and longer run times are required compared with steam sterilisation, because the moisture in the steam sterilisation process significantly speeds up the penetration of heat and shortens the time needed to kill microorganisms. This means that where endotoxin destruction is not required, dry heat has a more limited application as a sterilisation technology and is reserved for articles that cannot be straightforwardly sterilised by other methods. Dry heat sterilisation is not the most efficient sterilisation process, because air is a poor conductor of heat and can act to insulate the article intended to be sterilised. Therefore, the time-temperature combination and the verification of the effectiveness are important. Thus, the chapter has emphasised the importance of validation, alongside a description of the physical forces at work.

6.7 References

1. Ernst, R.R. (1977), 'Sterilisation by heat', in: Block, S.S. (ed.), *Disinfection, Sterilisation and Preservation*, Philadelphia: Lean and Febige.
2. Booth, A. (1998), *Sterilisation of Medical Devices*, Buffalo Grove, IL: Interpharm Press.
3. Welty, J.R., Wilson, C.E. and Elliott, R. (1976), *Fundamentals of Momentum, Heat, and Mass Transfer*, 2nd edition, New York: Wiley.
4. Burmeister, L.C. (1993), *Convective Heat Transfer*, 2nd edition, New York: Wiley-Interscience, p. 107.
5. Incropera, F.P., DeWitt, D.P., Bergman, T.L. and Lavine, A.S. (2007), *Introduction to Heat Transfer*, 5th edition, Chichester, UK: John Wiley & Sons.
6. Lienhard, J.H. (2008), *A Heat Transfer Textbook*, 3rd edition, Cambridge, MA: Phlogiston Press.
7. Halls, N.A. (1994), *Achieving Sterility in Medical and Pharmaceutical Products*, New York: Marcel Dekker, Inc.
8. Geankoplis, C.J. (2003), *Transport Processes and Separation Process Principles*, 4th edition, Upper Saddle River, NJ: Prentice Hall Professional Technical Reference.
9. Ludwig, J.D. and Avis, K.E. (1990), 'Dry heat inactivation of endotoxin on the surface of glass', *Journal of Parenteral Science and Technology*, 44: 4–12.
10. Darmady, E.M., Hughes, K.E., Jones, J. and Tuke, W. (1958), 'Sterilisation by conducted heat', *Lancet*, 11, 2(7050): 769–70.
11. Darmady, E.M. and Brock, B.B. (1954), 'Temperature levels in hot-air ovens', *Journal of Clinical Pathology*, 7(4): 290–9.
12. American Association of Operating Room Nurses (AORN) (1992), 'Recommended practices: Sanitation in the surgical practice setting', *American Association of Operating Room Nurses Journal*, 56(6): 1089–95.

7

Steam sterilisation

DOI: 10.1533/9781908818638.93

Abstract: This chapter examines sterilisation by steam (or moist heat). Steam sterilisation involves the use of steam under pressure, delivered at a particular temperature for an appropriate time in order to achieve the required lethality. This is normally achieved by using autoclaves. The mechanism by which steam sterilisation destroys microorganisms is examined. The chapter proceeds to describe autoclaves and how they function, paying particular attention to the parameters of time, temperature and air removal. The focus is on the validation of autoclave cycles in relation to thermometric monitoring and the use of biological indicators, and makes reference to reasons for cycle failure. It concludes with parameters necessary to assess the routine operation of steam sterilisation devices.

Key words: steam sterilisation, moist heat, autoclave, steam-in-place, biological indicator, *Geobacillus stearothermophilus*, thermocouple, vacuum, pressure, super-heat.

7.1 Introduction

The most widely used sterilisation method in the pharmaceutical industry is steam sterilisation in autoclaves, moist heat in the form of saturated steam under pressure. This is primarily applicable to the terminal sterilisation of products, stainless steel items and equipment not intended for single use. Sterilisation occurs as the latent heat of condensation is transferred to the load causing it to heat rapidly. Steam sterilisation is non-toxic, inexpensive, rapidly microbiocidal, sporicidal and efficient at heating and penetrating fabrics. It is because of the ability of heat to penetrate that steam sterilisation is widely used as a terminal process for drug products in glass ampoules, vials, syringes and plastic containers. It is also used for sterilising closures, filters, manufacturing equipment, cleaning equipment and product holding vessels. Whilst most medical and surgical devices used in healthcare facilities are made of materials that are heat stable and can therefore undergo heat processing, there has been a move towards low-temperature sterilisation methods, such as ethylene oxide and radiation in relation to certain materials and as the biopharmaceutical industry embraces single-use disposable items. However, for sterile medicinal products, steam sterilisation remains the most widely-used method for products that can be terminally sterilised.

In relation to the terminal sterilisation of pharmaceutical products, the European Agency for Medicinal Products (EMA) requires that:

> ... products intended to be sterile should be terminally sterilised ... where it is not possible to carry out terminal sterilisation by heating due to formulation instability, a decision should be made to utilise an alternative method. [1]

To assist with the decision-making process, the EMA provides a decision tree in which the first question is: 'can the product be sterilised by moist heat at 121°C for 15 minutes?' This means that if the product can be sterilised in this way, then this is the method of choice. The question in the EMA guidance, which follows from an answer of 'no', is: 'can the product be sterilised by moist heat with $F_0 = 8$ minutes achieving SAL of 10^{-6}?' The US FDA adopts a similar position [2]. This question in relation to the Sterility Assurance Level (SAL) and the F_0 concept, the sterilisation value or sum of lethality rate that will insure sterilisation or equivalent minutes at 121°C to achieve the SAL of 10^{-6}, are discussed within this chapter.

The inference from the FDA and EMA guidance is that only those products that cannot be terminally sterilised should be produced through aseptic filling (Chapter 14). The EMA document also implies that a temperature of 121°C for 15 minutes represents the process parameters of choice. There are some alternatives to this set of conditions, although this temperature-time combination remains the industry benchmark.

This chapter discusses this most widely used of terminal sterilisation methods: steam (or moist heat) sterilisation. In doing so, it provides an outline of the mechanisms of microbial destruction, discusses some of the operational issues with respect to autoclaves, and outlines the best practice approach for validation.

7.2 Microbial destruction

The oldest known agent for inactivation of microorganisms is heat. This important discovery is traceable to when people began boiling food as a means to avoid food poisoning. The mechanism by which populations of microorganisms are inactivated at high temperatures in the presence of steam (moisture) and in the absence of air is one where the energy input from the steam inactivates microorganisms by denaturation and coagulation of their intracellular proteins [3]. In addition, moist heat causes irreversible damage to macromolecules, primarily to cellular structural proteins. It is thought the destruction of cells by lysis may also play a role [4]. Sufficient temperature and time applied to an object cannot only destroy microorganisms in the vegetative state, but the optimal combinations can also inactivate microbial endospores.

The temperature at which denaturation occurs varies inversely with the amount of water present. It has been found that the presence of moisture significantly affects the coagulation temperature of proteins and the temperature at which microorganisms are destroyed. Therefore, sterilisation in saturated steam requires precise control of time, temperature and pressure. For this, specialised sterilisation devices are required.

7.3 Steam sterilisation devices

There are different devices used for steam sterilisation within the pharmaceutical facility. The most widely used is the autoclave.

Modern autoclaves are generally very reliable and computer controlled. The autoclave is essentially a pressure-cooker. Water boils at 100°C, at atmospheric pressure, whereas at lower temperatures it boils at lower temperatures, and at higher pressure it boils at higher temperatures. At a steam over-pressure of 1 bar (a non-SI unit of pressure, exactly equal to

100,000 Pascals, about equal to the atmospheric pressure at sea level) water boils at approximately 121°C. This allows the autoclave to produce temperatures above those that can ordinarily be achieved. For sufficient time, and with the correct conditions, such temperatures can destroy bacterial endospores.

When operating an autoclave, it is very important to ensure that all of the trapped air is removed before commencement of the sterilisation cycle. This is because hot air is a very poor medium for achieving sterility. Air can act as an insulator and prevent sufficient heat from reaching the microbial population. Autoclaves destroy microorganisms by direct steam contact at the required temperature and pressure for a specified time. Another important variable is uniformity of heat transfer. Therefore it is important that every item included in the autoclave load is subject to the same lethality [5].

The standard sterilising temperature in steam autoclaves is 121°C, but lower (e.g. 116°C) and higher (e.g. 134°C) temperatures are also used for certain cycles.

For autoclave operation there are four key parameters, steam, pressure, temperature and time (Figure 7.1). The ideal steam for sterilisation is dry saturated steam and entrained water (i.e. steam with a dryness fraction

Figure 7.1   An operator starting an autoclave cycle

≥97%) [6]. Dryness is important, because excess moisture carried (suspended or entrained) in the steam may cause wet loads. If an item is removed from an autoclave wet, it has probably not been correctly sterilised. Furthermore, for packaged items, moisture will affect the integrity of the packaging. The moisture content of the steam (dryness fraction) is measured as the weight of dry steam present in a mixture of dry saturated steam and entrained water.

In relation to these parameters, the operation of an autoclave typically follows the following sequence:

- a pump starts running to evacuate the chamber;
- the pump stops and steam is bled into the chamber to dilute the residual air and to pre-heat the load;
- this sequence of evacuation and steam bleeding may be repeated a further one or two times;
- a steam valve is opened and steam is charged into the chamber until a control sensor measuring temperature reaches its set point. At this point, the sensor sends a signal closing the steam valve. According to the location of the sensor versus the load and versus the steam inlet points, there may be some temperature over-shoot at the beginning of the sterilisation hold phase;
- the sensor also sends a signal to start a timer running. This timer is set to time out at the end of the sterilisation time prescribed in the specification;
- during the hold period, the load temperature may drop; to avoid it dropping below the lower end of the sterilisation specification, the temperature may be modulated by steam being bled into the chamber. Temperature modulation may be achieved through a control signal from a temperature sensor or from a pressure sensor;
- at the end of the hold period, all steam supply is cut off and the vacuum pump is triggered again to remove the steam;
- the vacuum is broken by introduction of air into the chamber via a bacteria retentive filter (nominally sterile air).

In the enclosed space of an autoclave chamber, it is relatively straightforward to create and demonstrate uniform conditions of temperature and pressure, notwithstanding the importance of load distribution and defined load patterns (Figure 7.2). Permanent records of temperature and pressure should be generated for all autoclave runs, and examined by a competent person.

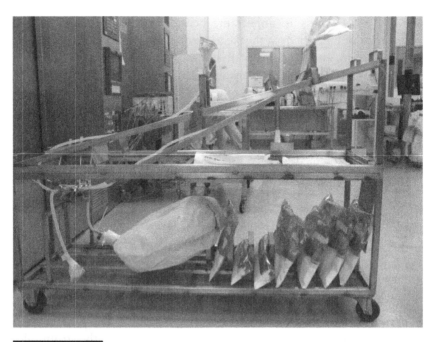

Figure 7.2 Typical autoclave load at a pharmaceutical facility

The two basic types of steam sterilisers (autoclaves) are the gravity displacement autoclave and the high-speed pre-vacuum steriliser. In the former, steam is admitted at the top or the sides of the sterilising chamber and, because the steam is lighter than air, this forces air out the bottom of the chamber through the drain vent. The gravity displacement autoclaves are primarily used to process laboratory media, water, pharmaceutical products, regulated medical waste and non-porous articles whose surfaces have direct steam contact. High-speed pre-vacuum sterilisers are similar to the gravity displacement sterilisers, except that they are fitted with a vacuum pump (or ejector) to ensure air removal from the sterilising chamber and load before the steam is admitted into the chamber.

In addition to autoclaves, the other commonly used devices for steam sterilisation are steam-in-place (SIP) units, sometimes called sterilise-in-place. These are used for the sterilisation of large items of equipment, where sterilisation is performed using steam with the equipment located in its normal fixed place. The principles are the same as steam sterilisation in autoclaves and most systems are fully automated [7].

Items of equipment subjected to SIP include assemblies and combinations of vessels, valves, process lines and filter assemblies [8]. The important consideration is that the equipment being sterilised must be able to withstand steam pressures sufficient to obtain a temperature of 121°C. With large equipment, the slowest point to reach 121°C may lag behind the fastest point by 10 or 15 minutes. Differences in lethality can therefore be huge and timing studies must be undertaken and cycles based on the predetermined slowest point [9].

The main advantage of SIP relies on the reduction of manipulations and aseptic connections that might compromise the integrity of the downstream equipment. SIP involves the use of specific components such as steam traps, pressure regulators and sterilising vent filters to evacuate air and condensate, and to cool down, dry and maintain the sterility of the equipment following sterilisation. Steam is ordinarily introduced at the top and drained from the bottom. This is because the production of condensate is the first step when high temperature steam meets cold stainless steel. Therefore condensate drains and traps are critical to the success of all SIP systems. At the conclusion of the hold period, the steam is pumped out of the system, and the system is then dried out by flushing through with nitrogen gas, which has been passed through a bacteria-retentive filter.

If there is the possibility of pharmaceutical preparations coming into contact with the equipment being sterilized by SIP, the steam supply should be what is termed 'pure steam', that is the condensate should comply with the pharmacopoeial requirements for Water for Injection, in relation to both chemical and microbiological requirements. Steam quality is discussed later.

7.4 Applications of steam sterilisation

There are generally two types of load encountered in pharmaceutical manufacture: aqueous fluid loads in sealed containers (pharmaceutical preparations for terminal sterilisation) and porous loads (items that may entrap air and inhibit the penetration of steam). Porous load items include processing equipment (i.e. filling pumps), container-closures and filters.

Sterilisation of aqueous fluid loads is achieved by contact of the external surfaces of the product containers with saturated steam, and then by heat transfer through the walls of the container to increase and maintain the temperature of the pharmaceutical preparation at the specified sterilisation temperature [10].

In contrast, the sterilisation of porous loads occurs by direct contact of the load items with good-quality steam. The temperature in the load items is raised and maintained at the specified temperature by transfer of the latent heat of steam to the load items as it condenses on their surfaces. Pure steam is necessary when load items are to be used in subsequent aseptic manufacture of sterile products, to ensure that chemical or physical contaminants are not transferred to the pharmaceutical preparation from materials or items of equipment that have come into contact with steam. Furthermore, poor-quality steam can hinder the diffusion of air from the load. Any trapped air can significantly reduce the rate at which any dense porous loads will heat. Therefore porous load sterilisers must be equipped with vacuum pumps to ensure that the air is removed from the chamber and the load before steam is admitted into the chamber.

In addition, such autoclaves are equipped with heated jackets to assist in drying of the load and to ensure that condensate does not form on the chamber walls during the hold period. Porous load autoclaves used in aseptic manufacturing facilities are generally of a double-door design. This allows them to be loaded from an area with a high specification for environmental control and cleanliness (i.e. an EU GMP Grade C/ISO 14644 class 8 cleanroom), and unloaded into a higher grade cleanroom used for aseptic processing (EU GMP Grade B/ISO 14644 class 7 cleanroom).

Many porous load items are not easy to sterilise. For example, air may be trapped inside or around many of the items. Trapped air leads to a failure to sterilise. This is normally only evident from biological indicator studies. The option of increasing the time or temperature to overcome this is dangerous. Good practice advice is that the only way to avoid air traps is to review and revise the load presentation and to repeat the validation [11].

7.5 Cycle development

When developing a steam sterilisation cycle, the specification needs to be decided at the outset. The required assurance of sterility is typically a SAL of 10^{-6}, although it is increasingly common for autoclaves which sterilise critical loads to be operated with the aim of achieving an SAL of 10^{-12}, in order to achieve 'overkill'.

The SAL is defined as the probability of there being no more than one viable microorganism in a non-sterile unit in a population of units (Chapter 11). This is dependent upon a number of variables. Sterilisation specifications can only relate specifically to the temperatures and times to which the microorganisms are actually exposed, and then only if the steam is saturated, and if air is absent [12].

Therefore, once the desired SAL has been selected, the most important part of cycle development concerns the required set of process parameters needed to achieve the SAL. This includes establishing the correct settings for the autoclave and for the condition of the product load, including the load size and the packaging used. The settings required will vary between different types of sterilisation devices. The parameters include the temperature control and the numbers and depths of vacuum pulses (required for air removal).

The most important part of the sterilisation cycle is the 'hold' period, at which the load to be sterilised is subjected to the required temperature for the required time. For this, the sterilisation device will have upper and lower tolerances for temperature and time. Here the lower specification limits are critical to sterilisation.

Time is easily controllable to high levels of accuracy and precision. A steam valve allows steam to enter the autoclave until the hold temperature is reached, the valve is then closed off and the process is controlled by a timer, which at the end of the specified hold period sends a control signal to activate the exhausts valves and cooling sequences. The hold time is usually specified in terms of whole minutes. However, temperature is less easy to control precisely. The temperature in the hold period in autoclaves is generally maintained by modulating valves that open to allow steam entry when the temperature, or pressure because these valves are more often than not controlled through pressure transducers, begins to drop towards the critical lower limit of the specification.

Therefore sterilisation specifications relate to the temperature and time that must be obtained within the product load. As indicated above, the standard conditions are 121°C for 15 minutes. However, alternative cycles can be developed through the use of the F_0 concept (the F sub-zero).

The F_0 concept concerns equivalent lethality. An F_0 of 8 minutes means that the process being conducted at whatever temperature (T°C) and time (θ minutes) is equivalent in terms of its lethality to 8 minutes at 121°C. This could be a higher temperature than 121°C for a shorter time, or a lower temperature than 121°C for a longer time. The lethality contributed during the heating up and cooling down periods, before and after the holding time at the specified temperature, may be integrated into the cumulative F_0 provided.

The F_0 for a particular temperature/time combination is an expression of the time required at 121°C to achieve the same lethality. Equivalent temperature/time combinations can be calculated using the following formula [13]:

$$F_T = F_0/L \qquad\qquad\qquad [7.1]$$

when $L = 10^{(T-121)/z}$ and $z = 10\,K$

For example, the F_0 equivalent to a heat treatment of 134°C for 10 minutes (effects of heat up and cool down times are disregarded in this example) can be calculated as:

(i) Determine L from $10^{(134-121)/10}$; i.e. $L = 10^{1.3}$

$10^{1.3}$ can be calculated by taking the $\log_{10}$ of 10 and multiplying by 1.3. The antilog of this function is equal to L.

- $\log_{10}$ of $10 = 1$; multiplied by 1.3 the function $\log_{10}L = 1.3$
- Antilog of $1.3 = 20 = L$

(ii) Determine F_0 from $F_T = F_0/L$, therefore $10 = F_0/L$

Rearranged to $F_0 = 10 \times L$, which is equivalent to 10×20 or 200 minutes.

A sterilisation specification based solely on F_0 (any temperature over any length of time, as long as the F_0 specification is achieved) generally does not work for preparations containing active pharmaceutical ingredients. This is for reasons of stability. However, the development of sterilisation specifications for porous loads affords a greater degree of freedom and is generally achievable.

With steam sterilisation, a sterilisation specification of an SAL of 10^{-6} must be achieved.

7.6 Validation of steam sterilisation cycles

For the validation of a new autoclave, new product, changed load configuration or new specification, the cycle is run using the parameters derived from process development on three separate occasions and tested for compliance with a variety of predetermined acceptance criteria. The initial phases of validation (Installation Qualification (IQ) and

Operational Qualification (OQ)) of autoclaves are principally focused on engineering specifications. The initial stages of validation typically involve the development of the physical aspects of the sterilisation device first, so that the required temperature can be uniformly achieved. The aspects of relevance to sterilisation occur during the Performance Qualification (PQ). These can be divided into assessment of temperature and biological kill. The purpose of biovalidation is to confirm that the lethality expected from the process does not significantly deviate from what is expected.

7.6.1 Temperature

The most important aspects of temperature are that it is sufficiently high, held for the required time and that it is uniform throughout the load in the chamber and throughout the holding period. This is achieved by:

■ heat distribution qualification in the empty chamber (OQ);
■ heat distribution qualification in the loaded chamber (PQ), where the composition and means of containment and manner of packing of the load has been precisely defined;
■ heat penetration qualification into loads within the chamber (PQ).

For this, assessment thermocouples are used and temperature charts generated.

7.6.2 Biological kill

Whilst time and temperature can be put into an equation to show theoretical kill, lethality can only be shown by biovalidation using biological indicators. Biovalidation is typically performed under worst case conditions of temperature and time. Here the lowest permitted temperature and time parameters in the sterilisation specification are used.

Steam sterilisation cycles are validated using biological indicators. The pharmacopoeias require that the microorganism *Geobacillus stearothermophilus* is used, which is a Gram-positive thermophilic (heat loving) bacteria characterised by an inner cell membrane and a thick cell wall. The microorganism is described in more detail in Chapter 17.

Gs. stearothermophilus is used due to its resistance to heat. It is also the most appropriate microorganism to demonstrate the achievement of an SAL of 10^{-6} for an autoclave. The important concepts for the use of biological indicators are the thermal death point, which is the lowest temperature at which all microorganisms are killed and the thermal death time, which refers to the minimum amount of time required to kill microorganisms at a given temperature. The time for destruction of 90% of the microbial population is the decimal reduction time (or D-value, at a given temperature).

The SAL is a function of the numbers of contaminating microorganisms per item and their resistance (as measured by their resistance or D-values) to the particular sterilisation treatment. A minimum D_{121}-value of 1.5 minutes is specified in the pharmacopoeias for the use of *Gs. stearothermophilus* biological indicators.

The range of D_{121}-values acceptable to the pharmacopoeia, for spores of *Gs. stearothermophilus* allowed as BIs for use in steam sterilisation, is 1.5–3.0 minutes. Thus, with a D_{121} at 1.5 minutes, an overkill sterilisation or biovalidation specification delivering an F_0 of 15 minutes would deliver 10 log inactivations or if there were 10^6 spores per biological indicator, 1 chance in 1 million of finding a survivor on any one biological indicator, 1 chance in 1000 of finding a survivor in 10 biological indicators, 1 chance in 100 of finding a survivor in 100 biological indicators, and so on.

Most autoclave sterilisation specifications are determined empirically and are based on inactivating 10^6 spores of *Geobacillus stearothermophilus*, using 10–20 replicate biological indicators in biovalidation cycles. Failure to inactivate biological indicators is normally due to inadequate air removal rather than inadequate conditions of temperature and time. Sometimes failures of revalidation can be attributed to using biological indicators with much higher D-values than those used for the initial validation, where the biological indicators used for the revalidation have a far higher resistance compared with those used for the initial qualification. This could occur, for example, if the initial qualification was performed using a biological indicator with a D-value of 1.5 minutes and the requalification executed using a biological indicator with a D-value of 3 minutes.

For the sterilisation of equipment, biological indicators on carriers are used. Ideally the carrier is made from the same or similar material as the item being sterilised (biological indicators on paper carriers for wrapped loads, which are the most porous materials and equipment loads; biological indicators on stainless steel discs for items of equipment made of metal, and so on). For the assessment of aqueous loads (i.e. with the terminal sterilisation of a product), spores of *Gs. stearothermophilus* in aqueous suspension are the presentation of choice. These consist of special ampoules that are suspended in the product itself [14]. A check should be made, in case the drug product itself inactivates spores of *Gs. stearothermophilus*, in which case a justification should be made to use water as an alternative to product.

Acceptance criteria for biovalidation of steam sterilisation processes are usually defined along the following lines [15]:

- *n* BI's will be placed in the load at locations defined in a drawing; it is usual for biovalidation to be performed with an arbitrary number of BIs between 10 and 100. In defining locations, it is common to place one BI alongside each thermal probe, in order to be able to relate thermal data to biological data. The number of indicators used must be justified and documented.

- Each BI will contain at least 10^6 viable spores of *Gs. stearothermophilus*.

- The load will be exposed to a defined autoclave treatment (the validation cycle, established thermometrically).

- Biovalidation will be considered satisfactory if no viable spores are recovered from the BIs after 7–14 days incubation at 55–60°C in a suitable microbiological growth medium. The acceptance criterion should be for no survivors (i.e. each BI must exhibit no growth at the end of incubation).

The destruction of the replicate BIs with 10^6 spores and a D-value 1.5 minutes, demonstrates that the thermal lethality delivered is not less than an F_0 of 12 minutes. By adopting the standard pharmacopoeial cycle 121°C for 15 minutes, the desired level of microbial destruction is easily achieved with a degree of overkill (in this case by 3 minutes).

For validation using biological indicators, the use of an overkill approach is common. The concept is to determine a specification that assures a 10^{-6} SAL or better for the BI population. This normally involves achieving a $12\text{-}\log_{10}$ reduction of the biological indicator population. However, this cannot be demonstrated experimentally due to the difficulties in creating a suitably large enough microbial population (here 10^8 is generally the maximum) and due to method limitations leading to imprecisions with the method of detection. Therefore, 'sterilisation' is a theoretical concept and one which can only be expressed probabilistically.

One method to achieve 'overkill' is with the so-called 'half-cycle' approach. Whilst this approach has no scientific foundation, it achieves a theoretical overkill. Trial runs are set up with BIs in a production steriliser and an exposure time is determined where all the BIs are killed. The sterilisation specification is derived by doubling this time, hence the term 'half-cycle approach'.

An alternative method is the bioburden approach, which is based on having detailed knowledge not only of the numbers of microorganisms contaminating the product prior to sterilisation but also their resistances. Here several representative items require testing using validated methods that can robustly show microbial recovery. This approach is difficult, given that to measure resistance requires the use of a specialist device called a Biological Indicator Evaluation Resistometer (BIER) vessel, which most facilities do not possess. It is uncommon to see the bioburden approach used for steam sterilisation validation. It is, nonetheless, used for gaseous sterilisation and for irradiation as the pertinent chapters in this book explain.

7.6.3 Requalification

Once validated, the requalification of steam sterilisation is usually undertaken at annual intervals or where significant changes to established loads are proposed [16]. This is because changes can occur with autoclaves, therefore the purpose of requalification is to determine if any unforeseen change has arisen that might affect the sterility assurance provided to the items being sterilised. It is important for requalification that the numbers, resistances and substrates for the BIs closely similar to those used in the initial validation.

Occasionally the requalification of biovalidation results in a failure. The reason for this could be related to the BI, in terms of the set used being of greater resistance than those used for the initial validation, mishandling of the BIs leading to cross-contamination, the composition of the load and its arrangement, or to something related to the function of the engineering of the autoclave, such as air remaining in the load or poor-quality steam being used [17]. All failures must be investigated and the steriliser should not be used until the root cause has been determined and successful sterilisation cycles achieved.

7.7 In-use evaluation

Autoclaves should be assessed each working day using the Bowie–Dick test, carried out before the first processed load. This test is used to detect air leaks and inadequate air removal, and consists of folded 100% cotton surgical towels that are clean and preconditioned, or a commercial alternative test kit. A Bowie–Dick-type test sheet should be placed in the centre of the pack. The test pack should be placed horizontally in the front and bottom section of the steriliser rack, near the door and over the drain, in an otherwise empty chamber and the steriliser then run. Air that is not removed from the chamber will interfere with steam contact and will lead to cycle failure, as discussed above [18].

Steriliser vacuum performance is acceptable if the sheet inside the test pack shows a uniform colour change. Entrapped air will cause a spot to appear on the test sheet, due to the inability of the steam to reach the chemical indicator. If the steriliser fails the Bowie–Dick test, the steriliser must not be used until it is inspected by the steriliser engineers and subsequently passes the test [19].

In addition, steam sterilisers are monitored for operational parameters using a printout. The user must assess the time, temperature and pressure for each cycle.

7.8 Flash sterilisation

Flash sterilisation is a modification of conventional steam sterilisation, either gravity, pre-vacuum or steam-flush pressure-pulse, in which the flashed item is placed in an open tray or in a specially designed, covered, rigid container to allow for rapid penetration of steam [20]. The method is not common to the biopharmaceutical industry due to the lack of biological indicators to monitor performance, the absence of protective packaging following sterilisation, and the risk of contamination of processed items during transportation. In short, it is not recommended.

7.9 Advantages and disadvantages of steam sterilisation

As with the other methods of sterilisation discussed within this book, steam sterilisation carries with it advantages and disadvantages. The primary advantages, provided the material or product can be subjected to the sterilisation process, are that steam sterilisation is non-toxic, inexpensive, rapidly microbiocidal, sporicidal and it works by rapidly heating and penetrating the load [21]. Penetration confers an important advantage compared with other sterilisation processes, some of which have poor penetrative ability or none at all. Like all sterilisation processes, steam sterilisation has some deleterious effects on some materials, including corrosion and combustion of lubricants, and changes to the shapes and increased hardening time with certain materials [22].

7.10 Conclusion

This chapter has examined steam sterilisation, moist heat in the form of saturated steam under pressure. Whilst steam sterilisation remains the most widely used method of sterilisation it is also prone to operational issues, often relating to the engineering design of the steriliser. The chapter has emphasised the concerns of time and temperature for achieving sterilisation and the risks surrounding air remaining in the autoclave load.

The importance of biovalidiation and the use of biological indicators has been discussed in detail. Regulatory authorities place considerable weight upon the regular and successful use of biological indicators and a robust validation study is often taken as the main indicator of sterility assurance. Within the biopharmaceutical and pharmaceutical sectors, considerable investment should be put into the design and execution of biovalidation studies.

7.11 References

1. EMEA (1998), *Note for Guidance on Development Pharmaceutics*, Brussels: European Agency for the Evaluation of Medicinal Products.
2. Akers, J.E. (1992), 'PDA response: FDA proposal to amend cGMP's entitles: Use of aseptic processing and terminal sterilization in the preparation of sterile pharmaceuticals for human and veterinary use', *PDA Journal of Parenteral Science and Technology*, 46: 65–8.
3. Lemieux, P. (2006), 'Destruction of spores on building decontamination residue in a commercial autoclave', *Applied and Environmental Microbiology*, 72(12): 7687–93.
4. Fuerst, R. (1983), *Forbisher's and Fuerst's Microbiology in Health and Disease*, Philadelphia, PA: W.B. Saunders & Co.
5. Agalloco, J. (2000), 'Steam sterilisation and steam quality. Commentary', *PDA Journal of Pharmaceutical Science and Technology*, 54(1): 59–62.
6. Association for the Advancement of Medical Instrumentation (2002), 'Steam sterilization and sterility assurance in healthcare facilities', Arlington, VA: ANSI/AAMI ST46:2000.

7. Cole, S.A. (2006), 'Steam sterilisation of filtration systems: practical considerations for in-line operation', *European Journal of Parenteral and Pharmaceutical Sciences*, 11(1): 15–22.

8. McClure, H. (1988), 'Sterilization in place: How to sterilize liquid filling equipment at point of contact', *Pharmaceutical Engineering*, 8: 14–17.

9. Kovary, S.J., Agalloco, J.P. and Gordon, B.M. (1983)' 'Validation of the steam-in-place sterilisation of disc filters housings and membranes', *Journal of Parenteral Science and Technology*, 37(2): 55–64.

10. Shuttleworth, K. (2000), 'The application of steam quality test limits', *European Journal of Parenteral and Pharmaceutical Sciences*, 5(4): 109–14.

11. Bruch, C.W. (1983), 'Biological indicators and degrees (probabilities) of sterilisation', *Developments in Industrial Microbiology*, 14: 3–16.

12. Enzinger, R.M. (1990), 'Sterility Assurance from post-filling heat treatment', *PDA Journal of Parenteral Science and Technology*, 44: 294–5.

13. Halls, N.A. (1994), *Achieving Sterility in Medical and Pharmaceutical Products*, New York: Marcel Dekker, Inc.

14. Halls, N.A. (1998), 'Resistance "creep" of biological indicators', in: Morrissey, R.F. and Kowalski, J.B. (eds), *Sterilisation of Medical Products*, vol. VII, Champlain, New York: Polysciences Publications Inc.

15. Brewer, J.H. and Briggs Phillips, G. (1968), 'Proper use of biological indicators in sterilisation', *Bulletin of the Parenteral Drug Association*, 22: 157–69.

16. Caputo, R.A. and Mascoli, C.C. (1980), 'The design and use of biological indicators for sterilisation-cycle validation', *Medical Device and Diagnostic Industry*, August: 23–43.

17. Allison, D.G., Gilbert, P. and Halls, N.A. (2001), 'Biological indicators: friends or foes?' *European Journal of Parenteral Sciences*, 6(4): 131–4.

18. Association for the Advancement of Medical Instrumentation (2006), 'Comprehensive guide to steam sterilization and sterility assurance in health care facilities', Arlington, VA: ANSI/AAMI ST79.

19. Association for the Advancement of Medical Instrumentation (2003), Technical Information Report on process challenge devices/test packs for use in healthcare facilities.

20. Rutala, W.A. (1991), 'Disinfection and flash sterilization in the operating room', *Journal of Ophthalmic Nursing and Technology*, 10: 106–15.

21. Adler, S., Scherrer, M. and Daschner, F.D. (1998), 'Costs of low-temperature plasma sterilization compared with other sterilization methods', *Journal of Hospital Infection*, 40: 125–34

22. Bucx, M.J., Veldman, D.J., Beenhakker, M.M. and Koster, R. (2000), 'The effect of steam sterilization at 134 degrees C on light intensity provided by fibrelight Macintoch laryngoscopes', *Anaesthesia*, 55: 185–6.

8

Gaseous sterilisation

DOI: 10.1533/9781908818638.111

Abstract: Gaseous sterilisation, as distinct from vapour sterilisation, is a common method for the sterilisation of medical devices. The ability to alter different process parameters allows the methods of gas sterilisation to be adapted for different types of devices, which confers advantages over steam sterilisation and radiation methods. The most common method of gas sterilisation is ethylene oxide (EO). This chapter outlines the application of EO, describes the way that it destroys microorganisms, and examines the important aspects required for developing, validating and operating sterilisation cycles. It also looks at two other types of gaseous sterilisation, ozone and chlorine dioxide gas. With ozone, the emphasis is upon the main application within the pharmaceutical industry, which is the sanitisation of pharmaceutical grade water systems. Chlorine dioxide gas is an underdeveloped technology and the description in this chapter, whilst capturing the pertinent points, is relatively brief.

Key words: gaseous sterilisation, ethylene oxide, ozone, chlorine dioxide, sterilisation, sterility assurance level, medical devices, plastic disposables, pharmaceuticals, microorganisms, biological indicators.

8.1 Introduction

There are different types of gaseous sterilisation. Sterilising gases include formaldehyde, ethylene oxide (EO), propylene oxide, ozone, peracetic acid, vapour hydrogen peroxide and chlorine dioxide [1]. Most common to sterile manufacturing is EO, which is used to sterilise many plastics, and vapour hydrogen peroxide, which is used to decontaminate barrier systems (i.e. isolators). Vapour sterilisation is addressed in a separate chapter. Gaseous sterilisation is distinct from vapour sterilisation because with gas, the condensation of the agent, is not a consideration in the execution of these processes.[1]

Gaseous sterilants are effective surface sterilising agents, in that they will sterilise the outside of a device, or the primary packaging in which the device is held [2]. Unlike other forms of sterilisation such as radiation or heat, the agent does not normally penetrate as well into the item being sterilised. The key parameters affecting the effectivity of gas sterilisation are active concentration, temperature, duration of exposure and relative humidity [3].

Aside from steam (moist heat) sterilisation, EO sterilisation is the most widely used method of sterilisation in the medical device and biopharmaceutical sectors. EO is commonly selected for objects sensitive to temperatures greater than 60 °C and/or to radiation. Due to its ubiquity, this chapter focuses foremost upon EO; with reference made to chlorine dioxide and ozone. In the past, other gaseous agents have been used, such as glutaraldehyde and formaldehyde. Due to the toxicological concerns associated with such agents, they are no longer used.

8.2 Applications

Materials that are processed using gaseous forms of sterilisation include plastics, optics and electrics. Of these materials, the processing of medical devices represents a substantial volume of the types of items sterilised. As with any sterilisation method, it is important to assess whether the process will be effective and the material to be sterilised will be compatible to the process. Before a gaseous sterilisation procedure is commenced, the following must be considered:

- product definition, in terms of physical, chemical, microbial and pharmacological properties, where appropriate;
- specifications for raw materials and components;
- determination of required Sterility Assurance Level (SAL) based on the use of the items being treated;
- compatibility of the process with the items to be treated;
- determination of acceptable limits of the major residues after gaseous sterilisation procedures;

- validation of analytical methods used with adequate calibration and qualification of measuring equipment, repeated enough times to assure reliable and meaningful results.

8.3 Ethylene oxide

Ethylene oxide (C_2H_4O), sometimes called oxirane, is an organic alkylating agent,[2] which functions as a very potent and highly penetrating gas [4]. It functions as a so-called 'cold sterilant', in contrast to methods of sterilisation by heat. As an industrial sterilant, EO is effective when sterilising paper, cloth and most types of plastics. It is compatible with most materials, even when repeatedly applied. EO is most commonly applied to medical devices and its use has increased with the growth of single-use sterile disposable materials, although not to the extent as with gamma radiation.

EO is capable of destroying most viruses, bacteria and fungi, including bacterial spores. The alkylating properties of EO provide it with its microcidal properties. These properties are primarily tertiary nitrogen groups and phosphoric acid esters of nucleic acid moieties. In functioning as a sterilant, EO does not require metabolic activation [5]. It reacts with protoplasm and DNA, causing the clotting of proteins, and deactivation of enzymes and other biologically important components of a living organism. The disinfectant effect of EO is similar to that of sterilisation by heat. In addition to DNA disruption, EO prevents normal cellular metabolism and ability to reproduce, which renders affected microorganisms non-viable [6].

The relationships of reaction temperature and concentration of gaseous EO to the time required for inactivation of bacterial spores is relatively complex, for the thermochemical death time does not always behave logarithmically, as in the case of death kinetics relating to moist heat sterilisation [7]. The microcidal effectiveness of EO is typically assessed using spores of the bacterium *Bacillus atrophaeus*, formerly described as *Bacillus subtilis var niger* [8,9]. Microbial kill is more effective on porous materials, such as paper and cloth, than on hard non-porous objects such as glass, metal and plastics.

The most common method of producing EO is by the direct oxidation of ethylene, a process first developed by the chemical company, Union Carbide. Validation of processes is normally undertaken to ISO 11135-1 [10] (this is examined below), with the critical attributes being the sterilising parameters of gas concentration, time of exposure, temperature of reaction, moisture, barriers to gas penetration and the degree of microbial resistance to the process.

An important concern when using EO is the presence of residuals, ethylene glycol and ethylene chlorohydrin, which can remain as toxic substances in the sterilised item. Ethylene chlorohydrin appears when chloride ions are present, and ethylene glycol is formed by an EO reaction with water [11].

Companies undertaking sterilisation using gas should have in place a policy and specification for acceptable residue levels, which are typically 1 mcg/mL or g for EO and 50 mcg/mL or g for ethylene chlorohydrin (ECH), as set out in ISO 10993-7 [12]. This standard specifies allowable limits for residual EO and ECH in individual EO sterilised medical devices, which have patient contact. The standard also addresses procedures for the measurement of EO and ECH, and methods for determining compliance so that devices may be released. The standard additionally categorises products based on the examination of toxicological risk of the residue to the patient, according to the length of the time the patient is likely to be exposed to the device [13].

8.3.1 *The ethylene oxide process*

The EO sterilisation process must consistently assure that all critical process parameters are delivered within the load, to a degree that assures the required SAL is achieved in a way that does not cause any deleterious effect on product or its sterile barrier package.

The two most common EO sterilisation methods are the gas chamber method and the micro-dose method. The former involves placing the items to be sterilised into a chamber and then flooding the chamber with a combination of EO and other gases used as dilutants, usually chlorofluorocarbons or carbon dioxide, which function as inert carrier gases. During this process, the time and temperature are controlled. In many countries, the use of chlorofluorocarbons is banned due to the environmental impact.

The gas chamber method requires a large chamber and uses a large quantity of EO. These results can create storage problems, and the operation of strict health and safety provisions to minimise operator exposure risks. Due to the carcinogenic properties of EO, the US OHSA (Occupational Safety and Health Administration) has set the permissible exposure limit (PEL) at 1 ppm, calculated as an 8-hour time weighted average.

Published by Woodhead Publishing Limited, 2013

The alternative method is the micro-dose sterilisation method. This method uses a specially designed bag, which eliminates the requirement to flood a larger chamber with EO. This method is also known as gas diffusion sterilisation, or bag sterilisation. The advantage of this method over the gas chamber method is that it minimises the amount of gas used; although the method cannot be used to process large quantities of product.

The effectiveness of the EO sterilisation cycle is dependent upon the following:

- chamber temperature;
- relative humidity;
- time of exposure;
- pressure/vacuum;
- concentration of the gas.

There is a proportional relationship with some of these variables, most particularly when the concentration for the EO increases, and within certain limits, the exposure time can be decreased [14]. Thus, first-order kinetics is followed [15].

The need to control these variables makes the process relatively complicated and seemingly more complicated than irradiation. Given that temperature is the most straightforward variable to measure and monitor, it is often used as the indicator of the worst-case location within the loaded steriliser, due to its complex relationship with microbial kill [16].

The physical and chemical nature of the environment is important, particularly humidity, as EO is more effective at achieving microbial kill under dry conditions [17]. EO treatment is generally carried out between 30 °C and 60 °C with relative humidity above 30% and a gas concentration between 200 and 800 mg/l. A sterilisation cycle lasts for at least 3 hours, and often for longer, depending upon the degree of aeration required, as discussed below.

The sterilisation cycle consists of:

- a preconditioning phase, which is the treatment of the product prior to the sterilisation cycle to attain a predetermined temperature and relative humidity throughout the load;
- the actual sterilisation run, which is the exposure to EO in a sealed chamber. The key step here is the gas time, which is the time elapsed from the start of EO injection into the sterilisation chamber until the desired gas concentration is attained;

- the removal of EO;
- a post-sterilisation aeration period.

The objective of the aeration period is to remove toxic residues, such as EO residues and by-products, such as ethylene glycol (formed out of EO and ambient humidity) and ethylene chlorohydrine (formed out of EO and materials containing chlorine, i.e. PVC, a common component of many plastics).

For aeration, there are different aeration technologies available, such as pulsed vacuum and heat addition, steam addition and removal, as well as combinations of different gases and pressure set points. Novel developments include microwave desorption. With each technology, sufficient time is required to ensure good efficacy and to aerate the devices, thus the EO cycle can be as long as 15 hours, although with modern processing equipment many cycles are far shorter. After the aeration stage, the cycle is complete and the load may be removed from the chamber.

Before undertaking an EO sterilisation study, the suitability of the material to the process must be considered. This includes considering the following points:

- the chemical nature of the components of the product;
- the physical nature of the product, such as long and/or narrow lumens that will represent barriers to gas permeation;
- the density of the materials through which gas must permeate;
- the nature of the primary and secondary packaging;
- whether there are dead air spaces within the package and within the load.

When running the sterilisation cycle, the following parameters must be controlled and recorded, with reference to validated cycle parameters:

- maximum permissible loading time;
- initial vacuum level and time taken to achieve it;
- holding time under vacuum, when used;
- steam addition, pressure, temperature or time, when used;
- steam holding time;
- gas injection, specifying pressure rise and time to achieve it;
- gas-hold time (minimum);
- gas concentration in chamber;

- weight of EO used;
- chamber temperature (minimum and maximum) during entire cycle;
- details of air washing at the end of the cycle;
- relative humidity.

8.3.2 Validation of ethylene oxide sterilisation cycles

When using gaseous systems, the initial validation is of great importance, as it provides assurance against the possibility of non-sterility. When preparing validation reports, key parameters should be established including temperature, relative humidity and gas concentration [18].

There are three microbiological approaches for process validation:

1. overkill method;
2. combined biologic indicator/bioburden method; and
3. bioburden method.

Of these, the overkill approach is the most robust and involves the use of biological indicators (*Bacillus atrophaeus*) with a defined spore population and D-value [19].

Validation begins with assessing the material in the steriliser and measuring physical variables. This is to establish the worst-case location or locations, and temperature fluctuations are commonly taken for this measure. Once the worst-case location(s) is identified for a given sterilisation cycle, validation studies are conducted with the goal of inactivating a known concentration of the biological indicator microorganisms in the worst-case location, using a specific loading pattern with a specific EO cycle with each variable defined and controlled.

Cycle lethality determination can be obtained from the half-cycle method, which consists of determining the minimum time of exposure at which there are no survivors from tested biological indicators.[3] According to this method, at least a 6-log reduction in population of microorganisms must be obtained for each biological indicator in the half cycle. Using the same process parameters, except exposure time, the full sterilisation cycle theoretically achieves at least a 12-log reduction by doubling the half-cycle time [20].

The validation of gaseous sterilisation procedures includes an assessment of:

- product bioburden, an assessment of 10 items from a minimum of 3 production lots;

- manufacturing area environment, to ensure that the clean environment in which the product is manufactured does not pose a contamination risk to the product;

- determination of time and humidity in the preconditioning area;

- determination of temperature, pressure, time and humidity in the chamber;

- ventilation of load after sterilisation;

- loading patterns;

- biological indicator survival;

- vendor certification, if the gaseous sterilisation treatment is carried out by an external contractor.

For initial validation, three cycles should be run for each test.

The most important aspect of the validation is the microbiological assessment. Here, microbiological qualification studies must be carried out under cycle conditions equivalent to, or marginally inferior to, the minimum acceptable conditions on a production cycle. Ideally, the studies should be carried out at or below the minimum acceptable relative humidity, gas concentration and temperature.

The microbiological assessment involves the use of biological indicators.[4] The pharmacopoeia recommended biological indicator *Bacillus atrophaeus*, with a concentration, according to the USP, of 1×10^6 spores. Significant spore survival results will indicate the need to increase the cycle lethality parameters.

Biological indicators should be evenly distributed in the load and should also include those locations where sterilisation conditions are assumed most difficult to achieve. The number of biological indicators used is typically 20 (or more) for chambers up to 5000 litres of usable chamber volume, and increasing in number thereafter for larger chambers. For the validation, the product should be packaged as it will normally be presented to the steriliser.

When assessing the effectiveness of biological indictor kill, this is either with a reference load, where the lethality of the cycle is shown by construction of a survivor curve, or alternatively by determining the minimum exposure time at which there are no survivors; and, once calculated, setting the routine cycle exposure time to at least double this time.

Published by Woodhead Publishing Limited, 2013

To demonstrate acceptability, it is common to run triplicate sub-lethal cycles at two different sub-lethal cycle times. The times of the sub-lethal cycles should be chosen so as to expect survival of 30% to 80% of the biological indicators (i.e. to achieve positive tests). The minimum acceptable number of cycles at each time point should be three.

In addition to using a biological challenge, it is also important to analyse gas concentration at periodic intervals during the distribution studies.

Requalification should be considered when a significant change occurs. Furthermore, an annual documented review of all manufacturing and sterilisation processes should be performed to demonstrate that nothing has changed that will affect the performance of the validated sterilisation process. In addition to the documentation review, a frequency must be set for a full physical and biological validation study. This is often carried out annually. This revalidation should consist of (at a minimum) bioburden testing, one sub-lethal cycle, one half-cycle and EO residual testing. If any significant changes are made in the product, packaging or manufacturing, a complete revalidation is required.

8.3.3 Routine operations

Once an EO sterilisation cycle has been validated, it should be operated at the set cycle parameters based on the worst-case conditions. This involves the assessment of critical parameters relating to time, temperature and humidity, and the verification of the gas concentration, which can be assessed by weight or according to Ideal Gas Law ($PV = RT$, where P = pressure, V = volume, T = temperature, and R = a constant; which in effect means that pressure, temperature and gas concentration cannot be controlled independently of one another).

The standard method of assessing whether an EO cycle has been successful, and for releasing a batch, is through parametric release. Parametric release relies solely on the recording and evaluation of the process parameters, because the equipment potentialities are enough to evaluate the impact of process parameters on microbiologic inactivation.

In some cases, biological release takes place whereby biological indicators are used in each run. Here biological indicators composed of the microorganism *Bacillus atrophaeus* are placed throughout the steriliser load and subjected to the sterilisation process. After the process, the biological indicators are removed from the load and placed into a special growth medium and subjected to ideal growth conditions for seven days. This latter approach is less common and provides little additional information, for if the cycles have been validated and shown to operate consistently, then it is uncertain what this extra information provides. Most operators of EO use parametric release.

Where parametric release is used, for conventional release compliance, the parameters that should be directly measured are the time of each phase, the pressure throughout the process and the headspace temperature. The remaining two critical parameters, humidity and EO concentration, can be quantified indirectly by thermodynamic calculation based on pressure rise and temperature.

It is also important to periodically assess the bioburden of the products to be sterilised. Such an assessment is undertaken as part of initial validation and then typically quarterly. Many factors can affect product bioburden, among which are changes in materials, vendors, manufacturing personnel, procedures or equipment, water systems used in manufacturing and seasonal changes [21].

The bioburden assessment should involve the testing of 10 items from a minimum of 3 production lots. Limits should be set, with reference to the initial validation studies and to any microorganisms recovered. The acceptance criteria, based on a risk assessment, should involve consideration of whether the routinely screened bioburden would present a significant challenge to the validated cycle parameters. In practice it is unlikely that 'natural' bioburden of the product would present a significant challenge, due to the type of biological indicators used (as outlined above), the successful sterilisation of which indicates considerable overkill.

The method selected for the routine determination of product bioburden levels must be validated to insure that it is effective in recovering microorganisms from the product and allows for adequate growth of the recovered microorganisms.

In addition to the assessment of the bioburden of the product, a sterility test should be conducted upon items of the product post-sterilisation. Again, this is something to be assessed as part of initial qualification and as a periodic routine assessment. A scientifically sound sampling plan should be deployed to ensure that a significant portion of the test set is examined for sterility from representative samples throughout the sterilisation load. The sterility test requires validating for the particular product examined. This is undertaken through the tests for bacteriostasis and fungistasis, an assessment of the inhibition of microbial growth.

8.3.4 Advantages and disadvantages

As with each of the sterilisation methods examined throughout this book, gaseous sterilisation has some advantages and disadvantages. In terms of advantages, a gas like EO is highly penetrative and will pass through most types of barrier packaging. A further advantage is that objects sterilised can be subject to repeat sterilisation cycles without any damage to the item. This gives gaseous sterilisation an advantage over radiation, which can cause embrittlement, particularly for repeat cycles, and with steam, where repeat applications can cause material damage.

EO is also advantageous because it is more flexible in relation to the degree that the operational parameters can be varied, than either steam or radiation. In assessing the thermal or moisture sensitivity of the specific material, the parameters of the EO cycle can be adjusted to preserve the integrity of the device.

Furthermore, EO can be used to sterilise a wide range of materials. Steam and gamma irradiation sterilisation can cause polymer degradation and changes to the physical or mechanical properties of the product, which can be detrimental for intended performance of the product [22].

A major disadvantage with a gas like EO is its toxicity, and toxins must be removed through strict adherence to the aeration step during the end of the sterilisation cycle. The gas is also potentially harmful to people (it is mutagenic and explosive); thus the process requires strict observance of health and safety. A further disadvantage, if the wrong material is selected or if the validation has not been carefully planned out, is the presence of residues that will lead to the build up of toxicity or can alter the nature of any chemicals treated with the process. Although EO is foremost a surface sterilant, gas residues can enter products, depending upon the nature of the material and the primary packaging used.

EO can also be harmful to the environment if the process uses chlorofluorocarbons, for these chemicals, if present, are released into the atmosphere as a by-product of the gas chamber method.

8.4 Ozone

Ozone is a natural form of activated oxygen and is formed when oxygen is exposed to a high-energy field. It is a triatomic molecule (O_3), consisting of three oxygen atoms. Ozone is much less stable than oxygen (O_2), breaking down, with a half life of about half an hour in the lower atmosphere, into oxygen. Ozone occurs naturally in the atmosphere and is produced during lightning storms and continuously occurring in the stratosphere due to action of ultraviolet (UV) light.

As a sterilant, ozone is classed as an oxidising agent, which means that it breaks down into oxygen molecules and oxygen atoms, which have high oxidation potential. First, ozone acts on the microbial cell membrane and damages the membrane structure so as to cause metabolism disruption. Second, the ozone infiltrates the cell membrane and destroys lipoprotein and lipopolysaccharide, changes permeability and causes cytolysis and cell death. As well as being effective against prokaryotic organisms, ozone is an effective protozoan cysticide [23].

Ozone is used across a variety of industrial settings to sterilise water and air, as well as a disinfectant for surfaces. It is also used to treat certain processed foods. Ozone is an effective sterilant due to its ability to oxidise most organic matter. The high reactivity of ozone means that waste ozone can be destroyed by passing over a simple catalyst that converts it back to oxygen. This means that the sterilisation cycle time is relatively short. However, the application of ozone is unsuited to many applications and, in terms of occupational exposure, is considerably more toxic (~160 times) than EO. When undertaking sterilisation, careful monitoring of ozone levels is required.

Ozone is produced using different methods. The most commonly used instrument is an ozone generator, which uses the corona discharge method. Here a 'hot spark' is applied to air to create ozone. A feed gas containing oxygen passes through a high-voltage field between a pair of electrodes and a dielectric; the oxygen is converted into ozone, similar to the reaction caused by a lightning storm. This method is very effective; although it is expensive when applied to a pharmaceutical water system due to the large quantities of ozone that need to be generated; for the ozone needs to be passed through the entire water distribution system and regular cycles of ozonisation are required to prevent recontamination. In addition, with water systems, there can be corrosivity problems resulting from the formation of nitric acid, which is caused by the reaction of water vapour with nitrogen in the feed gas.

With pharmaceutical grade water systems, the preference is to create dissolved ozone electrolytically from the water itself. In this case, a strong potential is applied to a set of electrodes and either the water is split or dissolved oxygen is converted and ozone created as a dissolved substance. Ozone generators employ a light source that generates a narrow-band UV light to produce ozone with a concentration of about 0.5% or lower. More effective variants are vacuum-ultraviolet (VUV) ozone generators.

Published by Woodhead Publishing Limited, 2013

Alternative production methods are cold plasma, where pure oxygen gas is exposed to plasma created by dielectric barrier discharge and electrolytic ozone generation, which splits water molecules into different chemicals, including ozone.

The ability of ozone to sanitise water results from its strong oxidation capacity against planktonic microorganisms in the water. The contact time (or dwell time) needed for reduction of a microbial population depends on the type of organism, other reactants in the water and the ozone concentration. The contact time is defined as the residual ozone quantity in a storage tank or loop multiplied by the time the ozone is in contact with the water. Since ozone is an undesirable addition to point of use pharmaceutical water, it is typically eliminated using a UV light source produced by an absorption photometer, operating at a wavelength of 254 nm,[5] or by degassification, which destroys the ozone after the disinfection process is complete. Once ozone reduction has been completed, the water must be tested to show that ozone levels are below a predetermined specification. Several on-line instruments are available for this process, including flow cell devices.

Another application of ozone is with Clean-in-Place (CIP) systems. With such systems, ozone is used to sanitise pipe works. Care is required because dissolved ozone is aggressive on certain materials and has been known to destroy piping and seals.

The main advantage with ozone is its speed, particularly with eliminating microbiological activity in the water at relatively low doses [24]. One research study showed that 0.1 mg/L of ozone will destroy 60,000 colony-forming units (cfu) of the bacterium *Escherichia coli* in 1 minute; whereas the same dose of chlorine would take up to 400 hours to achieve the same level of microbial destruction [25]. A further advantage, particularly in comparison with EO, is that ozone can be used without the need for handling hazardous chemicals, for the ozone is generated within the steriliser from medical grade oxygen.

The primary disadvantage with ozone is that the gas is toxic and is a very unstable gas. It also requires relatively expensive and specialised equipment to be produced, making it impractical for most biopharmaceutical facilities to use, an exception being larger pharmaceutical facilities that have ozone generators linked into their water systems for sanitisation purposes [26]. Preparing ozone at a specialist contractor and shipping is impractical, because ozone cannot be stored and transported due to its half-life and rapid decay into diatomic oxygen. It should be ideally used within the first 10 minutes of production to assure its strength, thus ozone must be produced and used at source.

Furthermore, ozone can damage some types of material. Because it is a powerful oxidizing agent, it will harm polyamide membranes, ion exchange resins and many elastomers.

8.5 Chlorine dioxide gas

Chlorine compounds are a significant type of microbiocidal halogen, and chlorine is widely used as a sporicidal disinfectant and as a sterilant in liquid form [27]. When in gaseous form, chlorine is normally in the form of chlorine dioxide, where it is a powerful surface sterilant. However, it has a poor ability to penetrate.

Chlorine dioxide (ClO_2) gas is a single-electron, transfer-oxidizing agent, similar to liquid bleach [28]. This makes it a highly active oxidizing agent and can thereby destroy the cellular activity of proteins [29]. Its deleterious effect on bacterial endospores is believed to be directed primarily towards the cell membrane rather than DNA [30]. As a means of gaseous sterilisation, it is not as widely used as EO or ozone. Indeed it was not registered as a sterilant in the USA until the mid-1980s. Theoretically, chlorine dioxide gas has some advantages over ozone in terms of requiring a lower dosage and in having a higher solubility in water.

Chlorine dioxide has been used to successful sterilise medical devices, laboratory equipment and to decontaminate cleanrooms and clean zones [31]. There are some applications with barrier devices, including isolators, as an alternative to the more commonly used hydrogen peroxide vapour. The gas has also been listed by the US Environment Protection Agency (EPA) as a recommended decontaminant to deal with anthrax spores [32]. In the sterilisation cycle, chlorine dioxide processing is similar to other decontamination cycles that rely upon the control of humidity or moisture. A specific gas concentration must be determined to ensure sporicidal efficacy [33].

The gas is either generated by a mix of chlorine gas and sodium chlorite solution; or by chlorine gas and technical grade sodium chlorite flakes (i.e. flowing chlorine gas through sodium chlorite canisters). As applied to sterilisation cycles, the gas has a chlorine-like odour and a green-yellow colour, which enables it to be monitored with an UV spectrophotometer, which can help provide a degree of process control of the decontamination cycle from beginning to end.

The key factors affecting the efficacy of chlorine dioxide gas as a sterilant are:

Published by Woodhead Publishing Limited, 2013

- concentration (mg/l);
- contact time;
- purity;
- relative humidity (the gas works better at higher levels);
- surface compatibility (the gas is effective on stainless, paper and epoxy);
- if crevices are present on surfaces (the gas has spoor penetration here).

Chlorine dioxide is not stable enough to be generated, bottled and shipped, therefore, it must be generated on site as needed. It is a very unstable substance and when it comes in contact with sunlight, it decomposes. The gas is typically generated by using a method in which solid sodium chlorite contained in small plastic cartridges is exposed to a chlorine–nitrogen (<3%) gas mixture. The reaction produces pure chlorine dioxide in nitrogen [34].

The instability is the main disadvantage with chlorine dioxide gas. Furthermore, when producing chlorine dioxide sodium chlorite and chlorine gas, safety measures must be taken, including providing sufficient ventilation. As well as being toxic, chlorine dioxide gas is also explosive.

8.6 Summary

This chapter has presented an overview of the main types of gaseous sterilisation methods, with a focus upon EO due to the wider use of this type for the sterilisation of medical devices. The important aspects of cycle development, the important validation steps and the requirements for routine assessment have been outlined.

Two other forms of gaseous sterilisation, ozone and chlorine dioxide, were discussed. With these technologies, EO is more commonly applied to plastic medical devices and ozone to water systems. Chlorine dioxide has a lower usage and its future application is more likely to be with water systems and with barrier technology used in cleanrooms.

8.7 Notes

1. In relation to sterilisation, gases are more penetrating, more uniform in concentration and less subject to variations in temperature and relative humidity than vapours. In contrast, vapours have different concentrations in

each phase. Furthermore, the kill rates in the gas and liquid phase appear to be substantially different, reflecting the different concentrations and available water in each phase. Thus, conventionally, gas and vapour are considered to be separate sterilisation processes.

2. Alkylation is the transfer of an alkyl group from one molecule to another.

3. Alternative methods are the survivor curve method and the fraction-negative method. These methods provide more detail pertaining to lethality kinetics.

4. For D-values for biological indicators used to measure gaseous sterilisation, the agent concentration, relative humidity and temperature must be indicated. For example, D_{900} ppm, 75% rH, 30 °C.

5. Ultraviolet light at a wavelength of 254 nm and a dosage of 30,000 microwatt seconds per square centimetre also has microcidal properties.

8.8 References

1. Rutala, W.A., Gergen, M.F. and Weber, D.J. (1998), 'Comparative evaluation of the sporicidal activity of new low-temperature sterilisation technologies: Ethylene oxide, 2 plasma sterilisation systems, and liquid peracetic acid', *American Journal of Infection Control*, 26: 393–8.

2. Bruch, C.W. (1961), 'Gaseous sterilisation', *Annual Review of Microbiology*, 15: 245–62.

3. Christensen, E.A. and Kristensen, H. (1991), 'Gaseous sterilisation', in: Russell, A.D., Hugo, W.B. and Ayliffe, G.A.J. (eds), *Principles and Practice of Disinfection, Preservation and Sterilisation*, 2nd edition, Oxford: Blackwell Scientific Publications Ltd, pp. 557–72.

4. McKetta, J.J. and Cunningham, W.A. (1984), *Encyclopaedia of Chemical Processing and Design*, Boca Raton, FL: CRC Press, p. 309.

5. Rutala, W.A. and Weber, D.J. (1999), 'Infection control: the role of disinfection and sterilisation', *Journal of Hospital Infection*, 43(Suppl): S43–55.

6. Plug, I.J., Holcomb, R.G. and Gomez, M.M. (2001), 'Thermal destruction of microorganisms', in: Block, S.S. (ed.), *Disinfection, Sterilisation, and Preservation*, Philadelphia: Lippincott, Williams & Wilkins, pp. 79–129.

7. Ernst, R.R. and Shull, J.J. (1962), 'Ethylene oxide gaseous sterilisation', *Applied Microbiology*, 10(4): 337–41.

8. Fritze, D. and Rudiger, P. (2001), 'Reclassification of bioindicator strains *Bacillus subtilis* DSM 675 and *Bacillus subtilis* DSM 2277 as *Bacillus atropaeus*', *International Journal of Systematic and Evolutionary Microbiology*, 51: 35–7.

9. Kereluk, K., Gammon, R.A. and Lloyd, R.S. (1970), 'Microbiological aspects of ethylene oxide sterilisation. Part II: Microbial resistance to ethylene oxide', *Applied and Environmental Microbiology*, 19(1): 152–6.

10. ISO 11135 (2007), 'Sterilisation of health care products – Ethylene oxide – Part 1: Requirements for development, validation and routine control of a sterilisation process for medical devices', Geneva: International Standards Organisation.

11. Buben, I., Melichercikova, V., Novotna, N. and Svitakova, R. (1999), 'Problems associated with sterilisation using ethylene oxide: Residues in treated materials', *Central European Journal of Public Health*, 4: 197–202.

12. ISO 10993 (2008), 'Biological evaluation of medical devices – Part VII: Ethylene oxide sterilisation residuals', Geneva: International Standards Organisation.

13. Centola, D.T., Ayoub, K.I., Lao, N.T., Lu, H.T.C. and Page, B.F.J. (2001), 'Variables affecting simulated use determination of residual ethylene oxide in medical devices', *Journal of the Association of Official Analytical Chemists International*, 84: 512–8.

14. Strain, P. and Young, W.T. (2004), 'Ethylene-oxide sterilisation aids speed to market – process developments reduce process times', *Medical Device Technology*, 15: 18–9.

15. Mosley, G.A., Gillis, J.R. and Whitbourne, J.E. (2002), 'Calculating equivalent time for use in determining the lethality of EO sterilisation processes', *Medical Device and Diagnostic Industry*, February: 101–5.

16. Oxborrow, G.S., Placencia, A.M. and Danielson, J.W. (1983), 'Effects of temperature and relative humidity on biological indicators used for ethylene oxide sterilisation', *Applied and Environmental Microbiology*, 45: 546–9.

17. Gilbert, G.L., Gambill, V.M., Spiner, D.R., Hoffman, R.K. and Phillips, C.R. (1964), 'Effect of moisture on ethylene oxide sterilisation', *Applied and Environmental Microbiology*, 12(6): 496–503.

18. Bayliss, C.E. and Waites, W.M. (1979) 'The combined effect of hydrogen peroxide and ultraviolet radiation on bacterial spores', *Journal of Applied Bacteriology*, 47: 263–9.

19. Heider, D., Gomann, J., Junghann, B.U. and Kaiser, U. (2002), 'Kill kinetics study of *Bacillus subtilis* spores in ethylene oxide sterilisation processes', *Zentral Sterilization*, 10: 158–67.

20. Sintani, H., Tahata, T., Hatakeyama, K., Takahashi, M., Ishii, K. and Hayashi, H. (1995), 'Comparison of the D10-value accuracy by the Limited Spearman-Karber Procedure (LSKP), the Stumbo-Murphy-Cochran Procedure (SMCP), and the Survival-Curve Method (EN), *Biomedical Instrumentation and Technology*, 29: 113–25.

21. Mosley, G.A. and Houghtling, C.W. (2005), 'Interpreting and understanding microbial data in validation of ethylene oxide sterilisation processes', *Biomedical Instrumentation and Technology*, 39: 466–82.

22. Gorna, K. and Gogolewski, S. (2003), 'The effect of g radiation on molecular stability and mechanical properties of biodegradable polyurethanes for medical applications', *Polymer Degradation Stability*, 79: 465–74.

23. Korich, D.G., Mead, J.R., Madore, M.S., Sinclair, N.A. and Sterling, C.R. (1990), 'Effects of ozone, chlorine dioxide, chlorine and monochloramine on *Cryptosporidium parvum oocyst* viability', *Applied and Environmental Microbiology*, 56: 1423–8.

24. IPSE (2001), ISPE Baseline Series, vol. 4, *Water and Steam Systems*, Appendix to 1st edition, section 11.8.6.2: Comparisons with chlorine, Florida: International Society for Pharmaceutical Engineering, p. 59.

25. Fetner, R.H. and Ingols, R.S. (1956), 'A comparison of the bactericidal activity of ozone and chlorine against *Escherichia coli* at 1°', *Journal of General Microbiology*, 15: 381–5.

26. Folchetti, N. (ed.) (2003), *Chemistry: The Central Science*, 9th edition, London: Pearson Education, pp. 882–3.

27. Bloomfield, S.F. (1996), 'Chlorine and iodine formulations', in: Ascenz, J.M. (ed.), *Handbook of Disinfectants and Antiseptics*, New York: Marcel Dekker, Inc, pp. 133–58.

28. Young, S.B. and Setlow, P. (2003), Mechanisms of killing *Bacillus subtilis* spores by hypochlorite and chlorine dioxide', *Journal of Applied Microbiology*, 95(1): 54–67.

29. Benarde, M.A., Snow, W.B., Olivieri, V.P. and Davidson, B. (1967), 'Kinetics and mechanism of bacterial disinfection by chlorine dioxide', *Applied Microbiology*, 15: 257–65.

30. Knapp, J. and Battisti, D. (2001), 'Chlorine dioxide', in: Block, S.S. (ed.), *Disinfection, Sterilisation, and Preservation*. Philadelphia: Lippincott, Williams & Wilkins, pp. 215–28.

31. Kowalski, J.B. (1998), 'Sterilisation of medical devices, pharmaceutical components, and barrier isolator systems with gaseous chlorine dioxide,' in: *Sterilisation of Medical Products*, Morrissey, R.F. and Kowalski, J.B. (eds), New York: Polyscience Publications, pp. 313–23.

32. Haas, C.N. (2001), 'Decontamination using chlorine dioxide', in: *Hearings on the Decontamination of Anthrax and other Biological Agents*, Committee on Science, United States House of Representatives. Available from: *www. house.gov/ science/full/nov08/haas.htm*. (Accessed 2012.)

33. Knapp, J.E., Rosenblatt, D.H. and Rosenblatt, A.A. (1986), 'Chlorine dioxide as a gaseous sterilant', *Medical Device and Diagnostic Industry*, 8: 48–50.

34. Jeng, D.K. and Woodworth, A.G. (1990), 'Chlorine dioxide gas sterilisation under square-wave conditions', *Applied and Environmental Microbiology*, 56(1): 514–19.

Published by Woodhead Publishing Limited, 2013

9

Hydrogen peroxide vapour sterilisation

DOI: 10.1533/9781908818638.129

Abstract: This chapter examines the use of hydrogen peroxide gas for the decontamination of cleanrooms and isolators. Hydrogen peroxide vapour is the method of choice for isolators. The gas is relatively low cost and it has efficient surface sterilisation properties and its microbiocidal properties are outlined. The main part of the chapter focuses on the development of decontamination cycles using hydrogen peroxide vapour. Cycle development involves the biological indicators prepared using the bacterium *Geobacillus stearothermophilus*. Strategies for using bioindicators are considered and actions to be taken for occurrences of failure are addressed.

Key words: hydrogen peroxide, VHP, HPV, isolator, cleanroom, *Geobacillus stearothermophilus*, biological indicator, steriliant.

9.1 Introduction

Hydrogen peroxide vapour is a gaseous form of hydrogen peroxide (H_2O_2). It is used as a low-temperature antimicrobial gas for the decontamination of enclosed and sealed areas such as laboratory workstations, isolators, cleanrooms and aircraft interiors [1]. Within the biopharmaceutical and healthcare sectors, the primary use is with isolators [2]. Decontamination in isolators with vaporised H_2O_2 has a number of advantages, such as the fact that the degradation products (water and oxygen) are non-toxic and can be removed easily after decontamination. Furthermore, there is a high degree of compatibility of H_2O_2 with materials commonly used in process areas, and the agent is of relatively low cost [3].

H_2O_2, in the gaseous state, is the prominent gaseous sterilant where the requirement is to sterilise or sanitise surfaces rather than to penetrate. This is an important point, as the gaseous agent will not penetrate most surfaces and it cannot sanitise the material held within. For effective sanitisation, the physical properties of the item being sterilised must be relatively smooth, impervious to moisture, and be of a shape that permits all surfaces to be exposed to the sterilant [4]. Alternatives to H_2O_2 are peracetic acid, although is now less commonly used, and chlorine dioxide gas, which is little developed [5].

There is more than one method by which H_2O_2 may be applied to surfaces and volumes, and the methods are often confused. The methods of application are:

■ *Aerosols* – Here a commercial system produces a fine mist (particle sizes between 8 and 10 microns) of 5% H_2O_2 in air, with <50 ppm silver ions, <50 ppm phosphoric acid, and <1 ppm Arabica gum as catalysts. Over time, the aerosols collapse, the H_2O_2 reacts, and then degrades to a safe state. There is little published validation of this method in hospital situations.

■ *Non-Condensing Vapour* – This is produced by a 4-step sequence: an enclosed volume is first dehumidified. Then 35% H_2O_2 is vaporised under controlled conditions of temperature, humidity and pressure, so there is no condensation. This state is maintained in the enclosure for a period of hours during which super lethal concentrations of H_2O_2 of several hundred ppm are maintained in air for disinfection. Finally, the enclosure is purged with air (catalytic aeration) so that the concentration of H_2O_2 is below the product exposure limit (as an indicator of safety).

Non-condensing vaporised H_2O_2 is referred to as VHP (which is trademarked) and as hydrogen peroxide vapour (HPV). H_2O_2 is a broad spectrum antimicrobial with virucidal, bactericidal, fungicidal and sporicidal activity. When used with barrier systems, HVP is a relatively rapid sterilisation technology [6]. HPV is normally supplied by a generator that delivers the vapour phase agent to an isolator body, transfer chamber or other enclosed device. The cycle has various stages, of which the most important is the maintenance of the required concentration of H_2O_2 during the biodecontamination process.

This chapter discusses the chemical composition of H_2O_2 vapour and discusses its use in the decontamination of isolators. Included within the discussion are the development of sanitisation cycles and the validation requirements using biological indicators (BI).

9.2 Chemical composition

H_2O_2 is the simplest type of peroxide, a compound with an oxygen–oxygen single bond [7]. It is a clear liquid, slightly more viscous than water and in dilute solution, appears colourless. The chemical is a strong oxidising agent, a substance that removes electrons from another reactant in a redox chemical reaction. Due to its oxidising properties, H_2O_2 is often used as a bleach to disinfect, or as a cleaning agent.

H_2O_2 is manufactured by the Riedl–Pfleiderer or anthraquinone process, which involves the auto-oxidation of a 2-alkyl anthrahydroquinone (or 2-alkyl-9,10-dihydroxyanthracene) to the corresponding 2-alkyl anthraquinone. This is achieved by bubbling compressed air through a solution of the derivatised anthracene, whereby the oxygen present in the air reacts with the labile hydrogen atoms (of the hydroxyl group), giving H_2O_2 and regenerating the anthraquinone [8]. Industrially, the manufacture is a straightforward process.

Flash vaporisation is the most common method of producing H_2O_2 gas for decontaminating enclosures for aseptic processing in the pharmaceutical industry. HVP is produced, using a generator, by the vaporisation of liquid H_2O_2 to give a mixture of HVP and water vapour [9]. Whilst the terms 'gas' and 'vapour' are used interchangeably in literature when describing HVP, it is more accurate to use the term 'vapour'. A gas is a single well-defined thermodynamic phase, whereas a vapour is a mixture of two phases, generally gas and liquid [10]. It is this point between the liquid and the gas phase that makes HVP effective as a sanitisation agent.

In practice, the concentration of HVP is maintained below a given condensation point, which is dependent on the area temperature. This has led it to be sometimes described as a 'dry' process. Its advantage over other gaseous sterilants is that it decomposes to water and oxygen, on contact with catalysts and in the environment on organic matter. These decomposed chemicals are relatively safe and so-called 'residue free' [11].

To produce HVP, the generators initially dehumidify the ambient air, then produce vapour H_2O_2 by passing aqueous H_2O_2 over a vaporiser, and circulate the vapour at a programmed concentration in the air, typically from 140 ppm to 1400 ppm. After the H_2O_2 vapour has circulated in the enclosed space for a pre-defined period of time, it is circulated back through the generator, where it is broken down into water and oxygen by a catalytic converter, until the concentration of gaseous H_2O_2 falls to a safe level (typically <1 ppm) [12].

9.3 Antimicrobial effectiveness

The broad spectrum efficacy of H_2O_2 vapour technology has been shown to be effective against a wide range of microorganisms, including bacteria, viruses, fungi, bacterial spores; as wells as parasite eggs [13]. The mode of action is due to direct interaction of the vapour with cellular components, including proteins. H_2O_2 produces both hydroxyl (HO*) and hydroperoxy (HOO*) radicals. Both components attack cell walls, and often destroy cells by causing them to collapse. As with most other disinfectants, bacterial spores are considered the most resistant organisms [14]. However, provided that contact is sufficient, the vapour is effective at deactivating endospores.

There are reported differences in the mode of action of H_2O_2 in the vaporised form and as a liquid, in terms of differences in microbial resistance [15]. For example, H_2O_2 vapour has been shown to break down microbial cell protein, including some protein-based toxins, while liquid H_2O_2 may possibly have a fixing reaction [16]. Whilst the vapour phase is a more effective agent, when applied to the biopharmaceutical sector HPV is used as a decontamination or sanitisation process, it cannot achieve sterilisation. With H_2O_2 vapour there are three major processing parameters that affect the inactivation of microorganisms, which are the gas concentration, the exposure time and the amount of saturation, a parameter influenced by the temperature and humidity level within the enclosure.

9.4 Barrier devices and isolators

Microbial contamination is of great concern within aseptic manufacture and with sterility testing [17]. A lower risk of product contamination can be achieved by isolating the people from the product. This is undertaken using Advanced Aseptic Processing (AAP) technologies [18], restricted access barrier systems (RABS), and isolators (these systems are discussed in greater detail in Chapter 14). Isolators provide a physical barrier, supported by unidirectional airflow (UDAF), which helps to ensure no airborne contamination can reach the product under normal operating conditions. In order to ensure that the levels of contamination within an isolator are kept to a minimum, isolators are normally operated under positive pressure and are subject to periodic decontamination [19].

Decontamination of isolators within the biopharmaceutical industry has evolved since the 1980s. Traditionally, formaldehyde was the gas of choice [20], but because of health and safety concerns it has been replaced by other gases, of which vaporised H_2O_2 is the most common method. As with other pharmaceutical equipment, the isolator system must be validated before it is used in any of the manufacturing process. The validation includes the development and verification of the sanitisation cycle (Figure 9.1).

H_2O_2 can also be used for the decontamination of cleanrooms, material pass-through hatches and hospital environments. Given the size of cleanrooms and the difficulty in achieving a complete and integral seal,

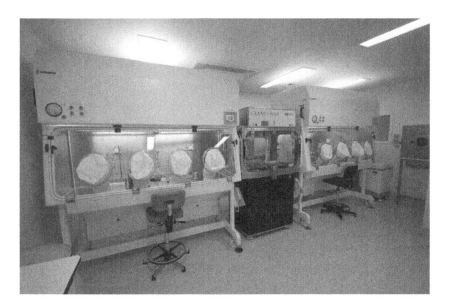

Figure 9.1 Sterility testing isolators connected to a gas generator

this can be a more complicated process than with barrier systems. However, when designed effectively, the vapour can fill the space in the room and, with adequate distribution is effective at working around corners in shadow areas and behind equipment and other obstructions [21].

9.5 HVP cycles

H_2O_2 vapour is used at different frequencies to decontaminate different types of areas. Isolators intended for aseptic processing are subjected to a decontamination process before start of the batch processing. For sterility testing isolators, the core isolator is sometimes subject to a lower frequency of sanitisation, although each sterility test load is sanitised each time; the appropriate frequency of the cycle is assessed through environmental monitoring. Cleanrooms are sanitised for specific events such as following maintenance.

It should be noted that gaseous disinfection is a final step that requires a necessary pre-cleaning step. All items entering the isolator should be sterilised or disinfected using a sporicidal disinfectant. This is because, as implied earlier, the H_2O_2 vapour can only sanitise the outermost layer of the items placed within the isolator. If there are high levels of soil, the vapour will not penetrate and the required level of sanitisation will not be achieved.

The generation and use of H_2O_2 vapour is carried out through an operational cycle. There are four key steps to the optimum H_2O_2 vapour disinfection process [22]:

1. vaporisation of liquid to small molecules (the gas phase delivery to target volume);

2. development of the gas concentration in the target environment to saturated vapour conditions, past dew point and transition into liquid phase. The maximum allowable H_2O_2 gas concentration is based upon the humidity level and the minimum surface temperature within an isolator or cleanroom. Thus, the temperature profiling of the isolator interior is critical to a successful decontamination cycle (as shown by temperature mapping during qualification);

3. micro-condensation formation on surfaces formed by merging molecules. Initially nuclei form on any surface contaminants, before full condensation occurs over the entire available surface, eventually forming a disinfectant monolayer (from gas to liquid phase);

4. re-evaporation of the surface condensate and removal of residual gas to target endpoint (safety level).

The production of vapour is achieved through the combination of a vapour generator and high velocity gas distribution nozzles and fans. These provide an even spread of HPV vapour, which can be introduced at the optimum combination to all areas of the isolator or cleanroom.

In developing a H_2O_2 vapour cycle, through the use of a gas generator, there are generally four key phases (there is some variation with the different technologies available). These are [23]:

1. *Dehumidification* – during dehumidification, the relative humidity is reduced to ~30%–40% by the circulation of sterile air in a closed loop. Humidity is removed from the area space via an integrated desiccant system. This is done to ensure that a 'dry' biodecontamination process is achieved (the H_2O_2 vapour is most effective in this state).

2. *Conditioning* – during conditioning, the decontaminant is produced by vaporisation of 35% liquid H_2O_2, using the generator, and introduced into the recirculating air stream to achieve the desired H_2O_2 concentration.

3. *Decontamination* – the decontamination phase proceeds almost identically to the conditioning phase, but at a steady state of injection and with recirculation flow rate in order to maintain the target concentration (generally 0.1–3.0 mg/L) for the desired exposure time. During the exposure time, H_2O_2 vapour concentrations are maintained at the target concentration level to provide an effective kill of microorganisms within the area space.

4. *Aeration* – during aeration, H_2O_2 is no longer introduced and the residual vapour is catalytically decomposed into water and oxygen by recirculation through an intrinsic platinum and palladium chemical destroyer. Aeration continues until H_2O_2 is reduced to an acceptable level. The typical time required for aeration is between 3 and 12 hours. Using catalytic aeration, the aeration phase can be shortened by more than 50%.

While designing the control system for HPV cycles, for cleanrooms and isolators, the following factors should be considered [24]:

1. The cycle should be designed in such a way that allows the complete air flow path to be subjected to decontamination, including the HEPA filters, valves, ducts and so forth.

2. The material properties of the load contents should be checked to ensure compatibility with the HPV.

3. With isolators, the room surrounding the isolator should be temperature controlled. Fluctuations in room temperature will cause fluctuations in the temperature of the isolator's exterior surface, leading to condensation on the isolator's interior surfaces.

4. The surface area of the load and the material is more important than the volume and contents of the load (essential for cycle development, as discussed below). Functionality must be designed in such a way that all moving parts inside the isolator are exposed to the gas. An intermittent movement of moving parts can be planned during a phase of cycle, if necessary. A glove-holding device and half-suit hangers should be used to keep gloves and half-suits from contacting any surfaces during decontamination.

5. The aeration cycle must be designed in such a way that residual concentration from the wrapped goods is reduced to a safe level.

6. Provisions should be made for holding the gloves in a position, which means that the inner portion of the gloves and sleeves are exposed to the gas during the cycle.

7. The opening and closing of the tunnel gate should be automated as required during or after the cycle.

8. Chemical and biological indicators are required during validation and for annual requalification.

In many instances, a small level of H_2O_2 will remain within the enclosed environment. This can cause a problem for environmental monitoring culture media, due to the inhibition of any microorganisms present. To overcome this, the media used should be verified to show that the wrapping is resistant or 1% pyruvate should be added to the media to act as a neutraliser (the chemical can tolerate as much as 15 ppm H_2O_2) [25].

9.6 Validating VHP cycles

As with any item of equipment, the validation of the equipment and the mechanism for sterilisation or decontamination is an important part of GMP. The validation of an isolator or a room using H_2O_2 vapour is similar to the approach taken for the validation of an autoclave. The 'load' (size and volume of materials) and the run time must be assessed in conjunction with each other. There is some variation according to the load, significantly the extent to which the vapour reaches all surfaces within the load, for the required contact time. Studies have shown that it is the increase in the concentration of the gas vapour that directly increases the microbial inactivation rate. For validation cycles, the maximum load, assessed in terms of total surface area, should, as a minimum, be evaluated. Since the half-life of the H_2O_2 gas decreases as the mass of the material in the load increases, the maximum fixed-load requirements should mean that any smaller load will also be decontaminated should the vapour distribution be consistent. However, some users elect to validate the smallest and largest loads.

The manufacturers of H_2O_2 gas generators provide standard tables for the determination of the gas concentration. These tables indicate the maximum allowable concentrations for isolators and cleanrooms and take into account temperature, relative humidity, load mass and flow rate. Using the tables, the most effective cycle parameters for the dehumidification, conditioning and sterilisation phases can be selected. From this, cycle development calculations, which utilise known (internal volume including the ductwork) and estimated (minimum surface temperature) isolator or cleanroom variables, will determine gas injection and airflow rates. Once calculated, these can be optimised for routine operations.

To demonstrate microbial kill, spores of *Geobacillus stearothermophilus* (ATCC 12980) are the BI of choice for the biovalidation of HVP processes. The BIs should have proven resistance against HPV and have a spore population of $\geq 1 \times 10^6$ [26]. *G. stearothermophilus* spores have demonstrated the longest D-value on exposure to H_2O_2 vapour. The sporicidal activity of H_2O_2 gas against various lots of *G. stearothermophilus* spore suspensions tends to follow first-order kinetics, where the reaction depends on the concentration of only one reactant, and a classic logarithmic death curve is produced (Figure 9.2) [27]:

With the use of BI, many users of H_2O_2 assess the point of microbial kill using fractional negative studies. This takes place after a set of initial gassing process set points have been chosen [28]. The fractional survivor study involves the timed removal of BI from the decontamination cycle at constant intervals, in order to determine the time point at which no further growth is observed after incubation of the exposed BIs in nutrient media (i.e. the theoretical point where death occurs). The cycle parameters (gas injection rate and duration) are adjusted until all placed indicators are inactivated [29]. Finally, an arbitrarily chosen safety margin (i.e. 20% additional time) is added to the cycle before starting the performance

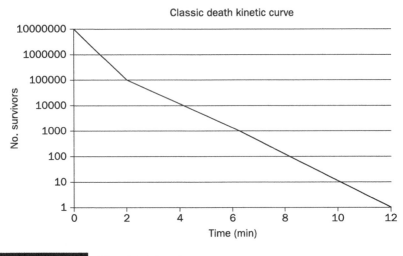

Figure 9.2 **Microbial death curve**

qualification. The target should be a demonstration of a 6-log reduction. Developed cycles should be undertaken multiple times in order to establish process robustness.

For performance qualification, BIs are normally used in triplicate so that the cause of any rogue BI (i.e. a lone survivor) can be investigated. Reasons for rogue survivors include the spores forming clumps or agglomerations, the spores becoming coated in debris, where catalytic or protective substances are present, or where the carrier substrate contains fissures into which some spores have become lodged.

There are some variations that can influence cycle effectiveness. For instance, increasing the temperature and/or decreasing the background humidity in an enclosure without increasing the gas concentration tends to decrease the overall microbial inactivation rate by reducing the saturation of the vapour [30]. Also the concentration of gas within an isolator will be reduced through a reaction with the various surfaces when the molecules come into contact with the vapour. Another variable is that the sporicidal activity of H_2O_2 vapour sporicidal activity varies, depending upon the surface type used for the BI carrier (i.e. paper or stainless steel discs).

In addition to BI, chemical indicators are normally used in cycle development. Chemical indicators are placed in representative locations. Indicators are exposed during the sanitisation cycles and later examined for variations in gas reach and penetration. The locations selected for the placement of both the chemical and BI should be based upon the physical configuration and the anticipated airflow characteristics of the enclosure. The selection of the locations should be documented.

9.7 Cycle failures

Occasionally, H_2O_2 cycles can fail, leading to BI exhibiting growth. Reasons for failure may include [31]:

- the robustness of the BI handling and media inoculation technique;
- physical operational parameters of the isolator or cleanroom (i.e. fan speeds, airflow velocities, instrument calibrations and valve damper positions). These parameters may affect gas distribution;
- strength and identify of the H_2O_2 solution;
- dirt or soiling protecting the BI.

Incidents of cycle failure require investigation through an out-of-specification procedure.

9.8 Conclusion

Vaporised H_2O_2 biodecontamination is used to achieve surface sterilisation of the exposed, clean and dry surfaces of components, containers and working areas of isolators and other devices used in pharmaceutical processing, as well as cleanrooms [32]. This chapter has introduced H_2O_2 vapour as a sanitisation agent and has outlined how the gas, if generated under controlled and optimal conditions, can effectively decontaminate the surfaces of materials held within an isolator or a cleanroom. For pharmaceutical and healthcare process isolators, the use of H_2O_2 vapour has become the standard method.

9.9 References

1. Kokubo, M., Inoue, T. and Akers, J. (1998), 'Resistance of common environmental spores of the genus Bacillus to hydrogen peroxide vapor', *Journal of Pharmaceutical Science and Technology*, 52: 228–31.
2. Agalloco, J. (1999), 'Barriers, isolators and microbial control', *Journal of Parenteral Science and Technology*, 53(1): 48–53.

3. Pflug, I.J. (1999), *Microbiology and Engineering of Sterilization Processes*, 10th edition, Minneapolis, MN: Environmental Sterilization Laboratory, University of Minnesota.

4. Midcalf, B., Mitchell Phillips, W., Neiger, J.S. and Coles T.J. (eds) (2004), *Pharmaceutical Isolators: A Guide to Their Application, Design and Control*, London: Pharmaceutical Press.

5. Klapes, N.A. and Vesley, D. (1990), 'Vapor-phase hydrogen peroxide as a surface decontaminant and sterilant', *Applied and Environmental Microbiology*, 56(2): 503–6.

6. Krause, J., McDonnell, G. and Riedesel, H. (2001), 'Biodecontamination of animal rooms and heat-sensitive equipment with vaporized hydrogen peroxide: Contemporary topics', *American Association for Laboratory Animal Science*, 40(6): 18–21.

7. Offermanns, H., Dittrich, G. and Steiner, N. (2000), 'Wasserstoffperoxid in Umweltschutz und Synthese', *Chemie in unserer Zeit*, 34(3): 150.

8. Campos-Martin, J.M., Blanco-Brieva, G. and Fierro, J.L.G. (2006), 'Hydrogen peroxide synthesis: An outlook beyond the anthraquinone process', *Angewandte Chemie International Edition*, 45(42): 6962–84.

9. Taizo, I., Sinichi, A. and Kawamura, K. (1998), 'Application of a newly developed hydrogen peroxide vapor phase sensor to HPV steriliser', *PDA Journal of Pharmaceutical Science and Technology*, 52(1): 13–18.

10. Scatchard, G., Kavanagh, G. and Ticknor, L. (1952), 'Vapor-liquid equilibrium. Part VIII: Hydrogen peroxide – water mixtures', *Journal of the American Chemical Society*, 74(15): 3715–20.

11. Holmdahl, T., Lanbeck, P., Wullt, M. and Walder, M.H. (2011), 'A head-to-head comparison of hydrogen peroxide vapor and aerosol room decontamination systems', *Infection Control and Hospital Epidemiology*, 32(9): 831–6.

12. Alfa, M.J., DeGagne, P., Olson, N. and Puchalski, T. (1996), 'Comparison of ion plasma, vaporized hydrogen peroxide, and 100% ethylene oxide sterilizers to the 12/88 ethylene oxide gas sterilizer', *Infection Control and Hospital Epidemiology*, 17: 92–100.

13. Heckert, R.A., Best, M., Jordan, L.T., Dulac, G.C., Eddington, D.L. and Skerritt, W.G. (1997), 'Efficacy of vaporized hydrogen peroxide against exotic animal viruses', *Applied and Environmental Microbiology*, 63: 3916–18.

14. McDonnell, G. and Russell, A.D. (1999), 'Antiseptics and disinfectants: Activity, action, and resistance', *Clinical Microbiology Reviews*, 12: 147–79.

15. Justi, C., Amato, R., Antloga, K., Harrington, S. and McDonnell, G. (2001), 'Demonstration of a sterility assurance level for a liquid chemical sterilization process', *Central Sterilization*, 9: 163–76.

16. Block, S.S. (1991), 'Peroxygen compounds', in: Block, S.S. (ed.), *Disinfection, Sterilization, and Preservation*, 4th edition, Philadelphia, PA: Lea and Febiger, pp. 167–81.

17. Friedman, R. (1998), 'Design of barrier isolators for aseptic processing: A GMP perspective', *Pharmaceutical Engineering*, 18(2): 28–33.

18. Rauschnabel, J. (2006), 'Zwischen Isolator und Sterilraum (Between isolator and sterile room) – Restricted Access Barrier System (RABS)', *Pharmazeutische Industrie*, 68(6): 767–73.

19. Sandle, T. (2004), 'General considerations for the risk assessment of isolators used for aseptic processes', *Pharmaceutical Manufacturing and Packaging Source*, Winter: 43–7.

20. Power, E.G.M. (1995), 'Aldehyde as biocides', *Progress in Medicinal Chemistry*, 34: 149–201.

21. French, G.L., Otter, J.A., Shannon, K.P., Adams, N.M., Watling, D. and Parks, M.J. (2004), 'Tackling contamination of the hospital environment by methicillin-resistant *Staphylococcus aureus* (MRSA): A comparison between conventional terminal cleaning and hydrogen peroxide vapour decontamination', *Journal of Hospital Infection*, 57: 31–7.

22. Drinkwater, J. and Buck, L. (2012), 'Gaseous disinfection of barrier systems', in: Sandle, T. (ed.), *The CDC Handbook: A Guide to Cleaning and Disinfecting Cleanrooms*, Surrey, UK: Grosvenor House Publishing, pp. 198–240.

23. Coles T. (1995), 'Experience in the design and use of isolator systems for sterility testing', *PDA Journal of Pharmaceutical Science and Technology*, 49(3): 140–4.

24. Khorzad, D. (2003), 'Design and operational qualification of a vapor-phase hydrogen peroxide biological indicator evaluator resistometer unit', *Pharmaceutical Technology*, 27(11): 84–90.

25. Ohresser, S. Griveau, S. and Schann, C. (2004), 'Validation of microbial recovery from hydrogen peroxide-sterilized air', *PDA Journal of Pharmaceutical Science and Technology*, 58(2): 75–80.

26. Kokubo M., Inoue T. and Akers J. (1998), 'Resistance of common environmental spores of the genus Bacillus to vapor hydrogen peroxide', *Journal of Pharmaceutical Science and Technology*, 52: 228–31.

27. Iglesias, P.A. and Ingalls, B.P. (2010), *Control Theory and Systems Biology*, Cambridge, MA: MIT Press.

28. Sigworth, V. and Moirandat, C. (2000), 'Development and quantification of H_2O_2 decontamination cycles', *PDA Journal of Pharmaceutical Science and Technology*, 54(4): 286–304.

29. Graham, G.S. and Boris, C.A. (1993), 'Chemical and biological indicators', in: Morrissey, R.F. and Phillips, G.B., *Sterilization Technology*, New York: Van Nostrand Reinhold, pp. 36–69.

30. Drummond, D.W. and Pflug, I.J. (1970), 'Dry heat destruction of bacillus subtilis spores on surfaces: effect of humidity in an open system', *Applied Microbiology*, 20: 805–9.

31. Kokubo, M., Inoue, T. and Akers, J. (1998), 'Resistance of common spores of the genus bacillus to vapour hydrogen peroxide', *PDA Journal of Pharmaceutical Science and Technology*, 52(5): 228–31.

32. Falagas, M.E., Thomaidis, P.C., Kossantis, I.K., Sgouros, K. and Samonis, G. (2011), 'Airborne hydrogen peroxide for disinfection of the hospital environment and infection control: A systematic review', *Journal of Hospital Infection*, 78(3): 171–7.

Sterilisation by filtration

DOI: 10.1533/9781908818638.143

Abstract: This chapter examines sterilising grade filters. These filters are membrane filters and function to retain microorganisms as a fluid (liquid or gas) is passed through the membrane. There are a number of complex and interactive factors that need to be considered when selecting and validating filters. These factors relate to physical and chemical characteristics of both the filter and product, and need to demonstrate the bacterial retentive properties of the filter through bacterial challenge studies, which involve the use of a diminutive challenge microorganism. The chapter sets out these factors, setting the theoretical aspects alongside practical considerations, mapping validation from small-scale development through to large-scale pharmaceutical processing.

Key words: filtration, membrane filters, hydrophilic, hydrophobic, *Brevundimonas diminuta*, extractables, leachables, pressure, temperature, integrity testing, adsorption.

10.1 Introduction

Filtration is a means of sterilising fluids (liquids or gases) through the removal, rather than the destruction or inactivation, of microorganisms. Liquids that would be damaged by heat (i.e. those containing proteins such as large molecule drug products) irradiation or chemical sterilisation, can only be sterilised by filtration [1]. Thus the sterilisation of liquids is a key step for aseptic manufacturing, as the means of passing the bulk product to the point where it will be dispensed into bottles (Chapter 14).

Due to the small pore size of the filters, the term 'microfiltration' is sometimes referenced in literature.

Sterilisation, in relation to filters, generally refers to the removal of bacteria and fungi. In processing of certain biologics, viruses must be removed or inactivated using nanofiltration. This requires a nanofilter with smaller pore size of 20–50 nm. The filtration of viruses falls outside the scope of this book.

The ideal characteristics of a sterilising grade filter is in selecting a filter that is compatible with the process. The filter must be non-toxic, able to be tested using the integrity test, and sterilisable (or provided pre-sterilised). Furthermore, the selected filter must not adsorb formula components or add extractables to the process; and it must, most importantly, remove the bioburden associated with the product [2].

The removal of microorganisms from fluids by passage through filters is a very complex process and is dependent upon interactions relating to the chemistry and surface characteristics of the membrane; the microorganisms (relating to species and population) and the suspending fluid. The mechanism of filtration involves sieving or surface retention [3]. The sterile filtration is also important for other parts of biopharmaceutical manufacturing, such as the sterilisation of gases, where the gas passes through a filter at the point of use.

Sterile filtration of liquids and gases in pharmaceutical manufacture is almost always performed using membrane filters. These are thin uniform porous sheets, which act as sieves that trap particles larger in size than the pores in the membranes. Other factors which prevent the passing through of particles include inertial impaction to the walls or surfaces of the pores and lodgement in crevices within the depth of the membrane [4].

This chapter discusses the different types of sterilising grade filters and their application within biopharmaceutical processing and also outlines some of the main requirements of a filter for the validation of sterile filtration.

10.2 Sterilising grade filters

The objective of filtration is for a fluid (gas or liquid) to be passed through the filter and for the filter to capture and retain particles. In relation to the 'sterile' aspect, the particles of concern are microorganisms, therefore the process of sterile filtration is one of bacterial retention [5].

The US Food and Drug Administration (FDA) define a sterilising filter as: 'one which when challenged with the microorganism *Brevundimonas diminuta* at a minimum concentration of 10^7 organisms per cm^2 of filter surface, will produce a sterile effluent' [6].

Filters are classified in different ways, one of which is by their removal rating, which relates to the size of microorganisms and particles that can be theoretically removed by the filter, rather than the actual size or shape of the filter. Bacteria retentive filters are required, as per cGMP, to have a maximum porosity of 0.22 μm. This maximum porosity is slightly smaller than the typical dimension of *Breviundimonas diminuta*, the microorganism used to validate sterile filtration, which is 0.3 μm [7]. Periodically, discussions take place within industry about the introduction of filters with a porosity requirement to 0.1 μm. To date, regulations do not require the use of a smaller pore size.

The porosity quoted for filters is not obtained by physical measurement of the dimensions of the pores. It is done on the basis of the pressure that is required to displace liquid from the pores (a 'bubble point') coupled to a formula that takes account of the pressure required, the surface tension of the liquid and the contact angle between the liquid and the surface of the pore. This formula assumes that filters are made uniformly from cylindrical pores, when in practice some pores are of different shapes. To compensate for this, filter manufacturers incorporate a correction factor.

The activity of bacteria-retentive filtration is, on one level, a type of sieving process. However, more complex processes come into play. Filtration is a combination of physical interception of particles that are too large to pass through the pore structure of the membrane, and indirect mechanisms such as inertial impaction and charge mediated adsorption. Particle retention is also affected by the particle shape and type, with shape affected by the fluid in which the particles are held. Osmotic pressure, for example, can alter the shape of particles.

To ensure proper functioning of the filter, the membrane filters are integrity tested post-use and, on occasions, pre-use. This testing is discussed below.

10.3 Application of sterilising grade filters

Different types of filter material are used within pharmaceutical manufacturing. Most applications use filters made from cellulose esters, polyvinylidine fluoride, polytetrafluoroethylene, nylon and other polymeric materials [8]. There are two types of membrane, hydrophobic ('water disliking') for use with gas filtration and hydrophilic ('water liking') for use with liquid filtration. With hydrophilic filtration, compounds have an affinity to water and are usually charged or have polar side groups to their structure that will attract water. With hydrophobic filtration, compounds are repelled by water and are usually neutral (no charge). These different types of filters are examined below.

10.3.1 Liquid (hydrophilic) filters

Liquid filters generally come in two forms, disc (sheet or plate) filters and cartridge filters. The traditional type of disc filter is less commonly used. With disc filters, the direction of fluid flow is from above the filter to below the filter. The membrane is placed between metal inlet and outlet plates, and because of its fragility it rests on a porous (often photo-etched) support plate. Sometimes disc filters may be serially stacked; in such instances each membrane requires its own support plate. Units are sealed by means of elastomeric O-rings. The problem with disc filters is that they are difficult to sterilise. Such filters cannot withstand major pressure differentials without tearing or moving relative to the O-rings. Therefore the deep pre-vacuums of the typical porous load steam sterilisation process are unsuitable.

In contrast, cartridge filters are more commonly used in pharmaceutical processing. These filters are located within cylindrical stainless steel housings or disposable in plastic housings. The compact presentation provides a large surface area. For example, a cartridge filter of 5 cm diameter and 25 cm length may contain up to 6500 cm^2 of pleated membrane surface.

The operational part of a cartridge filter is a rectangular sheet of membrane, pleated and folded into a cylindrical form. Since membranes are fragile and do not fold easily without tearing, the membrane is sandwiched between two support layers of a non-woven fabric. The pleated cylinder is positioned around one perforated plastic hollow tube (the core of the cartridge) and within another perforated plastic hollow tube (the cage). The whole assembly is held together by two end caps. The plastic parts are bonded together with low melting point thermoplastic sealants.

Published by Woodhead Publishing Limited, 2013

10.3.2 Gas (hydrophobic) filters

Sterile filtration of gases with hydrophobic membranes in cartridges has several applications, such as a supply of sterile air is required as an ingredient gas in fermentation processes, when a sterile inert gas is required to remove oxygen from a liquid preparation to ensure stability, when a sterile inert gas is required to fill the head space above a product to stop, slow or delay deleterious oxidative effects, and when sterile compressed air is required to actuate valves.

Hydrophobic sterilising-grade filters are also used as air vents on processing tanks. The objective is to maintain near ambient pressure in the tank while ensuring sterility. The tank vent filter removes viruses and microorganisms from the gas as it flows in or out of the tank. The construction of hydrophilic filters is basically the same as hydrophobic filters. Filtration is achieved through sieving and adsorption. Sieving is a physical mechanism of particle removal, where a particle is denied access through a pore or passageway that is smaller than the particle itself. Adsorption is a mechanism that relies on the chemical interaction between the particle and the filter matrix (where particles 'adhere' to the filter material).

Gas filtration poses problems because of the length of the filtration process and the potential for damage upon repeated use of the filter element.

10.4 Filter testing

There are several tests required to be undertaken on filters and the material passed through the filter. For sterile liquid filtration, a sample of the liquid must be taken prior to filtration and assessed for microbial bioburden. This applies to the point prior to product filling in relation to aseptic processing. In terms of the permitted microbial challenge to sterilising grade filters when used for processing, it is referenced by both FDA and within Europe through a CPMP Note ('Guidance on Manufacture of the Finished Dosage Form') [9]. For example, the CPMP guidance reads:

> For sterilisation by filtration the maximum acceptable bioburden prior to the filtration must be stated in the application. In most situations not more than 10 cfu/100 ml will be acceptable,

depending on the volume to be filtered in relation to the diameter of the filter.

The use of 10 cfu/100 ml provides a theoretical limit 180–800 times lower than the standard sterilising filter rating.

A further test relates to the porosity of filters. Porosity requires confirmatory testing, based on the pressure that is required to displace liquid from the pores (a bubble point value). The 'bubble point test' is applied to sterilising grade filters before and after use. For this test, a 'bubble point' value for the filters, derived from the filter manufacturer, is required. The test is undertaken either by testing the filter by increasing the pressure on a wetted filter until the wetting liquid is displaced (determination of an actual bubble point) or through increasing pressure to the level given by the filter supplier at the bubble point, and as long as the wetting liquid is not displaced the filter can be safely assumed to meet the requirement. Bubble point testing is generally undertaken using automatic filter integrity test equipment. This provides information about pressure decay values and diffusion or forward flow values, in addition to the bubble point [10].

With hydrophobic (gas) filters, water is used as the wetting fluid for integrity testing hydrophilic filters. However, surface tension may be too high to allow it to penetrate the pores of hydrophobic filters. The main alternate for hydrophobic filter testing is isopropanol, but this introduces the problem of removing alcohol residues (by blow drying with dry gas) and the problem of flammability. The second alternative for hydrophobic filters is the water intrusion integrity test. The test is similar to the bubble point test in that it measures the pressure required to force water into the pores [11].

10.5 Filter failures

Occasionally a filter failure will occur following pre- or post-use testing. Reasons for filter failure include:

- incorrect assembly in the housing;
- defective cartridges;
- membrane failure;
- grow-through of microorganisms (bacteria trapped in the filter which continue to grow.

The latter is generally unlikely to occur due to a lack of available nutrients. However, any bacteria that were forced through a damaged filter would present a problem to the filtrate. This is unlikely to occur provided that set times are in place for the length of the filtration activity.

Bacterial issues will be unlikely provided that the liquid presented to the filter is of a low bioburden. Therefore, good controls in place during processing are of importance. Each case of filter failure represents a process deviation and warrants an investigation.

10.6 Selection of sterilising grade filters

The selection of a membrane filter for a particular product or process is an important choice. This requires an assessment of the filter, the chemical nature of the product, and the physical demands that will be placed on the filter. The key considerations are as described below [12].

10.6.1 Flow rates

The filter system must be selected, on the basis of size, to provide flow rates (the time taken to filter a given volume of material) and volume (the amount of material to be passed through the filter) for the appropriate item of production equipment. Prior to the use of a filter for large-scale production, small-scale sizing and filterability tests are used as the basis for extrapolating or scaling-up filtration systems.

10.6.2 Pressure and temperature resistance in relation to membrane support layers, core, or cage, o-rings and housings

These relate to the sterilising filter and filter housing, whether manufactured from stainless steel or disposable plastic, and must be rugged enough to withstand the pressures and temperatures associated with the process. The evaluation should include an assessment of the minimum and maximum physical challenges linked with the process.

10.6.3 Assessment of hydrophilic or hydrophobic properties

Sterilising-grade filters for aqueous solutions are normally hydrophilic. With certain solvent or chemical liquids, hydrophobic filters are sometimes used.

10.6.4 Membrane composition

The filter system must be assessed to ensure that all product-contact surfaces of the filter and its constituent parts (i.e. the membrane, support layers, core, cage and end caps), o-rings, piping, hoses, seals, pumps and gaskets, can withstand the hydraulic, thermal and chemical challenges of the sterilisation and production processes.

10.6.5 Compatibility

The composition of the membrane must be compatible with the chemicals passed through the filter. This should be evaluated through the use of a small-scale pilot batch.

10.6.6 Sterilisation of the membrane filter

The filter must be able to withstand the sterilisation process without the process damaging the filter or leading to release of fibres or toxic substances. Sterilisation methods include steam sterilisation and gamma radiation.

10.7 Validation of sterilising grade filters

The purpose of sterile filtration validation is to prove that a particular filtration process generates a sterile filtrate. Validation of sterilising grade filters can be divided between tests of the bacteria-retentive properties and of physico-chemical interactions between the filter and the gas or liquid being sterilised [13]. Filters must be qualified by the user to demonstrate that their performance in processing will meet process requirements. These tests are as described below.

10.7.1 Physical and chemical compatibility

This has been discussed in the section on filter selection above. However, these considerations must also be established during the qualification phase prior to validation.

10.7.2 Binding and adsorption filter characteristics

These characteristics are measured during the qualification phase from both pre- and post-filtrate testing. It is important that the filter does not remove active ingredients, excipients, carriers, diluents, proteins, preservatives, or any other formulation component, otherwise the properties of the product will be affected and the yield will be reduced [14].

10.7.3 Bacterial retentive efficiency

The validation of bacterial retention requires, according to cGMP standards, the complete removal of a minimum challenge level of 10^7 colony forming units (cfu) of *Brevundimonas diminuta* (ATCC 19146) per square centimetre of membrane surface area [15]. This ensures that a sufficient challenge is given to the membrane, so that every pore is challenged and given the same opportunity to allow passage of the test microorganism [16].

The reason why *Brevundimonas diminuta* is used for this challenge is because the microorganism can be consistently cultured under controlled conditions to produce very small, monodispersed cells with a narrow size distribution. The cells are typically of $0.3 \times 0.6\,\mu m$ cylindrical dimensions. Under these conditions, the microorganisms represent a potential 'worst-case' challenge [17].

The most important aspect of validating bacterial retention efficiency concerns process-specific validation. The operating conditions of the test must simulate the actual pharmaceutical manufacturing process for a particular drug product. The purpose of this is to take account of interactions that may exist between the filter components, the mode of filter action, the physical conditions of the process and the physico-chemical characteristics of the pharmaceutical product solution. This requires the microorganism to be challenged into the product, provided that the product is not bactericidal; where the product is bactericidal and the formulation cannot be adjusted then a surrogate material should be used. It is important that the product challenged is of a low bioburden [18].

The validation also requires an assessment of the product contact time. The bacterial challenge using pharmaceutical product must be run for at least the same duration as a product batch will be run in processing. For example, if the batch requires 8 hours to filter, the challenge must be run for at least 8 hours. Another factor to take into account is the maximum process differential pressure and flow rates. These should be incorporated into the validation protocol. An adjustment which may be required is temperature. If the product is normally filtered at a high temperature and where this temperature may kill the challenge microorganism, then the temperature in the validation should be adjusted downwards so that the test microorganisms survive the process challenge in sufficient numbers [19].

It is also important that the microbiological passage test is performed as part of the development of new sterile formulations. Due to the specialised nature of the test, the assessment is normally performed only by the filter manufacturers, who then provide limits for secondary physical tests (i.e. bubble point, pressure decay, forward flow, and so forth). These can subsequently be applied to verify the pore size rating and integrity of the membrane filters [20].

Should the filter fail to retain microorganisms, an investigation is required. The retention of microorganisms by the filter is a combination of different factors. These include the filter polymer, the filter structure, the properties of the aqueous product including pH, viscosity, osmolarity and ionic strength, and the process conditions, including temperature, differential pressure and flow rate. The investigation may lead to process modifications or the selection of an alternative filter.

10.7.4 Integrity testing

Although the integrity test is an important part of pre- and post-use assessment of the selected filter, such testing should also feature during the initial validation, in order to determine if the filter can be satisfactorily tested prior to implementation.

10.7.5 Toxicity and extractables

To demonstrate that the filter must be non-toxic, it should be examined according to specified tests. The *European Pharmacopeia* does not specify such tests; however, there are applicable chapters in the *United States Pharmacopeia*, which should be followed. These are: chapter 'Biological Reactivity Tests,' *in vitro*; and chapter 'Biological Reactivity Tests,' *in vivo*. In addition, filters must be free of bacterial endotoxins and, depending upon the process requirements, free from beta glucan (these are tests normally undertaken by the manufacturer and certified).

The validation of membrane filters must also address the possibility of products leaching harmful 'extractables' out of the plastics [21]. This type of validation is formulation-specific. In addition to the potential adverse effect of extractables on the filtered product, the presence of extractables may be related to degradation of the filter, which will affect its ability to perform as intended. Extractables are chemical entities, both organic and inorganic, that will extract from the filter into the product under controlled conditions. Consideration must also be given to leachables. Leachables are chemical entities, both organic and inorganic, that could migrate into the drug product following contact with the filter [22].

With filters used for the sterile filtration of gases, the FDA requirement for bacteria-retention is for filter suppliers to undertake the same test as with the microorganism suspended in water. It can be reasoned that hydrophobic filters have all the bacteria-retentive mechanisms of hydrophilic filters plus some more mechanisms, therefore if they meet the standard when wet they will more than fit the bill when dry.

10.8 Conclusion

This chapter has outlined sterilising grade filters and has shown that the filtration process, particularly in relation to filter selection and validation, is a complex area. This is due to the different physical and chemical factors that affect how fluids pass through filters, and due to the requirement to demonstrate bacterial retention. In validating filters, it is not necessary to test every type of product combination with each type of membrane filter. For different formulations of product, a bracketing approach can be used, provided that a suitable justification is provided. Often those products having the highest and lowest concentrations of the active ingredient are selected.

This chapter, in outlining filter selection and validation, has inferred that sufficient time and resources should be spent on research and development before a filter is introduced for a process. Thereafter the performance of the filter should be reviewed regularly and a risk assessment undertaken before an existing filter is applied for a new product formulation.

10.9 References

1. Levy, R.V. and Jornitz, M.W. (2006), 'Types of filtration', *Advances in Biochemical Engineering/Biotechnology*, 98: 1–26.
2. Jornitz, M.W. (2006), *Advances in Biochemical Engineering/Biotechnology. Sterile Filtration*, vol. 98, Ch. 6, Berlin: Springer Verlag.
3. Halls, N.A. (1994), *Achieving Sterility in Medical and Pharmaceutical Products*, New York: Marcel Dekker, Inc.
4. Meltzer, T.H. (1987), *Filtration in the Pharmaceutical Industry*, New York: Marcel Dekker, Inc.
5. MacDonald, W.D., Pelletier, C.A. and Gasper, D.L. (1989), 'Practical methods for the microbial validation of sterilizing-grade filters used in aseptic processing', *Journal of Parenteral Science and Technology*, 43(6): 266–70.
6. Pall, D.B., Kirnbauer, E.A. and Allen, B.T. (1980), 'Particulate retention by bacteria retentive membrane filters', *Colloids and Surfaces*, 1: 235–56.
7. Cundell, A.M. (2004), Microbial testing in support of aseptic processing', *Pharmaceutical Technology*, June, 56–64.
8. McKinnon, B.T. and Avis, K.E. (1993), 'Membrane filtration of pharmaceutical solutions', *American Journal of Health-System Pharmacy*, 50(9): 1921–36.
9. European Medicines Agency (1996), *cGMP Note for Guidance on Manufacture of the Finished Dosage Form*, Re-issue 5–6, London: EMA.
10. Jornitz, M.W. and Meltzer T.H. (2003), *Filtration Handbook – Integrity testing*, Bethesda, USA: Parenteral Drug Association.
11. Dosmar, M., Wolber, P., Bracht, K., Tröger, H. and Waibel, P. (1992), 'The water pressure integrity test – A new integrity test for hydrophobic membrane filters', *Journal of Parenteral Science & Technology*, 46(4): 102–6.
12. PDA Technical Report #26 (1998), 'Sterilizing filtration of liquids', *Journal of Pharmaceutical Science and Technology*, 52 (1 Supp).
13. Aranha, H. and Meeker J. (1995), 'Microbial retention characteristics of 0.2-microns-rated nylon membrane filters during filtration of high viscosity fluids at high differential pressure and varied temperatures', *PDA Journal of Pharmaceutical Science and Technology*, 49(2): 67–70.
14. McBurnie, L. and Bardo, B. (2004), 'Validation of sterile filtration', *Pharmaceutical Technology*, Filtration Supplement, 10(8): S13–22.
15. Carter J. (1996), 'Evaluation of recovery filters for use in bacterial retention testing of sterilizing-grade filters', *PDA Journal of Pharmaceutical Science and Technology*, 50(3): 147–53.
16. Lee, S.H., Lee, S.S. and Kim, C.W. (2002), 'Changes in the cell size of *Brevundimonas diminuta* using different growth agitation rates', *PDA Journal of Pharmaceutical Science and Technology*, 56(2): 99–108.

17. Hunter, D. (2006), *Bacterial Challenge & Correlation to Integrity Test Data For Sterilising Grade Pharmaceutical Air & Liquid Filters*, London: Dominic Hunter Group.

18. American Society for Testing and Materials (ASTM) (1993), *Standard Test Method for Determining Bacterial Retention of Membrane Filters Utilized for Liquid Filtration*, ASTM Standard F838–05, Philadelphia: ASTM

19. Lee, S.H. and Kim, C.W. (2002), 'Microbial retention characteristics of sterilizing-grade membrane filters with alginate substituted for oil-based products', *PDA Journal of Pharmaceutical Science and Technology*, 56(5): 248–54.

20. Schroeder, H.G. and DeLuca, P.P. (1980), 'Theoretical aspects of filtration and integrity testing', *Pharmaceutical Technology*, 4: 80–5.

21. Kao, Y.H., Bender, J., Hagewiesche, A., Wong, P., Huang, Y. and Vanderlaan, M. (2001), 'Characterization of filter extractables by proton NMR spectroscopy: studies on intact filters with process buffers', *Journal of Pharmaceutical Science and Technology*, 55(5): 268–77.

22. Weitzmann, C. (1997), 'The use of model solvents for evaluating extractables from filters used to process pharmaceutical products', *Pharmaceutical Technology*, April: 44–60.

Other methods of sterilisation

DOI: 10.1533/9781908818638.157

Abstract: This chapter examines emerging methods of sterilisation which may, in the future, become established methods for the sterilisation of pharmaceutical products, medical devices or healthcare materials. The technologies described are X-rays, ultrasonification, supercritical gases, ultraviolet light, pulsed light, microwaves, infrared radiation, plasma and formaldehyde steam. This chapter has attempted to select methods which have a reasonable chance of becoming more widely used. Due to the confusion between sterilisation and disinfection, reference is also made to microbial reduction processes which cannot be classified as sterilisation processes. This distinction is made so that the reader can appreciate the differences between the two processes.

Key words: sterilisation, X-rays, ultrasonification, supercritical gases, ultraviolet light, pulsed light, microwaves, infrared radiation, plasma and formaldehyde steam.

11.1 Introduction

This chapter addresses other methods of sterilisation outside of the primary methods detailed in the previous chapters and prior to moving onto examining aseptic processing. The methods described are either not in common use, due to their specificity, they are under-developed or they are not common to mainstream pharmaceutical or healthcare facilities. It is uncertain if the methods described will become mainstream sterilisation technologies and we do not attempt to enter into speculative debate, but merely to describe the novel technologies currently being referenced in literature at the time of writing.

In addition to describing novel sterilisation technologies, reference is made to disinfection processes, which are sometimes mistaken for sterilisation technologies. These are highlighted so that the reader is aware of what is, unfortunately, a common confusion. In making the distinction, the chapter briefly describes some of these disinfection methods.

All emerging technologies need to meet a number of criteria in order to be considered as suitable methods for the sterilisation of a product. These criteria are [1]:

- whether the product can withstand the sterilisation conditions;
- if the process can achieve the necessary assurance of sterility;
- whether terminal sterilisation of the product can be achieved within the final packaging;
- if toxic chemical residues are created as a by-product of sterilisation;
- understanding the physical and chemical conditions required to achieve sterilisation.

In addition, novel sterilisation technologies:

- need to be sufficiently advanced to be used on a practical scale;
- the technology must be able to be validated, to show microbial kill;
- the technology must be affordable;
- the technology must be safe to use;
- the processing time must meet with production requirements.

To assist with the introduction of new technologies, the international standard ISO 14937 'Sterilisation of health care products – General requirements for characterisation of a sterilising agent and the development, validation and routine control of a sterilisation process for medical devices' [2], provides useful guidance for the development and validation of alternative technologies. Although the focus of the standard is on medical devices, the general principles are sufficiently useful to be applied to any product requiring sterilisation [3]. Here we discuss some of the emerging or developing sterilisation technologies.

11.2 Ultraviolet light

Ultraviolet (UV) light is electromagnetic radiation with a wavelength shorter than that of visible light, but longer than those associated with X-rays, in the range 10 nm to 400 nm, and with energies from 3 eV to 124 eV. UV light falls into three broad groups, based on wavelength: UV-C, wavelengths in the range 100 to 280 nm; UV-B for wavelengths between 280 to 315 nm; and UV-A for wavelengths between 315 to 400 nm. For sterilisation, it is short-wavelength UV radiation (UV-C) that is harmful to microorganisms [4]. Though frequently referred to as 'non-ionising radiation', the shortest UV wavelengths do bring about some ionisation. An alternative term is 'natural light sterilisation'.

The lethal effects of UV towards microorganisms were discovered at the end of the nineteenth century and the first practical application of UV was in the disinfection of water [5]. The term 'disinfection' is important, for although UV light can sterilise, this is not easily demonstrated. This remains the use to which UV is most commonly associated today and it is such technology for treating water that is relatively well accepted.

UV lamps for sterilisation are low-pressure mercury-vapour lamps, which emit about 86% of their light at 254 nm. This wavelength coincides well with one of the two peaks of the germicidal effectiveness curve (i.e. effectiveness for UV absorption by DNA). One of these peaks is at about 265 nm and the other at about 185 nm. Although 185 nm is better absorbed by DNA, the quartz glass used in commercially available lamps, as well as environmental media such as water, are more opaque to 185 nm than to 254 nm.

UV light at these wavelengths causes adjacent thymine molecules (pyrimidine bases) on DNA to dimerise; if a sufficient number of these defects accumulate within a microorganism's DNA, its replication is inhibited, which means that the organism's enzyme-mediated repair processes no longer functions [6], thereby rendering the microorganism harmless, even though they may not be killed outright.

The effectiveness of UV depends on a number of factors: the length of time a microorganism is exposed to UV; power fluctuations of the UV source that impact the EM wavelength; the presence of particles or shaded areas that can protect the micro-organisms from UV; and a microorganism's ability to withstand UV during its exposure. The efficacy of UV surface treatment is further influenced by surface topography. Crevices, and similar features, of dimensions comparable to the size of microorganisms (i.e. of a few microns) may shield microorganisms from potentially lethal UV rays and enable them to survive.

UV light is harmful to humans and, in any application, serious consideration must be given to protecting personnel from exposure to it. The eyes are particularly susceptible and the condition arising from exposure to UV, referred to as 'welder's eye', is both painful and ultimately sight threatening. Exposure of skin to UV results in delayed reddening and, at sufficiently high doses, UV can have profound effects on the immune system that can lead to severe and potentially lethal consequences. However, all such harmful effects can be completely avoided by careful design of containment measures to eliminate stray UV through the use of shields and non-reflective surfaces. Other disadvantages of UV are that it requires a reliable source of electricity and is not very effective in areas of high relative humidity. As a consequence, UV irradiation is neither a practical nor effective method outside of the sanitisation of water systems [7].

11.3 Pulsed light

Some studies have been undertaken using bursts of broad spectrum white light, delivered at high intensities, to sterilise products within their final containers. Pulsed light is typically generated from a xenon source to produce flashes of white light over short durations [8]. The most common application is for treating food, and for this a standard cycle is with light of a wavelength of 200 nm to 1000 nm, and operated so that the pulse duration is no longer than 2 ms.

The antimicrobial effects (both photochemical and photothermal effects) are due to the light containing a considerable proportion of UV light (in essence, the technology functions in a similar way to the description of UV light above) in that the pulsed UV light causes formation of pyrimidone dimers in DNA, resulting in genetic damage to cells and their ultimate destruction [9]. The advantage of such technology is that it will not cause a significant temperature rise in the product. However, the technology is not applicable for products sensitive to photodegradation.

The technology is not widely used and most of the research remains orientated towards the food industry as a surface treatment [10]. However, studies which have been undertaken in relation to the pharmaceutical sector have shown that the technology can achieve 6-log microbial kill of vegetative microorganisms and microorganisms in the endospore state in vials of Water-for-Injection [11]. Other research, of potential relevance to the pharmaceutical industry, has been with methods to disinfect (rather than 'sterilise') water systems [12]. The major limitation with this type of technology for terminal sterilisation is the potential drug degradation risk.

11.4 Microwaves

Microwave sterilisation is a thermal process and microwaves are radio-frequency waves, which are generally used at a frequency of 2450 Megahertz (MHz). For sterilisation, microwaves deliver energy to a product under pressure and controlled temperature to achieve the inactivation of bacteria. Here microwaves interact with polar water molecules and charged ions. The friction resulting from molecules aligning in rapidly alternating electromagnetic fields generates the heat [13]. The destruction of microorganisms is caused by thermal effects in a similar way to dry heat methods of sterilisation [14].

Microwave heating has the potential to be developed as a sterilisation method, particularly for empty glass vials [15]. Other applications are as a means of disinfection. Microwaves are used in medicine for disinfection of soft contact lenses, dental instruments, dentures, milk, and urinary catheters for intermittent self-catheterisation, with some success and such development may well go further.

The advantage with microwave technology is that it is relatively quick, easy, reliable, and it is unlikely to contaminate the product with trace metals or cause precipitation [16]. The disadvantage is that microwaves must only be used with products that are compatible (i.e. those that do not melt). The effectiveness of microwave ovens for different sterilisation and disinfection purposes is affected by variables that include the presence of water, the presence of 'cold spots' and the microwave power delivered to the product [17].

11.5 Infrared radiation

With infrared sterilisation, articles to be sterilised are placed in a moving conveyer belt and passed through a tunnel that is heated by infrared radiators to a temperature of 180°C. The articles are exposed to that temperature for a set time period and 7.5 minutes at 180°C has been shown to achieve a 6-log reduction in bacterial spores. The infrared is produced by specially designed carbon emitters subjected to a high level of heat or, alternatively, a ceramic heating element. Infrared radiation has the potential to destroy bacterial spores.

The types of articles that can be sterilised include metallic instruments and glassware. The process requires special equipment, and hence it is not widely used. Some of the possible advantages of infrared technology include short sterilisation cycle times, low energy consumption, no cycle residuals, and no toxicological or environmental effects [18]. The technology could be developed as an alternative dry heat technology for sterilisation of selected heat-resistant instruments; however, research in this field remains limited.

11.6 Ultrasonics

Ultrasonication is, at least in theory, a means of sterilisation, although it is not one which has been particularly well developed and it is probably best considered as a disinfection method. To kill bacteria, an ultrasonic process uses sound waves with a frequency of more than 20,000 cycle/second (25 kiloHertz), based on exposure times greater than 1 hour. The high frequency sound waves disrupt cells, causing permanent damage [19].

11.7 Supercritical gases

The application of supercritical gases (i.e. carbon dioxide) is of interest for sterilisation, because it has been shown to have anti-microbial effects at high pressures while still being otherwise non-toxic, inflammable, non-hazardous, chemically inert and relatively inexpensive. A supercritical fluid is any substance at a temperature and pressure above its critical point, where distinct liquid and gas phases do not exist. In terms of anti-microbial properties, the increased diffusitivity properties of supercritical CO_2 allow it to cross the cellular membranes of microbes and extract necessary nutrients [20]. The CO_2 also has the potential to react with water within the microbial cells and subsequently form carbonic acid. The acid lowers the internal pH of the cell and deactivates pH sensitive cellular components [21].

At relatively low pressures and temperatures, carbon dioxide transitions to a supercritical state, often referred to as a dense phase gas. To work effectively, a supercritical gas requires a chemical modifier, such as ethanol, distilled water or hydrogen peroxide, which aid in the inactivation of microorganisms. The properties of supercritical CO_2 lend themselves to deep penetration of substrates, which enables the gas to destroy bacterial cells [22]. The effectiveness of supercritical gases is affected by different temperatures (40–105°C), CO_2 pressures (200–680 atm) and treatment times (25 minutes to 6 hours), the combination of which lead to different sterilisation cycle parameters [23].

As the technology stands, not all supercritical gas processes are sporicidal, and thus many only act as disinfectants. However, as research into the technology continues, the potential for supercritical gases to become established sterilisation methods could be harnessed.

11.8 Formaldehyde steam

Low-temperature steam with formaldehyde can be used as a low-temperature sterilisation method. The process involves the use of formalin, which is vaporised into a formaldehyde gas that is passed into the sterilisation chamber. A formaldehyde concentration of 8–16 mg/l is generated at an operating temperature of 70–75°C. The sterilisation cycle consists of a series of stages that include an initial vacuum to remove air from the chamber and load, followed by steam admission to the chamber with the vacuum pump running to purge the chamber of air and to heat the load. This is followed by a series of pulses of formaldehyde gas, followed by steam. Formaldehyde is removed from the steriliser and load by repeated alternate evacuations and flushing with steam and air [24].

Theoretically, the cycle time for formaldehyde gas is faster than that for other gaseous processes such as ethylene oxide. The process has a further advantage in that there are no temperature and humidity parameters to adjust. The main disadvantage is that formaldehyde is a mutagen and a potential human carcinogen. Consequently, much of the industrialised world has moved away from using formaldehyde [25].

11.9 X-rays

X-radiation (composed of X-rays) is a form of electromagnetic radiation. X-rays have a wavelength in the range of 0.01 to 10 nanometres, corresponding to frequencies in the range 30 petahertz to 30 exahertz

(3×10^{16} Hz to 3×10^{19} Hz) and energies in the range 100 eV to 100 keV. X-rays are shorter in wavelength compared with UV rays and longer than gamma rays. X-rays are sometimes referred to as Röntgen radiation [26]. X-rays have strong penetration capabilities because, like gamma rays, they consist of photons and react with the material being processed in a similar manner [27].

X-rays can be generated by an X-ray tube. This is a vacuum tube that uses a high voltage to accelerate the electrons released by a hot cathode to a high velocity. The high velocity electrons collide with a metal target, the anode, creating the X-rays. The use of a machine makes the application of X-ray sterilisation similar to the electron beam method.

X-rays have the same basic effect on microbial cells as gamma rays and electron beams [28]. This is due to the interaction of radiation with cellular DNA (which causes depolymerisation) and the physical and biochemical effects of the radiation on other cell structures such as RNA, proteins, cell membranes and enzymes [29].

Despite the long history of X-ray applications in medicine and industry, their application for medical device sterilisation is relatively new. The use of X-rays for sterilisation has been limited due to the high expenditure associated with the under-developed application of the technology. However, introduction of high-power, reliable accelerators and the economics of large X-ray sterilisation facilities are starting to become comparable with similar capacity gamma sterilisation facilities. X-ray installations, like gamma radiation, are typically designed to sterilise products in their final shipping configuration primarily because of their deep penetration capabilities.

11.10 Plasma

Plasma is a state of matter similar to gas, but where a certain portion of the particles within the gas are ionised, to the extent that plasma is often regarded as the fourth state of matter. Heating a gas may ionise its molecules or atoms (reduce or increase the number of electrons in them), thus turning it into plasma, which contains charged particles (positive ions and negative electrons) [30]. Plasma is a 'cold sterilisation' technology, because only the very lightweight electrons in the atoms are excited, and not the heavier nuclei. For reasons not yet fully understood, these non-radical plasmas can kill or inactivate certain cells, with microcidal kill more effective on planktonic communities than microorganisms bound to a surface. Several plasma products are believed to play a role in this process; these products include reactive oxygen species, reactive nitrogen species, UV radiation and charged particles.

Plasma theoretically works well as a surface sterilant. The efficacy of plasma for surface modification and cleaning is due to the energy of the plasma particles and/or the UV light they emit, as well as from chemical interaction of plasma constituents with surface molecules. The two commercially available methods deactivate microorganisms by ionising either peracetic acid or hydrogen peroxide to create low temperature gas plasma. The sterilisation process can be accomplished at temperatures lower than 50°C and the cycle time for this process can range anywhere from 75 minutes to 4 hours.

The main application for plasma has been in relation to food microbiology, using cold plasma to remove bacteria from fruit and vegetables without spoiling them. Another area is in medicine. The use of atmospheric pressure non-thermal plasmas has been evaluated for a number of biomedical applications, including wound healing, blood coagulation, skin regeneration, tooth bleaching and apoptosis of cancer cells. In time, such technology may become more commonplace in the pharmaceutical industry.

11.11 Nitrogen dioxide

Nitrogen dioxide (NO_2) has tended to be studied, not as a sterilant, but as a common component of air pollution. This body of knowledge has contributed with the development of NO_2 as a sterilant. Prior research has shown that DNA in mammalian cells is degraded via single-strand breaks upon exposure to NO_2 gas. Little has come of this development to date, although there has been some research directed towards the use of nitrogen dioxide for the sanitisation of isolators as an alternative to hydrogen peroxide.

11.12 Non-sterilising processes

There are a number of processes which reduce microbial populations, but are not sterilisation processes. A brief overview is provided, to emphasise the distinction as to what can be and what cannot be considered a sterilisation process.

11.12.1 Disinfection

Of all of the terms sometimes confused with 'sterilisation', disinfection is the most often misinterpreted term. A disinfectant is one of a diverse group of chemicals which reduces the number of microorganisms present (most efficiently on an inanimate object). Disinfectants form part of a wider group of anti-microbial agents called biocides and have bactericidal or bacteriostatic properties. To be defined as a disinfectant, a chemical does not need to be sporicidal and thus a disinfectant is not a sterilant. Disinfection, which is aimed at reducing a microbial load by a set value, is not synonymous with sterilisation [31]. Nevertheless, chemicals which are often classed as disinfectants that can be used for chemical sterilisation include glutaraldehydes and formaldehyde. Further detail on disinfectants is provided in Chapter 16.

11.12.2 Metals

Many heavy metals have antimicrobial properties and act as microcides. Metals such as silver, iron and copper can be used for environmental control, disinfection of water, reusable medical devices or incorporated into medical devices [32]. However, these are not sterilants and are best classified and discussed as disinfectants, so are thus outside the scope of this book.

11.12.3 Freeze drying

Freeze drying, also known as lyophilisation or cryodesiccation, is a dehydration process typically used to preserve a perishable material or make the material more convenient for transport. Product is contained within vials, with partially inserted closures (stoppers). The freeze-drying process works by freezing the material and then reducing the surrounding pressure to allow the frozen water in the material to sublimate directly from the solid phase to the gas phase. Within the lyophiliser the liquid in the vial is frozen and a vacuum is drawn. As the water from the solid (frozen) phase sublimes directly into vapour, the dosage form dehydrates. At the end of the cycle, the vacuum is broken and the closures are automatically rammed home.

Lyophilisation is not a sterilisation process, although it has the effect of inhibiting the action of microorganisms and enzymes through the

Published by Woodhead Publishing Limited, 2013

reduction in water activity, a measure of the energy status of the water in a solid. Higher water activity substances tend to support more microorganisms. Bacteria usually require at least 0.91, and fungi at least 0.7) [33]. At low water activity, microbial cell enzymes will not function and microbial cell growth is not possible. This does not necessarily kill the microorganism and, in fact, freeze drying is a method that can be used to conserve microbial strains in the presence of cryopreservation fluid [34].

However, the process can be vulnerable to microbiological contamination. The main vulnerability to microbiological contamination of that part of the overall process done within the lyophiliser is clearly at the point where the vacuum is broken and air enters. Replacement air must be filtered to become sterile but other undiscovered means of air contamination from leaks or bypasses cannot be discounted.

11.12.4 Pasteurisation

Pasteurisation is not a sterilisation process; its purpose is to destroy all pathogenic microorganisms. However, it will not destroy bacterial spores due to the limitation of time and temperature. Pasteurisation is generally limited to the food and beverage industries.

11.12.5 Flushing and rinsing

Procedures for flushing and rinsing (i.e. using sterile or low bioburden water) are appropriate for bioburden reduction and, in some cases, endotoxin removal. They are difficult to validate, in terms of demonstrating that microorganisms which adhere to surfaces can be reliably removed, and are not a means of sterilisation.

11.13 Conclusion

This chapter has described some of the novel sterilisation technologies that are either being developed or have attracted interest in the literature. It is unclear how many of these will become established within the pharmaceutical and healthcare sectors. To do so, such technologies need to be demonstrably effective at destroying microorganisms; they must not unduly damage the material being sterilised and they must be cost-effective. To meet all of these criteria is challenging.

11.14 References

1. Dewhurst, E. and Hoxey, E. (2003), 'New and emerging sterilisation technologies', in: Hodges, N. and Hanlon, G., *Industrial Pharmaceutical Microbiology*, Basingstoke, UK: Euromed Communications, pp. 14.1–21.
2. ISO (2009), International Standards Organization. ISO 14937:2009. Sterilisation of health care products – General requirements for characterisation of a sterilising agent and the development, validation and routine control of a sterilisation process for medical devices, Geneva: International Standards Organisation.
3. Perkins, J.J. (1983), *Principles and Methods of Sterilisation in Health Sciences*, 2nd edition, Charles C., Springfield, IL: Thomas Publishers, Ltd, pp. 95–166; 286–311.
4. Kowalski, W.J., Bahnfleth, W.P., Witham, D.L., Severin, B.F. and Whittam, T.S. (2000), 'Mathematical modeling of ultraviolet germicidal irradiation for air disinfection', *Quantitative Microbiology*, 2(3): 249–70.
5. Wolfe, R.L. (1990), 'Ultraviolet disinfection of potable water', *Environmental Science and Technology*, 24(6): 768–73.
6. Morris, E.J. (1972), 'The practical use of ultraviolet radiation for disinfection purposes', *Medical Laboratory Technology*, 29(1): 41–7.
7. Gruendemann, B.J. and Mangum, S.S. (2001), *Ultraviolet Irradiation and Lights, in Infection Prevention in Surgical Settings*, Philadelphia, PA: WB Saunders & Co, pp. 32–5.
8. Demirci, A. and Panico, L. (2008), 'Pulsed ultraviolet light', *Food Science and Technology International*, 14: 443–6.
9. Demirci, A. and Krishnamurthy, K. (2008), 'Pulsed ultraviolet light', in: Zhang, H.Q., Barbosa-Cánovas, G., Balasubramaniam, V.M., Dunne, P., Farkas, D. and Yuan, J. (eds), *Nonthermal Processing Technologies for Food. Technologists*, Ames, IA: Blackwell Publishing.
10. Jun, S., Irudayaraj, J., Demirci, A. and Geiser, D. (2003), 'Pulsed UV-light treatment of corn meal for inactivation of *Aspergillus niger*', *International Journal of Food Science and Technology*, 38: 883–8.
11. Dunn, J., Burgess, D, and Leo, F. (1997), 'Investigation of pulsed light for terminal sterilisation of WFI filled blow/fill/seal polyethylene containers', *PDA Journal of Pharmaceutical Science and Technology*, 51(3): 111–15.
12. Demirci, A. and Krishnamurthy, K. (2006), 'Disinfection of water by flow-through Pulsed ultraviolet light sterilisation system', *Ultrapure Water Journal*, 24(1): 35–40.
13. Guan, D., Gray, P., Kang, D.H., Tang, J., Shafer, B., *et al.* (2003), 'Microbiological validation of microwave-circulated water combination heating technology by inoculated pack studies', *Journal of Food Science*, 68(4): 1428–32.
14. Cope, F.W. (1976), 'Superconductivity – A possible mechanism for non-thermal biological effects of microwaves', *Journal of Microwave Power and Electromagnetic Energy*, 11(3): 267–70.
15. Wu, Q. (1996), 'Effect of high-power microwave on indicator bacteria for sterilisation', *IEEE Transactions on Biomedical Engineering*, 43(7): 752–4.

16. Keller, M.D., Bellows, W.K. and Guillard, R.L. (1988). 'Microwave treatment for sterilisation of phytoplankton culture media', *Journal of Experimental Marine Biology and Ecology*, 117(3): 279–83.

17. Najdovski, L., Dragas, A.Z. and Kotnik, V. (1991), 'The killing activity of microwaves on some non-sporogenic and sporogenic medically important bacterial strains', *Journal of Hospital Infection*, 19: 239–47.

18. Mata-Portuguez, V.H, Pérez, L.S. and Acosta-Gío, E. (2002), 'Sterilisation of heat-resistant instruments with infrared radiation', *Infection Control and Hospital Epidemiology*, 23(7): 393–6.

19. Stach, D.J., Cross-Poline, G.N., Newman, S.M. and Tilliss, T.S. (1995), 'Effect of repeated sterilisation and ultrasonic cleaning on curet blades', *Journal of Dental Hygiene*, 69(1): 31–9.

20. Zhang, J., Burrows, S., Gleason, C., Matthews, M.A., Drews, M.J., *et al.* (2006), 'Sterilizing *Bacillus pumilus* spores using supercritical carbon dioxide', *Journal of Microbiology Methods*, 66(3): 479–85.

21. Dillow, A.K., Dehghani, F., Harkach, J.S., Foster, N.R. and Langer, R. (1996), 'Bacterial inactivation by using near- and supercritical carbon dioxide', *Proceedings of the National Academy of Sciences USA*, 96: 10344–8.

22. Spilimbergo, S. and Bertucco, A. (2003), 'Non-thermal bacterial inactivation with dense CO_2', *Biotechnology and Bioengineering*, 84(6): 627–38.

23. Hemmer, J.D., Drews, M.J., LaBerge, M. and Matthews, M.A. (2007), 'Sterilisation of bacterial spores by using supercritical carbon dioxide and hydrogen peroxide', *Journal of Biomedical Materials Research, Part B: Applied Biomaterials*, 80(2): 511–8.

24. Kanemitsu, K., Kunishima, H., Imasaka, T., *et al.* (2003), 'Evaluation of a low-temperature steam and formaldehyde sterilizer', *Journal of Hospital Infection*, 55: 47–52.

25. Kanemitsu, K., Imasaka, T. and Ishikawa, S. (2005), 'A comparative study of ethylene oxide gas, hydrogen peroxide gas plasma, and low-temperature steam formaldehyde sterilisation', *Infection Control and Hospital Epidemiology*, 26: 486–9.

26. Novelline, R. (1997), *Squire's Fundamentals of Radiology*, 5th edition, Harvard, IL: Harvard University Press.

27. del Regato, J.A. (1985), *Radiological Physicists*, New York: American Institute of Physics.

28. Ginoza, W. (1967), 'The effects of ionizing radiation on nucleic acids of bacteriophages and bacterial cells', *Annual Reviews of Nuclear Science*, 17, 469–512.

29. Morrissey, R.F. (2002), 'Radiation sterilisation: past, present, and future', *Radiation Physics and Chemistry*, 63(3–6): 217–21.

30. Sturrock, P.A. (1994), *Plasma Physics: An Introduction to the Theory of Astrophysical, Geophysical and Laboratory Plasmas*, Cambridge, UK: Cambridge University Press.

31. Sandle, T. (2003), 'Selection and use of cleaning and disinfection agents in pharmaceutical manufacturing', in: Hodges, N and Hanlon, G., *Industrial Pharmaceutical Microbiology Standards and Controls*, Basingstoke, UK, Euromed Communications.

32. Weber, D.J. and Rutala, W.A. (1995), 'Use of metals and microbicides in the prevention of nosocomial infections', in: Rutala, W. (ed.), *Disinfection, Sterilisation, and Antisepsis in Healthcare*, New York: Polyscience Publications, pp. 271–85.

33. Fennema, O.R. (ed.) (1985), *Food Chemistry*, 2nd edition, New York: Marcell Dekker, Inc, pp. 46–50.

34. Heckly, R.J. (1985), 'Principles of preserving bacteria by freeze-drying', *Developments in Industrial Microbiology*, 26: 379–95.

Depyrogenation and endotoxin

DOI: 10.1533/9781908818638.171

Abstract: This chapter examines the process of depyrogenation, the removal or inactivation of bacterial endotoxin. Depyrogenation refers to a distinct and specialised set of processes that are different to sterilisation. This chapter outlines the different types of depyrogenation and then focuses on two types most applicable to pharmaceutical processing: dry heat inactivation of endotoxin and the removal of endotoxin through rinsing. These two different processes are illustrated through case studies, with an emphasis upon the essential validation requirements.

Key words: depyrogenation, bacterial endotoxin, dry heat, rinsing, endotoxin removal, endotoxin inactivation, validation.

12.1 Introduction

Chapter 2 outlined the importance of the risk of pyrogenic substances to sterile drug products and described the most common type of pyrogen, and the one of greatest risk, as bacterial endotoxins [1]. In relation to this earlier discussion, this chapter addresses depyrogenation, which is the elimination of all pyrogenic substances, including bacterial endotoxin, and is generally achieved by complex processes of removal or inactivation (or destruction)[1]. Depyrogenation is an important part of the manufacture of pharmaceutical products and is distinct from sterilisation, which refers to the destruction of living cells. However, the process does not necessarily destroy microbial by-products and toxins. Endotoxin is extremely heat stable and is not destroyed by standard sterilisation cycles (i.e.

autoclaving). Depyrogenation may be achieved through filtration, distillation, chromatography or inactivation.

In pharmaceutical production, it is necessary to remove all traces of endotoxin from drug product containers, as even small amounts will cause illness in humans. This is important because endotoxicity is not necessarily lost with loss of viability of microorganisms, as would be achieved through a successful sterilisation process [2]. Lipopolysaccharide (LPS) is not destroyed to any significant extent by sterilisation treatments such as steam sterilisation, gamma radiation, ethylene oxide or hydrogen peroxide. LPS also passes through $0.22\,\mu m$ bacteria retentive filters. Therefore, additional and different processes are required for depyrogenation within the pharmaceutical facility.

This chapter provides an overview of depyrogenation methods and then proceeds to examine two case studies in more detail. The first case study concerns endotoxin inactivation by dry heat and the second concerns endotoxin removal through water rinsing.

12.2 Different types of depyrogenation

There are various mechanisms by which depyrogenation is achieved. Some methods are more widespread than others and have different levels of success. The choice between methods partly relates to the material or object that is subjected to the depyrogenation method, in terms of the applicability of the method and whether or not the material can be subjected to it; here, as with moist heat sterilisation, products filled aseptically cannot be subjected to depyrogenation methods by heat [3]. The methods of depyrogenation are described below [4, 5].

12.2.1 Ultrafiltration

Ultrafiltration is a variety of membrane filtration in which hydrostatic pressure forces a liquid against a semi-permeable membrane ($0.025\,\mu m$ ultrafilters). Suspended solids and solutes of high molecular weight are retained, while water and low molecular weight solutes pass through the membrane; so, in a sense the ultrafilter functions as a molecular sieving process [6]. Ultrafiltration is not necessarily a method of depyrogenation, although it can be designed to be so. There are several different kinds of ultrafilters, with different nominal molecular weights.

Through this method of filtration by weight, endotoxin can be excluded by molecular weight using an ultra-fine filter, which blocks molecules of 10,000 Daltons or greater (the size of the LPS molecule). This is often coupled with a 0.1 μm filter. Ultrafiltration can be used as a method for removing endotoxin from liquids. The maximum efficiency is generally by up to 4-$\log_{10}$ [7].

12.2.2 Reverse osmosis

Reverse osmosis primarily functions as a size-excluding filter operating under highly pressurised conditions. The process will block 99.5% of endotoxin and ions and salts, whilst allowing water molecules through. In the USA, reverse osmosis is used to make Water-for-Injections (WFI), whereas to meet the *European Pharmacopoeia* requirement, this highest grade of pharmaceutical process water can only be produced by distillation [8].

12.2.3 Affinity chromatography

Affinity chromatography includes methods such as DEAE sepharose or polymyxin-B. Ion exchange chromatography is the most common depyrogenation method for removing endotoxin bound to proteins. The process binds endotoxin by using a positive charge to attract the negatively charged endotoxin molecules and then allowing for its elution. However, such processes are affected by the pH range, temperature, flow rate and amount of electrolytes in the solution [9].

There are some difficulties associated with this technology. These includes handling and usage problems such as packing columns, channelling, low flow rates, long regeneration times, compressibility and limited chemical stability [10].

12.2.4 Dilution and rinsing

Dilution and/or rinsing refers to either washing away endotoxin or reducing it down to an acceptable level through the use of 'pyrogen free' or low-endotoxin water, such as WFI [11]. The effectiveness of this technique is dependent upon how strongly endotoxin is bound to a surface.

12.2.5 Water and distillation

Endotoxins are a concern for pharmaceutical water systems. The vast majority of aquatic bacteria found in water are Gram-negatives. The risk increases as water undergoes greater processing, where bacteria are destroyed, thereby increasing the potential risk of endotoxins. The environmental endotoxin produced by the Gram-negative bacteria in water is highly heterogeneous and the potency varies according to bacterial species and strain; and by solubility and molecular weight. The more potent endotoxins are those of the highest molecular Lipid-A weight and those which are most disaggregated. In water, endotoxin has a tendency to aggregate to form vesicles (membranous structures). The size of these vesicles is dependent upon the type of the LPS structure and the pH, salt concentration and purity of the water. In pure water, the size is typically between 20,000 and 100,000 Daltons. Such environmental aggregates of endotoxin have a high affinity to surfaces.

The highest grade of pharmaceutical water is produced by distillation, which removes endotoxin (Figure 12.1). With this process, stills function by turning water from a liquid to a vapour and then from vapour back to

Figure 12.1 Distillation units

Published by Woodhead Publishing Limited, 2013

liquid. Endotoxin is removed by the rapid boiling, which causes the water molecules to evaporate and be passed into a separate system, whilst the relatively larger LPS molecules remain behind [12].

12.2.6 Adsorption

Adsorption includes the water treatment step of activated carbon beds, where endotoxin is absorbed into charcoal, or depth filters. Carbon beds function by attracting negatively charged endotoxin molecules to the carbon bed. This mechanism is only efficient to a small degree and is affected by a range of environmental factors [13].

12.2.7 Hydrophobic attachment

With hydrophobic attachment, certain materials, like polyethylene, can be used to bind endotoxin [14]. This method is used for specific biotechnology processes.

12.2.8 Acid or base hydrolysis

Acid or base hydrolysis destroys the eight carbon sugar (2-keto-3-deoxyoctonic acid) that links the Lipid-A component of endotoxin (the part that triggers the pyrogenic response) to the core polysaccharide and causes physiochemical changes that decrease pyrogenicity. The separated Lipid-A loses its pyrogenic activity. An example of this is the treatment of a substance by adding 0.05 M HCl for 30 minutes at 100°C (acid hydrolysis) or 0.5 M NaOH for 30 minutes at 50°C (base hydrolysis). It is possible, with alkaline hydrolysis, that the level of endotoxin may initially rise as part of the separation process [15].

The hydrolysis methods are frequently used for depyrogenating glassware. The efficiency of this process is often connected to the cleanliness of the glassware prior to treatment.

12.2.9 Oxidation

Oxidation works by peroxidation of the fatty acid in the pyrogenic Lipid-A region of the endotoxin molecule, for example, using hydrogen peroxide or ozone [16]. These methods are inappropriate for pharmaceutical products.

12.2.10 Ionising radiation

Theoretically, ionising radiation will inactivate endotoxin, although this is a very slow and inconsistent process, and one which is difficult to validate [17].

12.2.11 Ethylene oxide

Ethylene oxide functions by nucleophilic substitution in the glucosome of Lipid-A on the endotoxin molecule. It is not the most efficient depyrogenation process and where endotoxin inactivation occurs this is normally a side effect of sterilisation, rather than a specific depyrogenation step [18].

12.2.12 Moist heat

Moist heat, such as conventional autoclaving will not destroy endotoxin and, by the nature of destroying Gram-negative bacteria, can actually contribute to increasing endotoxin levels through cell lysis. However, the combination of a chemical additive, such as hydrogen peroxide, and physical variations, such as using 'super heat' for 5 hours at 121°C with a pressure of 20 psi and at a pH of 3.8, are sometimes effective. However, the destruction of endotoxin is difficult to achieve and only small log reductions will be obtained, when compared with dry heat. In essence, it is not a recommended method for depyrogenation [19].

12.2.13 Dry heat

Dry heat destroys endotoxin through the physical destruction of the endotoxin molecule. Dry heat processes achieve this by convection (transfer of heat by movement of fluid or air), conduction (transfer of heat from adjacent molecules) or irradiation (emission of heat by electromagnetic radiation) [20].

A depyrogenation oven or tunnel is used for this purpose. A defined endotoxin reduction rate is a correlation between time and temperature

[21]. To depyrogenate glassware, a temperature of 250°C and a holding time of 30 minutes is typically applied to achieve a reduction of endotoxin levels by a factor of 1000 [22].

Having outlined a variety of methods of depyrogenation (above), this chapter proceeds to examine the two most widely used methods of depyrogenation in the pharmaceutical industry: dry heat and rinsing.

12.3 Case study 1: Dry heat depyrogenation

A widely used method for endotoxin inactivation is dry heat. This process is commonly applied to glass vials, which are required for sterile parenteral manufacture. This is through the use of a specially designed oven or a tunnel. These devices require validating and this is performed along the conventional lines of design qualification, installation qualification, operational qualification and performance qualification [23].

Dry heat depyrogenation is a complex process, which is still poorly understood and there is contradictory research data [24]. The phenomenon that complicates the picture is that inactivation may approximate to Second-order chemical kinetics with a high initial rate of inactivation [25], then a tail off to nothing (following what Ludwig and Avis (1990) describe as a 'biphasic destruction curve') [26]. There is a logarithmic reduction until 3-logs of endotoxin have been eliminated and then a varied 'slow down' when the inactivation of endotoxin ceases to decrease at a log-step rate. This is partially why the criteria for a successful depyrogenation validation is set at 3-logs in the *United States Pharmacopeia*, and why some manufacturers set to achieve a 4-log reduction in order to overcome the risk of residual endotoxin. The time and temperature combination is of importance [27].

The regulatory standard for validation of an endotoxin inactivation (depyrogenation) process is that it should be capable of reducing an endotoxin challenge through 3-$\log_{10}$ reduction [28]. Oven temperatures above 180°C will inactivate endotoxin through 3-$\log_{10}$, provided that the time of exposure is sufficient. The *United States Pharmacopeia* recommends 250°C for 30 minutes and peak temperatures approaching 350°C are achieved in tunnels. Based on these data, it is worth noting that each valid depyrogenation process is also an overkill sterilising process.

D-values for pure endotoxin, the time required to achieve 1-log_{10} reduction in activity, at 170°C are as high as 20 minutes, which would suggest that 3-log_{10} reductions are achievable in 60 minutes. However, due to the complexity of the kinetics this is not necessarily true. What this means in practice is that at any particular depyrogenating temperature there will be some degree of inactivation in some period of time or other, but beyond that point there will be no further inactivation by holding the material at that temperature.

To ensure that this limit works, there is also a requirement to clean materials prior to dry heat depyrogenation with WFI otherwise, at least in theory, an item contaminated with 10 000 Endotoxin Units (EU) could enter a validated endotoxin inactivation process and still emerge with 10 EU intact and ready to contaminate the product.

All work with the validation of depyrogenating processes must be done empirically with endotoxin challenges. This is not easy, as the amount of endotoxin dried on an item, depending on the material of the item, may not be the maximum amount that can be recovered. Also the amount that can be recovered after treatment may only be a fraction of the amount that remains. Validation of endotoxin inactivation is a complex experimental area and requires a great deal of knowledge and a lot of well considered controls to be included [29].

For the validation of depyrogenation, devices are challenged using a known level of a high concentration of *Escherichia coli* endotoxin. The preparation used is a freeze-dried extract from the Gram-negative bacterial cell wall, LPS. The preparation is similar to the Control Standard Endotoxin (CSE) used for routine testing, although the concentration, once reconstituted, is far greater [30].

The testing of a depyrogenation device, at performance qualification, first involves running the device with a full set of containers in 'normal operation'. Simultaneously, the depyrogenation device is temperature mapped using thermocouples, which will indicate where the 'cold spots' (areas of the lowest temperatures) are within the device. The run is then repeated using endotoxin challenges at these colder areas, alongside thermocouples. A rationale should be in place for how many challenge vials to use per validation run; a number of less than 10 would be an inappropriate challenge. One problem to consider, before undertaking such a study, is how to identify the inoculated vials once they enter the tunnel, given that many tunnel sterilisers have a capacity for 20 000 bottles.

There are two approaches for adding the endotoxin challenges [31]:

Published by Woodhead Publishing Limited, 2013

1. using a high potency endotoxin spike directly onto the surface of the container to be depyrogenated; allowing this to dry or to freeze dry and then placing it into the depyrogenation device;

2. using vials of high concentration endotoxin and substituting these for the containers.

These prepared items are described as Endotoxin Indicators [32].

Of the two methods, the former is the one that is commonly employed and is generally expected from regulators. The second approach is sometimes regarded as not being a representative challenge. In both cases, the endotoxin challenge is typically 1000 EU or greater. The level of the challenge is determined by using control vials that are not subjected to the depyrogenation cycle. These are tested alongside the test vials on completion of the depyrogenation run. It is not necessary to recover all of the endotoxin from the control vials, and it is acknowledged that recovering endotoxin is very difficult. It is only necessary to recover a level of endotoxin to show that the necessary log reduction has been achieved. Therefore, if a 3-log reduction was required and 1000 EU was the theoretical challenge per container, but only 500 EU per container was recovered, then provided the test vials showed less than 0.5 EU/device recovery, then the 3-log reduction would have been achieved.

When carrying out a depyrogenation study, pyrogen-free pipettes and glassware must be used throughout. Exposed vials should also be covered with a pyrogen-free covering, such as Parafilm™. The vials that are challenged with endotoxin require preparation the day before the validation run. The endotoxin should be applied to the base of the vial and the vials dried, so that there is no visible endotoxin, under a unidirectional airflow cabinet. Typically, a 0.1 ml inoculum can take 8 hours to dry onto the surface of the glass. In order to increase the recovery of endotoxin, Novitsky recommends freeze-drying the challenge (rather than air-drying) [33], although this is not practical for all organisations to undertake. Other techniques include using an elevated temperature to increase the rate of drying.

Pre-validation work should be conducted to determine the maximal time interval between spiking the vials and placing them into the depyrogenation device, and at what temperature they are required to be stored at, with 2–8°C being typical. Work must also be carried out to determine the 'expiry time' of vials that have passed through the depyrogenation device, that is, how long the vials can remain before they are required to be tested. Typically, this time should not exceed 24 hours [34].

Once the depyrogenation cycle has been completed, the spiked containers or endotoxin vials are removed and tested using the LAL assay where the remaining level of endotoxin is assessed. This is performed by adding a known level of pyrogen-free water to the control and test vials. The amount of water should be sufficient to cover the base of the device and allow rinsing. The vials will require different techniques in order to remove the endotoxin from the glass surface. These are typically variations of vortex mixing and ultrasonication; the actual times required for optimal endotoxin recovery will need to be assessed by the user. A dispersing agent or buffer may also be used in place of pyrogen-free water.

An aliquot is then tested against an endotoxin standard series, consisting of a minimum of 3-log concentrations of endotoxin. The standard series is to be prepared using the same lot of endotoxin used to challenge the vials.

The control vials will require dilution prior to testing, and the level of dilution will depend upon the expected level of endotoxin to be recovered. Negative control vials are also required. Normally two types of negative controls are used. The first set consists of un-inoculated vials, which are not put into the depyrogenation device. The results from these will indicate if any residual endotoxin is present. The second set consists of vials that have passed through the depyrogenation device. These are tested in the event that the elevated temperature inside the depyrogenation device has resulted in the leaching of any interfering substances. Both types of negative controls should show no detectable endotoxin, or at least a low level of residual endotoxin of below the calculated 3-logs. The negative control vials are tested in the same way as the spiked test vials.

In order to claim depyrogenation, the device must show a 3-log reduction of endotoxin of a 1000 EU or more challenge (as per USP) [35].

There are several factors that introduce variability into depyrogenation studies and may affect the success or otherwise of the study. These include:

- the material being challenged, e.g. a glass vial behaves very differently to an aluminium cap (Figure 12.2);

- for glass, the type of glass the challenge vials are made from: Type I or Type II glass;

- the type of depyrogenation device and its efficiency. One key difference between dry heat ovens is the HEPA filter type and housing. Some filters shed a high number of particles during temperature transition (the rate of temperature change). Generally, the faster the temperature increases, the more particles are generated. This phenomenon is also affected by degree of airflow uniformity and pressure balance. Some of these particles may contain endotoxin or interfere with the LAL assay [36];

- the method used to dry the endotoxin to the container being tested;

- the mechanism of the depyrogenation device; devices that dry heat depyrogenate using infrared are more effective;

- different manufacturers endotoxin varies based on the extent of natural or artificial 'contaminants'. This is dependent upon how pure the endotoxin is (whether other cellular components are present) and whether the endotoxin containers 'fillers', i.e. glycol. These factors may increase or decrease the time taken to achieve heat inactivation.

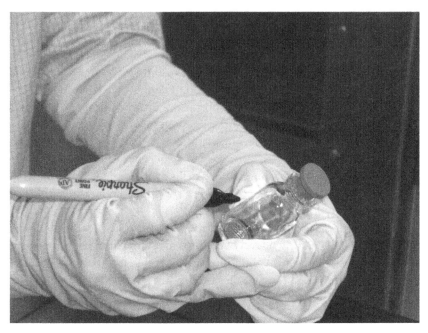

Figure 12.2 A depyrogenated glass vial complete with rubber closure

Published by Woodhead Publishing Limited, 2013

12.4 Case study 2: Removal of endotoxin through rinsing

An effective method of endotoxin removal is by rinsing a material with WFI, for example, as applied to rubber stoppers for vials prior to sterilisation. Rinsing is applied to vessels and major pieces of equipment used for sterile parenteral manufacture. The case study in this section focuses on rubber stoppers, which form part of the container-closure mechanism of a product vial.

Although the preparation of most rubbers and plastics does not readily lead to endotoxin contamination, subsequent processing can make them susceptible. Such follow-on risks include human handling, dust, dirty packaging material, rinsing with endotoxin contaminated water and environmental microbial contamination. Therefore, demonstrating that such devices for packaging materials are endotoxin-free is of importance, after the final rinse cycle has been completed, and a regulatory expectation. The advantage of 'ready to sterilise' components to pharmaceutical users cannot be underestimated, although the user must still test some lots initially and carry out a thorough audit of the manufacturer in order to have confidence in such systems.

Endotoxin removal by washing is a highly variable process. The process consists of a number of water rinses applied to product vials or container closures (typically elastrometric/rubber stoppers). The final rinse is WFI, normally 'hot', i.e. above 50°C. After the washing cycle, the components undergo sterilisation or depyrogenation. Even if the components are undergoing depyrogenation, it is important to understand the capabilities of the system in reducing what is sometimes referred to as the 'pyroburden', so that the user can have a level of confidence that the depyrogenation will be achieved (i.e. the pyroburden challenge is not too great).

The time between washing and sterilisation should be kept to a minimum, because any residual moisture on the components could lead to microbial growth.

As with dry heat depyrogenation, the rinsing process requires validating. Again, a known level of endotoxin is applied to the component undergoing washing. This validation is more difficult to perform and the results are more varied than studies on dry-heat devices.

Different factors, which affect the variability, are:

■ the concentration of the endotoxin applied;
■ the material of the closure may have a high affinity for endotoxin;

- binding sites may be limited due to 'pile up' of endotoxin of higher concentrations as saturation occurs (see below);
- presence of detergent or surfactant residues;
- rinsing procedures can be variable, especially for large vessels and tanks;
- representative sampling and placement of closures in the load;
- the method used to apply the endotoxin;
- the method used to extract the endotoxin.

The main way in which endotoxin is removed from a stopper is by the direct spiking of surfaces. The spiking of container closures is very difficult due to the material used (i.e. natural rubber or polybutadiene[2]) and the fact that endotoxin, once it enters pores on the surface, is very difficult to remove due to binding.

Typically, the endotoxin spike applied to rubber is of the lowest level that can be applied and where a 3-log reduction can still be measured. The reason for this is that where a very high level of endotoxin is used, there is a danger of simply applying endotoxin on top of endotoxin and it is the presence and absence of this, rather than the endotoxin actually adsorbed into the rubber surface, which is measured (a phenomenon called 'saturation'). These situations do not reveal anything about the actual depyrogenation process or, according to Williams (1995) [37]:

> The higher the level of endotoxin application, the less relevant the removal of it becomes to the removal of pyroburden levels of endotoxin.

The appropriate practice is not to increase the level of endotoxin in order to achieve a 3-log reduction, but to improve the sensitivity of the recovery method. Improvements to method recovery can be achieved through the addition of surfactants; increased agitation (by vortexing) and ultrasonication.

A simplified method for challenging the closures is outlined below.

12.4.1 Method

1. Add a low level endotoxin challenge to a number of closures (typically 10).
2. Keep a minimum of two closures aside to act as positive test controls.

3. Identify the closures in some way, i.e. using a different colour rubber, binding the stopper together with nylon, or making a small nick into the stopper surface.

4. Add the spiked closures into the standard load.

5. Subject the closures to the washing cycle.

6. Remove the spiked closures and return aseptically to the test laboratory.

7. The washer machine should be run through the cycle again or steam sanitised to remove any residual endotoxin.

8. The spiked closures and controls are then examined against a standard series to determine the endotoxin challenge and log-reduction. The test controls may require dilution depending upon the standard series used and theoretical challenge applied.

9. Other factors that affect LAL test variability, such as pH, remain of concern.

Having outlined an approach to the validation of rinsing, a question arises as to whether rinsing can really be validated and assured? The answer is that the sampling statistics are likely to be poor, the test method is inaccurate, and probably there is not very much endotoxin present to begin with. This is an area that the regulators have looked at but there is no consistent standard, although it is implicit that a 3-$\log_{10}$ reduction should be achieved by washing, just as it should be by heat inactivation. From this, satisfactory validation of washing processes is not easy to demonstrate, or conversely, it can be easy, depending on the rigour of the validation design and the minutiae of process knowledge.

Questions of concern that arise include:

■ Where should the endotoxin 'spike' be placed on the material or item being washed? The sensible location on vial stoppers must be that part of the stopper that potentially could come into contact with the product.

■ How much endotoxin should be 'spiked' on items or materials? We can envisage that if too much is added, i.e. 1 000 000 EU/component, it could be too easily removed and may reveal little about the washing method used. Alternatively, too little may not even allow demonstration of a 3-$\log_{10}$ reduction.

■ How effective are washing processes? Air bubbles can cling to the surfaces of rubber stoppers and create areas that do not interact properly with the washing process.

■ How effective are washing machines? Batch washing machines generally work on a siphonage principle such that removed materials (including endotoxin) are flushed upwards out of the washer rather than allowing the removed materials to settle back on the washed items. Continuous (semi-continuous washers), commonly used for glassware and linked to depyrogenating tunnels, hold items upside down throughout the washing process; the final water rinse is frequently recycled to be the first wash, and probably adds less endotoxin than a lower grade of water would.

12.5 Conclusion

This chapter has presented an overview of different types of depyrogenation and has examined, in more detail, two mechanisms of depyrogenation, dry heat inactivation and endotoxin removal. These are common processes found in many pharmaceutical production facilities; although with the latter, the purchase of 'ready to sterilise' container closures is becoming increasingly common and is in a lower risk strategy.

For both dry heat and endotoxin removal, the archetypal questions relate to the number of validation runs and frequency of re-validation surface. The number of validation runs is contemporaneously taken to be three. The frequency of re-validation is to be determined by the user and this is typically annually. Both methods of depyrogenation require the use of endotoxin indicators. Increasingly, the same levels of control are being applied to endotoxin indicators as to biological indicators, in terms of preparation and verification of their suitability.

It should not be forgotten, on achieving successful depyrogenation, that the pyroburden that presents a risk to pharmaceuticals is derived from a combination of raw materials, water, active ingredients, environment and primary packaging materials [38]. Therefore, risks of endotoxin or other pyrogenic contamination can arise from multiple sources and not simply from the final containers alone.

12.6 Notes

1. It is important to note that some scientists regard depyrogenation purely as endotoxin destruction or inactivation, and endotoxin removal as a distinct and unrelated process. Nevertheless, it is more common for the term to cover both inactivation and removal, and this chapter adheres to this convention.
2. Other elastic or rubber containers include polyisoprene, styrene, nitrile butadiene and polychloroprene.

12.7 References

1. Erridge, C., Bennett-Guerrero, E. and Poxton, I.R. (2002), 'Structure and function of lipopolysaccharides', *Microbes and Infection*, 4: 837–51.
2. Baines, A. (2000), 'Endotoxin testing', in: Baird, R.M., Hodges, N.A. and Denyer, S.P. (eds), *Handbook of Microbiological Quality Control*, London: Taylor & Francis, pp. 144–67.
3. Weary, M. and Pearson, P. (1988), 'A manufacturer's guide to depyrogenation', *Biopharm*, 1(4), 2–7.
4. Sandle, T. (2004), 'Three aspects of LAL testing: Glucans, depyrogenation and water system qualification', *Pharmaceutical Microbiology Interest Group News*, 6: 3–12.
5. Tours, N. and Sandle, T. (2008), 'A comparative study of different methods of endotoxin destruction', *Pharmaceutical Microbiology Interest Group News*, 30: 4–8.
6. Abramson, D., Butler, L.D. and Chrai, S. (1981), 'Depyrogenation of a parenteral solution by ultrafiltration', *Journal of Parenteral Science and Technology*, 35(1): 3–7.
7. Brown, S. and Fuller, A.C. (1993), 'Depyrogenation of pharmaceutical solutions using submicron and ultrafilters', *Journal of Parenteral Science and Technology*, 47(6): 285–7.
8. Hou, K.C. and Zaniewski, R. (1990), 'Depyrogenation by endotoxin removal with positively charged depth filter cartridge', *Journal of Parenteral Science and Technology*, 44(4): 204–9.
9. Malchesky, P.S., Zborowski, M. and Hou, K.C. (1995), 'Extracorporeal techniques of endotoxin removal: a review of the art and science', *Advance in Renal Replacement Therapy*, 2(1): 60–9.
10. Petsch, D. and Anspach, F.B. (2000), 'Endotoxin removal from protein solutions', *Journal of Biotechnology*, 76: 97–119.
11. Gorbet, M.B. and Sefton, M.V. (2005), 'Endotoxin: The uninvited guest', *Biomaterials*, 26(34): 6811–17.
12. Meltzer, T.H. (1995), *Pharmaceutical Water Systems*, Littleton, CO: Tall Oaks Publishing, pp. 739–44.
13. Anspach, F.B. (2001), 'Endotoxin removal by affinity sorbents', *Journal of Biochemical and Biophysical Methods*, 49(1–3), 665–81.
14. Xing, Z., Pabst, M.J., Hasty, K.A. and Smith, R.A. (2006), 'Accumulation of LPS by polyethylene particles decreases bone attachment to implants', *Journal of Orthopaedic Research*, 24(5): 959–66.
15. McCullough, K.Z. and Novitsky, T J. (1985), 'Detoxification of endotoxin by acid and base', Ch. 8. PDA Technical Report No. 7, Philadelphia, PA: Parenteral Drug Association, Inc.
16. Anderson, W.B., Mayfield, C. and Dixon, D.G. (2003), 'Endotoxin inactivation by selected drinking water treatment oxidant', *Water Research*, 37: 4553–60.
17. Bertók L. (1999), 'A new possibility for enhancing natural immunity: a radiation-detoxified endotoxin', *Orvosi Hetilap*, 140(15): 819–27.
18. Hudson, C.T. and Nase, R. (1985), 'Inactivation of endotoxin by ethylene oxide sterilisation and Cobalt T60 irradiation', Ch. 14, PDA Technical Report No. 7, Philadelphia, PA: Parenteral Drug Association, Inc.

Published by Woodhead Publishing Limited, 2013

19. Fujii, S., Takai, M. and Maki, T. (2002), 'Wet heat inactivation of lipopolysaccharide from *E. coli* Serotype 055:B5', *PDA Journal of Pharmaceutical Science and Technology*, 56(4): 220–7.
20. Baird, R. (1988), 'Validation of dry heat tunnels and ovens', *Pharmaceutical Engineering*, 8(2): 31–3.
21. Avis, K.E., Jewell, R.C. and Ludwig, J.D. (1987), 'Studies on the thermal destruction of *Escherichia coli* endotoxin', *Journal of Parenteral Science and Technology*, 41: 49–56.
22. Guy, D. (2003), 'Endotoxins and depyrogenation', in: Hodges, N. and Hanlon, G. (eds), *Industrial Pharmaceutical Microbiology: Standards and Controls*, Passfield, UK: Euromed Communications, 12.1–15.
23. Tours, N. and Sandle, T. (2008), 'Comparison of dry-heat depyrogenation using three different types of Gram-negative bacterial endotoxin', *European Journal of Parenteral and Pharmaceutical Sciences*, 13(1): 17–20.
24. Akers, M.J., Ketron, K.M. and Thompson, B.R. (1982), 'F Value requirements for the destruction of endotoxin in the validation of dry heat sterilization/depyrogenation cycles', *Journal of Parenteral Science and Technology*, 36(1): 23–7.
25. Tsuji, K. and Lewis, A.R. (1978), 'Dry-heat destruction of lipopolysaccharide: Mathematical approach to process validation', *Applied and Environmental Microbiology*, 36: 715–19.
26. Ludwig, J.D. and Avis, K.E. (1990), 'Dry heat inactivation of endotoxin on the surface of glass', *Journal of Parenteral Science and Technology*, 44(1): 4–12.
27. Tsuji, K. and Harrison, S.J. (1978), 'Dry-heat destruction of lipopolysaccharide: dry-heat destruction kinetics', *Applied and Environmental Microbiology*, 36: 710–14.
28. Agalloco, J.P. and Carleton, F.J. (2007), *Validation of Pharmaceutical Processes*, 3rd edition, New York: CRC Press, p. 233.
29. Novitsky, T.J., Schmidt-Gengenbach, J. and Remillard, J.F. (1986), 'Factors affecting the recovery of endotoxin adsorbed to container surfaces', *Journal of Parenteral Science and Technology*, 40: 284–6.
30. Nakata, T. (1993), 'Destruction of typical endotoxins by dry heat as determined using LAL assay and pyrogen assay', *Journal of Parenteral Science and Technology*, 47(5): 258–64.
31. Anon. (1989), 'Preparation and use of endotoxin indicators for depyrogenation process studies', *Journal of Parenteral Science and Technology*, 43(3): 109–12.
32. Sandle, T. (2007), 'Some considerations on the use of endotoxin indicators in depyrogenation studies', *Pharmaceutical Microbiology Forum Newsletter*, 13(10): 2–11.
33. Novitsky, T.J. (1996), 'Limulus Amebocyte Lysate (LAL) assays in automated microbial identification and quantitation', in: Olson, W.P. (ed.), *Automated Microbial Identification and Quantitation*, New York: CRC Press, pp. 277–98.
34. Plant, I. (1993), 'Destruction of typical endotoxins by dry heat as determined using LAL assay and pyrogen assay', *Journal of Parenteral Science and Technology*, 47(5): 258–64.

35. Hecker, D., Witthaeur, D. and Staerk, A. (1994), 'Validation of dry heat inactivation of bacterial endotoxins', *PDA Journal of Parenteral Science and Technology*, 48(4): 197–204.
36. Melgaard, H. (1988), 'Filter shedding and automatic pressure balance in batch depyrogenation ovens', *Pharmaceutical Engineering*, 8(6), 37–43.
37. Williams, K. (1995), 'Differentiating endotoxin removal from inactivation in vial component depyrogenation validations', *Pharmaceutical Technology*, October.
38. Sandle, T. (2011), 'A practical approach to depyrogenation studies using bacterial endotoxin', *Journal of GXP Compliance*, 15(4): 90–100.

Published by Woodhead Publishing Limited, 2013

Cleanrooms, isolators and cleanroom technology

DOI: 10.1533/9781908818638.189

Abstract: This chapter examines cleanrooms and clean air devices. Cleanrooms are special environments where a number of environmental parameters are controlled, including levels of airborne particles and they are designed to create spaces where contamination levels are minimised. Cleanrooms are used in most pharmaceutical manufacturing facilities and for the manufacture and filling of all sterile products. The chapter introduces cleanrooms and describes how they are certified and classified. It also explains the key aspects of the physical operation of cleanrooms and discusses ongoing monitoring requirements.

Key words: cleanrooms, clean air, unidirectional air, particles, particle counting, environmental monitoring, viable counts, agar, HEPA filtration, HVAC systems.

13.1 Introduction

Many biopharmaceutical and pharmaceutical processes and manufacturing steps take place in cleanrooms, and all sterile product manufacturing must, according to regulations, be undertaken within a cleanroom. This is in order to minimise product contamination, for if the product becomes contaminated, the level of contamination may be to the extent that the contaminating microorganisms are resistant to the sterilisation process or, in the case of aseptic filling, cannot be removed or eliminated. In this regard, the FDA states in its 21 CFR Part 820.70 'Production and process controls', section 'c', that [1]:

> Where environmental conditions could reasonably be expected to have an adverse effect on product quality, the manufacturer shall establish and maintain procedures to adequately control these environmental conditions.

Cleanrooms and clean zones are typically classified according to their use, the main activity within each room or zone, and confirmed by the cleanliness of the air through the measurement of particles. In addition to air cleanliness, certain environmental parameters must be met. Furthermore, the construction and use of the room is in a manner to minimise the generation and retention of particles. The classification is set by the cleanliness of the air.

The cleanliness of the air is controlled by an HVAC system (Heating, Ventilation and Air-Conditioning). Cleanrooms are used in several industries, including the manufacture of pharmaceuticals and in the electronics industry. For pharmaceutical cleanrooms, air cleanliness is either based on EU GMP guidance for aseptically filled products, where EU GMP alphabetic notations are adopted; or by using the International Standard ISO14644, where numerical classes are adopted.

The management of cleanrooms in the twenty-first century requires risk-based approaches, which are encouraged by the FDA. Risk-based approaches involve identifying risks, assessing their impact by accounting for the severity of the risk and the likelihood of its occurrence, and then either accepting the risk or eliminating it. Where a risk cannot be eliminated or reduced to a satisfactory level, the risk should be monitored. It is around such detection systems that cleanroom environmental monitoring is based [2].

This chapter discusses cleanrooms and clean zones. Clean zones are special areas within the cleanroom designed to provide cleaner environments either through the localised provision of clean air or through the use of barrier technology (i.e. an isolator system). The chapter addresses the issues of cleanroom certification, design and operations.

13.2 Cleanrooms and contamination control

The objective of cleanrooms is to maintain a clean air space and to avoid the product being contaminated from particles (including microorganisms) being carried in the air stream. There are many sources of contamination [3]. The atmosphere contains dust, microorganisms, condensates and gases. Manufacturing processes will also produce a range of contaminants. Wherever there is a process which grinds, corrodes, fumes, heats, sprays, turns, etc., particles and fumes are emitted and will potentially contaminate the surroundings (Figure 13.1).

People in clean environments are the greatest contributors to contamination through emitting body vapours, dead skin, microorganisms, skin oils, and so on. The average person sheds 1000 million skin cells per day, of which 10% have microorganisms on them. This statistic alone demonstrates the importance of personnel working within cleanrooms wearing cleanroom clothing and wearing this clothing correctly [4]. Most cleanroom microorganisms are suspended in the air, originating from

Figure 13.1 Operator working on an aseptic filling line

Published by Woodhead Publishing Limited, 2013

people. If they settle on a dry surface, they are unlikely to survive. However, microorganisms can be transferred by people touching surfaces.

Second to people, the key contamination source is water. This is an important issue, for water is the main ingredient in many products, and is used widely throughout the main process areas. Water is a risk because it is both a growth source for microorganisms and a vector for contamination transfer. Other sources of contamination relate to equipment and the items and consumables transferred into a cleanroom.

Whilst air can potentially be a source of contamination, it is also the means to ensure that cleanrooms are clean. We require personnel to operate our processes, so we need an air supply. Even in clean rural areas, air is contaminated with about 10^8 particles of 0.5 μm and more per m^3; many of these will be microorganisms, depending on the nature of the area and the season of the year: so air is a contamination problem. However, in the pharmaceutical industry, air flow is the answer to many contamination problems, as discussed in relation to the physical monitoring of cleanrooms below.

There are four principles applying to control of air borne microorganisms in clean rooms:

1. *Filtration* – through the use of HEPA filters. The air entering a cleanroom from outside is filtered to exclude dust, and the air inside is constantly recirculated through High Efficiency Particulate Air (HEPA) filters. This is controlled through an HVAC system.

2. *Dilution* – to ensure that particles generated in cleanrooms, in addition to those which pass the filters, are carried away by diluting the clean area with new 'clean' air.

3. *Directional Air Flow* – to ensure that air blows away from critical zones, as particles and microorganisms cannot 'swim upstream' against a directional air flow. For this, some cleanrooms are kept at a higher air pressure so that if there are any leaks, air leaks out of the chamber instead of unfiltered air coming in.

4. *Air Movement* – whereby rapid air movement is important, for as long as particles and microorganisms stay suspended in the air they are not really a problem. It is only when they settle out that they become an actual cause of contamination.

These principles are key to cleanroom design.

Other ways by which contamination is controlled within cleanrooms are:

Published by Woodhead Publishing Limited, 2013

- Staff enter and leave through airlocks and wear protective clothing such as hats, face masks, gloves, boots and coveralls.

- Equipment inside the cleanroom is designed to generate minimal air contamination. There are even specialised mops and buckets. Cleanroom furniture is also designed to produce a low amount of particles and to be easy to clean.

- Contamination control requires personnel to practice aseptic techniques, to wear specially designed clothing; and to behave in ways to minimise contamination.

- Common materials such as paper, pencils and fabrics made from natural fibres are excluded from the cleanest working areas, including areas used for aseptic filling.

- Cleanroom HVAC systems also control the humidity to low levels, such that extra precautions are necessary to prevent electrostatic discharges.

- Opportunities for contamination are minimised (i.e. not leaving water puddles on the floor).

- Cleanrooms should be regularly cleaned and disinfected using approved techniques and validated disinfectants (Chapter 16).

13.3 Cleanroom classification

There are two main ways by which cleanrooms are classified, either to EU GMP [5] or to ISO 14644 [6], which are used by the FDA. Somewhat confusingly, EU GMP refers to ISO 14644 for cleanroom classification but uses its own grading system for routine operations; and the FDA refers to ISO 14644 for both classification and for routine operations. EU GMP uses letters to denote cleanroom grades and the ISO standard uses numbers for cleanroom classes. The descriptors indicate how clean a cleanroom is, based on the permitted maximum number of particles allowed within a cubic metre of air. There are differences between the two standards, in relation as to whether cleanrooms are operating in the static or dynamic states.

Static conditions are listed in Table 13.1:

For static conditions (or 'at rest'), there is a difference between European, ISO and US standards in terms of meaning:

- EU GMP defines the static state as a room without personnel present, following 15–20 minutes 'clean up time', but with equipment operating normally.

- ISO defines 'at-rest' as all required equipment being installed and operating, but with no personnel present.
- The FDA guidance for aseptic filling indicates that equipment must not be running.

Dynamic conditions, are listed in Table 13.2:

Dynamic conditions (or 'operational') are defined as rooms being used for normal processing activities with personnel present and equipment operating. Here there is agreement between the standards.

In order to ensure that cleanrooms and their HVAC systems are functioning correctly, cleanrooms are classified at different intervals (ISO classes 5 and 7 (EU GMP Grade A and B) six-monthly, and other cleanrooms annually). Classification of cleanrooms is confirmed in the dynamic state by taking non-viable particulate readings at a defined number of locations for $0.5\,\mu m$ size particles (some users additionally elect to monitor for $5.0\,\mu m$ size particles).

The sampling locations for the classification of a cleanroom are derived from the formula in ISO 14644-1. Establishment of the sampling locations is based on the area of the room.

Table 13.1 EU GMP and ISO 14644 equivalence table, static state

EU GMP	ISO 14644-1
A	4.8
B	5
C	7
D	8

Table 13.2 EU GMP and ISO 14644 equivalence table, dynamic state

EU GMP	ISO 14644-1
A	4.8
B	7
C	8
D	9

The formula is:

$$NL = \sqrt{A}$$

where NL is the minimum number of sampling locations (rounded up to a whole number) and A is the area of the cleanroom or clean zone in m^2 for which the square root is taken.

Once the number of samples has been calculated, samples are to be taken at approximately equal distance apart, by dividing the clean area into a grid, whilst taking into account fixed equipment. Samples are to be taken approximately 1 m from the floor or at the height of the work activity. Only one sample is required to be taken from each location, unless there is only one location in the clean area, and in this case three samples are required. A sample is a minimum of 20 counts/readings for a minimum sample volume of 2 litres. A 95% UCL is applied when there is less than 9 sample locations in a clean area.

'Particle' in the context of a cleanroom is a general term for sub-visible matter. Airborne particles refers to particles suspended in air. The unit of measurement for particles is the micrometre (or 'micron'). This is symbolised as μm. The micron is a unit of length equal to one millionth (10^{-6}) of a metre. Air contains a variety of different particles of a range of different sizes. These are particles of dust, dirt, skin, microorganisms and so on. An ISO Class 5/EU GMP Grade A cleanroom is designed not to allow more than 100 particles (0.5 μm or larger) per cubic foot of air.

Regarding cleanrooms, the regulatory standards discussed below focus on two sizes of particles, which are selected due to the potential risk they pose. These are:

■ 0.5 μm size particles, which are close in size to many microorganisms;

■ 5.0 μm size particles, which are close in size to skin flakes, to which many microorganisms are bound.

With European GMP, there is concern with both types of particle size. With the FDA, the primary focus is upon the 0.5 μm size.

Particle counting is performed using a variety of optical particle counters, which are aerosols passed through a focused light source, where the scattered light is converted into electrical pulses to allow the counting of particles. These are designed to detect the number of particles of a given size from a given volume of air. Some particle counters may be connected to a Facility Monitoring System (FMS).

Particle counters draw air in using a pump at a controlled flow rate. The air is passed into a sensor area and through a light beam created by a laser diode. The amount of light reflected from each particle is measured electronically, as an electronic pulse. The larger the particle, then the larger the amount of reflected light observed (the greater the height of the light pulse). This allows the particle counter to 'count' the number of particles in a given volume of air (as the number of light pulses) and to assess the size of the particles counted.

Once a room has been assigned a classification, certain environmental parameters (physical and microbiological) are to be met on a routine basis. For viable monitoring it is normal for the microbiologist to set action levels based on an historical analysis of data. The frequency of the assessment of these other parameters should be assessed based on a risk management approach. This approach should consider the room use and the risk to the product. Factors to consider may include room activities, exposure risk, room temperature, process stage, duration of process activities, water exposure and so on.

13.4 Cleanroom operating conditions

Cleanrooms have three different 'states' of use, which are as built, static and dynamic [7].

'Built' refers to the condition of a newly built cleanroom, with the operational qualification having been completed, at the point it is handed over to the user for performance qualification. 'Static' conditions is the room without personnel present, following 15–20 minutes 'clean up time', but with equipment operating normally. 'Dynamic' conditions (or 'operational') are defined as rooms being used for normal processing activities, with personnel present and equipment operating. The dynamic condition is the most relevant to assess, as this reflects the conditions within which the product is processed.

13.5 Measuring the physical operation of cleanrooms

A number of aspects of the physical operation of cleanrooms and clean air devices require monitoring, in order to demonstrate that environmental control is maintained [8, 9].

Published by Woodhead Publishing Limited, 2013

13.5.1 Air filtration

HEPA filters are designed to control the number of particles entering a clean area by filtration. These filters were invented and developed during World War II as parts of atomic bomb research for containment of radioactive aerosols [10]. HEPA filters function through a combination of three important aspects. First, there are one or more outer filters that work like sieves to stop the larger particles of dirt, dust and hair. Inside those filters, there is a concertina – a mat of very dense fibres – which traps smaller particles. These pre-filters are designed to remove 90% of particles from the incoming air. The inner part of the filter uses three different mechanisms to catch particles as they pass through in the moving airstream. At high air speeds, some particles are caught and trapped as they smash directly into the fibres, while others are caught by the fibres as the air moves past. At lower air speeds, particles tend to wander about more randomly through the filter (via Brownian motion) and may stick to the fibres as they do so. Together, these three mechanisms allow HEPA filters to catch particles, which are both larger and smaller than a certain target size.

There are different grades of HEPA filters, based on their 'efficiency ratings'. One of the most commonly used HEPA filters is the H14 filter, which is designed to remove 99.997% of particles from the air. To use an example, if air contains about 3×10^8 particles per m^3, and there is one pre-filter and one HEPA Filter:

■ Pre-filter leaves about 3×10^7 per m^3, as a challenge to the HEPA filter.
■ The terminal HEPA filter leaves about 10^3 per m^3.

In addition to assessing the efficiency of HEPA filters, they are also subject to leak testing. Because potential leakage is not confined to the filter media, there is a requirement to perform an *in situ* filter integrity test. This is commonly called the DOP test after Di-octyl phthallate, one of the first substances used as an aerosol challenge for this test. Alternative fluids with similar particle-size distribution, such as BP-grade paraffin and Poly-Alfa-Olefins (PAOs), are now commonly used. The chemical is used in conjunction with an aerosol generator, a device used in conjunction with an aerosol photometer, which creates a polydispersed sub-micron aerosol to challenge integrity of HEPA filters and containment of safety cabinets.

The accepted standard is that the tolerable leakage of an aerosol challenge should be not more than 0.01% (note, this is not the reciprocal

Figure 13.2 An isolator within a cleanroom

of the filter efficiency). This is measured using an aerosol photometer, a device which determines particle concentration in air by measuring the mass concentration of scattered light [11].

13.5.2 Air changes

Each cleanroom grade has a set number of air changes per hour that the room must achieve. Air changes are provided in order to dilute any particles present to an acceptable concentration. Particles are then removed through air ventilation. Any contamination produced in the cleanroom is, theoretically, removed within the required time appropriate to the room grade. This is important, because particles would otherwise build up in enclosed spaces if there were no ventilation.

The minimum ventilation rate expected in pharmaceutical cleanrooms is 20 air changes per hour; the modern requirement is up to twice as many as this, and up to 75 for a changing room, and the air in a cleanroom is replaced at least every 3 minutes. In contrast, an office might have 2–3 air changes per hour. Monitoring air changes is necessary, because the recirculation of filtered air is important for maintaining control of the clean area. Air change rates stated are the minimum and should be calculated from supply air volume and room volume measurements.

13.5.3 Clean-up times

Connected to air changes is the time taken for a clean area to return to the static condition, appropriate to its grade, in terms of particulates after an incident, when a high level of particles has occurred. Clean-up times are sometimes referred to as 'recovery tests'. The conducting of clean-up times is an optional test to be considered at the time of room classification, following substantial changes to room design, for newly built clean rooms or as part of an investigation. Typically, cleanrooms should 'clean up' within 15–20 minutes.

13.5.4 Positive pressure

In order to maintain air quality in a cleanroom, the pressure of a given room must be greater relative to a room of a lower grade. This is to ensure that air does not pass from 'dirtier' adjacent areas into the higher grade cleanroom. Pressure differentials are expressed in Pascals, used to describe the relative pressures from a higher grade area into a lower one. Generally this is 15–20 Pascals, although some areas of the same grade will also have differential pressure requirements due to specific activities, such as where dust is generated through the weighting of powders [12].

13.5.5 Temperature and humidity

EU GMP Grade B rooms have set requirements for temperature and humidity. These are monitored for operator comfort and to avoid a high temperature–humidity situation, which may result in the shedding of microorganisms. Other clean areas have a temperature appropriate to the process step (e.g. if the process requires a cold room at 2–8°C).

Lighting should be adequate, uniform and anti-glare, to allow operators to perform process tasks effectively. A range of 400 to 750 lux is recommended.

13.5.6 Airflows

An assessment of airflows is a requirement for sterile manufacturing, to assess the ISO class 5 (Grade A zone) and the surrounding ISO class 7 (Grade B) room. Within cleanrooms, the air is normally operating at a turbulent flow, where air enters the room with non-uniform velocity, or with turbulent flow. With clean air devices, the object is to have unidirectional airflow (UDAF). Airflows, for critical activities in relation to UDAF devices, should be studied in order to show that air turbulence does not interfere with critical processes. This is undertaken by visualising the airflow with the use of smoke [13].

13.5.7 Air velocity

The air velocity of clean air devices is an important parameter, as this demonstrates if contamination is being blown away from the critical zone. Airflows are monitored using an anemometer. The air velocity is designed to be sufficient to remove any relatively large particles before they settle on to surfaces. The acceptance criterion, according to EU GMP and FDA regulations, is a speed of 0.45 m/s ± 20%. The FDA Guide requires airflow measurements to be taken at 6 feet from the filter face and 'proximal to the work surface'. The EU GMP Guide requires readings to be taken at the working height.

13.6 Clean air devices and isolators

Within many cleanrooms, various clean air devices are used. The terminology of ISO 14644-7 'Cleanrooms and associate controlled environments – Part 7' is 'Separative Devices', which is used to collectively describe clean air hoods, gloveboxes, isolators and mini-environments (Figure 3.2). These devices include laminar airflows, more commonly described as UDAF devices in the context of pharmaceutical manufacturing, given that 'true' laminarity cannot be easily demonstrated, Biosafety Cabinets, Restrict Access Barrier Systems (RABS) and isolators. Such devices normally operate at EU GMP Grade A/ISO Class 5. The term 'cabinet' is used more widely within Europe and the term 'hood' used more widely in the USA [14].

Whereas most cleanrooms operate with a turbulent airflow, clean air devices are designed to minimise turbulence, which creates dust and dirt collection pockets by operating with the air blowing in one direction (hence unidirectional), where the design feature is to move air away from the critical activity to ensure that any contamination is blown away to a less critical area.

With UDAF devices, these are either constructed with horizontal flow or vertical flow. Specially designed UDAFs are biosafety cabinets. These are 'self-contained' enclosures to provide protection for personnel, environment and/or products when working with hazardous microorganisms. The cabinets provide protection by creating an air barrier at the work opening and by HEPA filtration of exhaust air. Class I cabinets protect the operation or the product from personnel contamination, whereas Class II cabinets protect personnel, environment and products.

For some UDAF devices, gloves are fitted in order to restrict the number of personnel interventions. Such devices are described as Restrict Access Barrier Systems (RABS). These stand partway between a conventional UDAF and an isolator. Another special type of cabinet is the powder containment cabinet. These are compact containment cabinets with inward airflow and HEPA filtration that provide protection for operators and the environment from powders generated by processes, such as compounding of pharmaceuticals.

Another type of clean air device is an isolator, which is superior to a cleanroom in that the contamination risk is reduced through the construction of a barrier between the critical area (sometimes called the 'micro-environment') and the outside environment. Thus, an isolator utilises constructional and/or aerodynamic means to enclose a controlled workspace. Isolators are used for sterility testing, aseptic filing and other applications where a clean environment is required [15].

In basic construction, isolators have either a flexible film barrier or a rigid physical barrier (Figure 13.3). The controlled workspace may be positive or negative pressure relative to the background environment and the airflow inside may be unidirectional or non-unidirectional (turbulent). In addition to its physical and dynamic components, all pharmaceutical isolators require a means to achieve sanitisation of the controlled workspace and the items in it and entering it [16]. The most widely used method of sanitisation is using hydrogen peroxide vapour (Chapter 9).

A variation of an isolator is a glovebox, which is an enclosure fitted with sealed gloves, that allows external manual manipulations in controlled or hazardous environments.

Other aspects of cleanroom design, which contribute towards the maintenance of a clean air space and operations, are described below.

Figure 13.3 An operator preparing a flexible film isolator

13.6.1 Pass through hatches

Many cleanrooms contain pass-through hatches. These are hatches with double doors that protect critical environments while allowing transfer or materials to or from adjoining rooms. They are typically installed within the walls of cleanrooms. The hatches allow materials to be transferred with minimal loss of room pressure and without the need for personnel movement between rooms.

13.6.2 Airlocks

An airlock is an airtight room which adjoins two cleanrooms. The airlock acts as a buffer zone between two independent areas of unequal pressure. A pressure differential of $\geq 15\,Pa$ is typically maintained between the inner room and the air lock; and between the air lock and the external area (Section 13.5.4).

13.7 Ongoing monitoring

In addition to formal classification, non-viable air monitoring is required at other times, such as described below.

13.7.1 Batch fill monitoring

Where aseptic filling takes place, there should be continuous monitoring of airborne particle counts at ISO class 5/EU GMP Grade A and at ISO class 7/EU GMP Grade B [17].

13.7.2 Routine monitoring

There should be a routine programme for cleanroom particle count monitoring. This examination of air borne particle counts is for the same sizes of particles required for the classification: 0.5 (and in addition, 5.0 μm for EU GMP regulated sectors). This is undertaken using an optical particle counter. Particle counters are used to determine the air quality by counting and sizing the number of particles in the air [18].

In addition to particulate monitoring, cleanrooms should also be assessed for numbers and incidences of microorganisms [19]. Viable monitoring is designed to detect levels of bacteria and fungi present in defined locations/areas during a particular stage in the activity of processing and filling a product. Samples are taken from walls, surfaces, people and the air, each of which represents a potential contamination source. Viable monitoring is designed to detect microorganisms and answer the questions: how may? how frequent? when do they occur? why do they occur?

Viable monitoring is undertaken using a substance called agar (a jelly-like growth medium) in different-sized Petri dishes. Sometimes mechanical devices are used to pull in a defined quantity of air (an air sampler). The unit of measurement for viable monitoring is the colony forming unit (cfu). This is a measure of viable bacterial or fungal numbers. It contrasts to direct microscopic counts where all cells, dead and living, are counted, for the cfu is only a measurement of viable cells, where growth is dependent upon a specific culture medium and under specific growth parameters of time, humidity, atmosphere and temperature.

The environmental monitoring programme is normally controlled by a microbiology department, who establish the appropriate frequencies and

| Table 13.3 | Environmental monitoring methods |

Method	Air	Surface	Personnel
1	Active air sampler (cfu/m^3)	Contact plate (cfu/25 cm^2)	Finger plate for hands (cfu/5 fingers) Contact plate for gowns (cfu/25 cm^2)
2	Settle plate (cfu/90 mm over × time)	Swab (cfu/surface)	

Note: cfu = Colony Forming Unit.

durations for monitoring based on a risk assessment approach. The sampling plan takes into account the cleanliness level required at each site to be sampled.

Viable microbiological monitoring is normally performed using the methods listed in Table 13.3.

With these methods:

- Settle plates detect any microorganisms which might gravitate or fall onto an exposed plate located in a defined area. They are particularly useful within UDAF units. EU GMP recommends a 4 hour exposure.

- Active (or volumetric) air sampling is a quantitative method. Air samples measure the number of microorganisms in a given volume of air (1 m^3).

- Contact plates allow a defined area of approximately 25 cm^2 (at a defined pressure) to be measured, whereas swabs only give an indication of the bioburden on a given area and can over estimate counts due to the formation of microcolonies or aggregates. Contact plates are more appropriate where the surface is flat and where lower contamination is expected (i.e. ≤50 cfu) [21 22]. Contact plates used for surfaces cleaned with disinfectants must contain an appropriate neutraliser. Contact plates are equivalent to RODAC (Replicate Organism Detection and Counting) plates. The plate provides a 'mirror image' of the contamination and positional information [23].

- Swabs are used for sampling irregular surfaces or where high levels of contamination are expected (i.e. ≥50 cfu). Generally, swabs provide only a qualitative indication of a surface bioburden.

In addition to the above classic methods, there are several developments with rapid methods that utilise the concept of Process Analytical Technology (PAT) in order to streamline air sampling. Technologies are now available which deploy fluorescence sensor technology to count both non-viable and viable particles. The prospect for 'real time' viable counting offers the potential to strengthen contamination control and to avoid many of the concerns and limitations of conventional methods [24].

The frequency of viable microbiological monitoring should be based on a criticality risk assessment of cleanrooms. For aseptic filling operations, monitoring is normally performed for each operating shift. Here samples of air are taken at defined time intervals during the fill and surfaces samples are taken at the end of the fill. Each individual present in the fill should also be monitored using finger plates. For lower-grade cleanrooms, monitoring should be by risk assessment, which should be based on an examination of each cleanroom based on different factors within the room.

Although compendia publish guideline alert and action levels for microbiological and particulate monitoring, regulators expect that, after a facility has been operating for a period of time, for monitoring levels to be set by the user to more closely reflect the actual environmental conditions [25].

Individual results from microbiological monitoring are rarely of significance when examining the totality of data gathered. What is of importance is the direction of the trend that the data is taking over time and the monitoring levels applied to indicate deviations from the norm. The key purpose of data gathering is environmental control, rather than simply environmental monitoring, or the act of gathering data and not analysing it. Further to this, all microorganisms from samples above the action level from samples should be characterised to species level.

13.8 Conclusion

The importance of well-maintained and functioning cleanrooms cannot be underestimated. Cleanrooms are an essential feature of contamination control and are required to reduce the risk that the product to be sterilised or filled or assembled aseptically is done so under conditions that will minimise the transference of microorganisms. In outlining the requirements for cleanroom construction and design, and for the continued monitoring, this chapter has shown cleanrooms and clean air devices to be complex areas. No single chapter can cover all of the required aspects; instead this chapter provides an introduction to cleanrooms and containment controlling devices.

13.9 References

1. Food and Drug Administration. Code of Federal Regulations: Title 21 – Food and Drugs. Ch. 1, Sub-ch. H: Medical Devices. Part 820: Quality System Regulation. Sub-part g: Production and Process Controls. 820.70 Production and process controls, Rockville, MD: Food and Drug Association, undated.
2. Whyte, W. and Eaton, T. (2004), 'Microbiological contamination models for use in risk assessment during pharmaceutical production', *European Journal of Parenteral and Pharmaceutical Sciences*, 9(1): 11–15.
3. Halls, N. (2004), 'Effects and causes of contamination in sterile manufacturing', in: Hall, N. (ed.), *Microbiological Contamination Control in Pharmaceutical Clean Rooms*, Boca Raton, FL: CRC Press, pp. 1–22.
4. Sharp, J., Bird, A., Brzozowski, S. and O'Hagan, K. (2010), 'Contamination of cleanrooms by people', *European Journal of Parenteral and Pharmaceutical Sciences*, 15(3): 73–81.
5. Euradlex (2009), *The Rules Governing Medicinal Products in the European Community*, Annex 1, Brussels: European Commission.
6. ISO Standard 14644 – Cleanrooms and associated controlled environments – Part 1: 'Classification of air cleanliness', Part 2: 'Specifications for testing' and Part 4: 'Cleanrooms and associated controlled environments', Geneva: International Standards Organisation.
7. Sandle, T. (2003), 'General considerations for the risk assessment of isolators used for aseptic processes', *Pharmaceutical Manufacturing and Packaging Sourcer*, Winter: 43–7.
8. Schicht, H.H. (2002), 'HVAC requirements and design concepts for facilities manufacturing non-sterile dosage forms', in: *Utilities Used by the Manufacturer of Pharmaceuticals*, Pharmaceutical Inspection Cooperation Scheme PIC/S, Geneva: Pharmaceutical Inspection Convention PIC (ed.), pp. 187–206.
9. Ramstorp, M. (2000), *Introduction to Contamination Control and Cleanroom Technology*, Weinham: Wiley, VCH.
10. EN 1822 (2009), High efficiency particulate air filters (EPA, HEPA and ULPA): Part 1: 'Classification, performance testing and marking', Part 2: 'Aerosol production, measuring equipment, particle counting statistics', Part 3: 'Testing flat sheet filter media', Part 4: 'Determining leakage of filter elements (scan method)', Part 5: 'Determining the efficiency of filter elements', Idem, ibid., November.
11. Whyte, W. (2001), *Cleanroom Technology: Fundamentals of Design, Testing and Operation*, Chichester, UK: John Wiley & Sons.

12. Whyte, W. (1992), *Cleanroom Design*, Chichester, UK: John Wiley & Sons.
13. Ross, S. and Sandle, T. (2007), 'Air pattern analysis of a filtration transfer', *Pharmaceutical Microbiology Interest Group News*, 26: 3–4.
14. Sandle, T. (2004), 'General considerations for the risk assessment of isolators used for aseptic processes', *Pharmaceutical Manufacturing and Packaging Sourcer*, Winter: 43–7.
15. Martin, P. (2010), 'The use of barrier isolator technology for a sterile anti-cancer drug', in: Agalloco, J.P. and Akers, J., *Advanced Aseptic Processing Technology*, USA: Informa Healthcare Books.
16. Midcalf, B., Phillips, W.M., Neiger, J.S, and Coles, T.J. (2004), *Pharmaceutical Isolators: A Guide to Their Application, Design and Control*, London: Pharmaceutical Press.
17. Food and Drug Administration (2004), *Guideline on Sterile Drug Products Produced by Aseptic Processing*. Rockville, MD: Food and Drug Association.
18. Vincent, D. (2002), 'Validating, establishing and maintaining a routine environmental monitoring program for cleanroom environments: Part I', *Journal of Validation Technology*, 8(4): 25–32.
19. Johnson, S.M. (2004), 'Microbiological environmental monitoring', in: Hodges, N. and Hanlon, G., *Microbiological Standards and Controls*, London: Euromed Communications.
20. Sandle, T. (2011), 'Environmental monitoring', in: Saghee, M.R., Sandle, T. and Tidswell, E.C. (eds), *Microbiology and Sterility Assurance in Pharmaceuticals and Medical Devices*, New Delhi: Business Horizons, pp. 293–326.
21. Niskanen, A. and Pohja, M. (1977), 'Comparative studies of sampling and investigation of microbial contamination of surfaces by the contact plate and swab methods', *Journal of Applied Bacteriology*, 42: 53–63.
22. Favero, M., *et al.* (1968), 'Microbiological sampling of surfaces', *Journal of Applied Bacteriology*, 31: 336–43.
23. Brummer, B. (1976), 'Influence of possible disinfectant transfer on *staphylococcus aureus* plate counts after agar contact sampling', *Applied and Environmental Microbiology*, July: 80–4.
24. Miller, M.J., Lindsay, H., Valverde-Ventura, R. and O'Conner, M.J. (2009), 'Evaluation of the BioVigilant IMD-A, a novel optical spectroscopy technology for the continuous and real-time environmental monitoring of viable and nonviable particles, Part I: Review of the technology and comparative studies with conventional methods', *PDA Journal of Parenteral Science and Technology*, 63(3): 244–57.
25. Lovegrove-Saville, P. and Perry, M. (2000), 'Setting environmental alert and action limits', *Pharmaceutical Microbiology Interest Group News*, 3, December.

Aseptic processing and filling

DOI: 10.1533/9781908818638.209

Abstract: This chapter describes aseptic processing, whereby a sterile product is assembled through the filling of a sterile bulk product into a sterile container. Unlike terminal sterilisation, products filled or assembled aseptically cannot be subjected to any further sterilisation. This means that aseptically filled products are those most at risk of contamination. The main sources of microorganisms within sterile product manufacturing facilities is discussed. The design and operational considerations of aseptic processing and some of the different types of aseptic filling operations, such as blow-fill-seal, are outlined. Included within the design discussion is reference to cleanrooms, and within the discussion on operations reference is made to personnel and aseptic practices. This chapter concludes by describing the advantages of single-use sterile disposable technology used for making aseptic connections and for product holding.

Key words: aseptic filling, asepsis, filling machine, cleanroom, blow-fill-seal, opthalmics, solid dose forms, contamination control, personnel, gowning, single-use sterile disposable technology.

14.1 Introduction

The first part of this book described methods of terminal sterilisation, where a product can be sterilised in its final container and different parametric attributes can be considered to assess the sterility assurance level and, thus, the probability of non-sterility can be assessed mathematically. Due to their inherent nature, some products cannot be subjected to the methods of terminal sterilisation described in the previous chapters. Such products are instead produced by aseptic filling.

With aseptic manufacture, the dosage form and the individual components of the containments system are sterilised separately and then the whole presentation is brought together by aseptic methods, which ensure that the existing sterility is not compromised. Thus aseptic filling involves the handling of sterile materials in a controlled environment, in which the air supply, materials and equipment are regulated to control microbial and particulate contamination to acceptable levels. Aseptic filling is subject to a greater contamination risk than terminal sterilisation, since the same level of sterility assurance cannot be built into the process.

Aseptic filling requires close coordination and complex interaction between personnel, sterilised product, the fill/finish equipment system, cleanroom and support facilities, and sterilised filling components (Figure 14.1). Virtually any solution, powder or suspension can be aseptically filled, although there are strict regulatory guidelines that need to be met prior to the selection of aseptic filling as opposed to terminal sterilisation (these are outlined below).

Aseptic filling ranges from hand filling operations for small quantities, to complex filling machines which operate at speeds of up to 300 units per minute and higher. The term 'aseptic filling' can embrace everything from the assessment of incoming raw materials, intermediate processing, utility validation and so forth. These areas, whilst essential elements of pharmaceutical manufacturing, fall outside the scope of this book.

This chapter focuses on the design and operation of aseptic filling. Much of this is addressed in general terms in relation to the filling of aqueous drug products. Reference is made to other forms of aseptic filling, such as solid dosage forms and blow-fill-seal. The sources of contamination that pose a potential risk to aseptically filled products, and to the trajectory within the biopharmaceutical industry towards the use of single-use disposable technology as a contamination control measure, are considered.

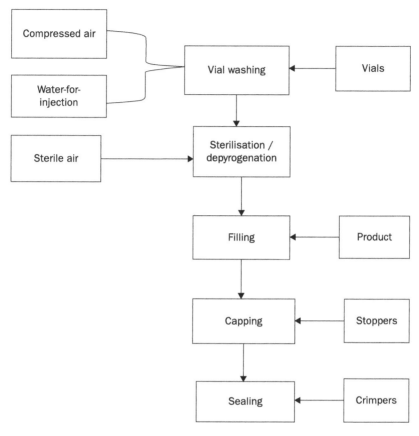

Figure 14.1 Diagram showing the main steps involved for aseptic filling

14.2 Selecting aseptic manufacture in place of terminal sterilisation

The decision as to which method should be employed for the manufacture of sterile products is towards terminal sterilisation wherever possible. This is due to the greater assurances from terminal sterilisation, as well as meeting European and FDA regulatory requirements. The FDA states its preference for terminal sterilisation in its 2004 guide relating to aseptic filling: 'Guidance for Industry Sterile Drug Products Produced by Aseptic Processing – Current Good Manufacturing Practice'. The inference is that terminal sterilisation is the method of first choice and falls back on aseptic manufacture only if terminal sterilisation is conclusively shown to be unsuited to the product [1].

With Europe, the European Medicines Agency issued guidance in 2000: 'Decision trees for the selection of sterilisation methods' [2]. The guide emphasises that 'products intended to be sterile should be terminally sterilised ... where it is not possible to carry out terminal sterilisation by heating due to formulation instability, a decision should be made to utilise an alternative method'. It should be noted that heat liability of a packaging material itself cannot be considered as an adequate justification for not utilising terminal sterilisation for otherwise heat stable products. Consequently, the first step in establishing the processing conditions, and therefore the design of the manufacturing facility, is to determine whether terminal sterilisation will be required.

14.3 Regulatory aspects

Aseptic processing is highly regulated and there is considerable guidance in the US Code of Federal Regulations (CFR 21, i.e. CFR 21 Sub-part C (211.42)), FDA documents, and in the EU GMP the 'Rules and Guidance for Pharmaceutical Manufacturers and Distributors' [3]. Nonetheless, regulatory guidance limits the basic principles expected of pharmaceutical manufacture and there are aspects that are open to interpretation or become part of 'current' Good Manufacturing Practice (cGMP).

The principal sources of guidance are:

- FDA Guidance for Industry 2004 on Drug Products Produced by Aseptic Processing [4];

- USP Microbiological Control and Monitoring of Aseptic Processing Environments [5];

- ISO 13408 Aseptic Processing of Healthcare Products [6];

- ISO 14698-1. 'Cleanrooms and associated controlled environments – Biocontamination control', Part 1: 'General principles and methods' [7]; ISPE Baseline Guide to Sterile Manufacturing Facilities [8].

Refer to Chapter 3 for more details of regulatory guidance.

14.4 Aseptic processing risks and sources of contamination

There are several sources of contamination within cleanrooms (Chapter 13). These sources of contamination present a concern for aseptic processing. There are parts of the process where the sterility of the product could be compromised as a result of the interaction of people or of the environment, such as manually connecting a bulk vessel of filter-sterilised liquid to a filling machine, filling a filter-sterilised liquid into a sterilised vial, and so forth [9].

The sources of microbiological contamination within clean environments are water, air, surfaces (both within the room and from equipment) and personnel. The potential for microorganisms from these to contaminate cannot be completely eliminated, since they are often inherent features of the manufacturing process. They can, nonetheless, be controlled.

In reviewing these contamination sources, people are the most significant source of contamination, although they are a highly variable and unpredictable source [10]. Microorganisms are shed from hair, skin, eyes and mucous membranes. Microorganisms are either deposited into the air stream or can spread through contact. Control of microbiological contamination from personnel sources is achieved by a combination of product-containment technologies (i.e. unidirectional airflow air, isolators and solid barriers) personnel-containment equipment (clothing) and discipline (Figure 14.2) [11].

Water is a common feature in pharmaceutical processing, as an ingredient, a cleaning agent, a diluent for disinfectants, steam supply, etc. The concern with water in cleanrooms is that it not only provides a means for microorganisms to survive, but also provides the opportunity for the numbers of microorganisms to increase. However, in most aseptic processing suites, water is excluded and there will only be rare and occasional sources such as from a vessel leak, or possibly from a disinfectant residue. However, water is an ingredient in most pharmaceutical formulations and is commonplace in processing areas leading up to the point of aseptic filling. The risk from water is partly controlled through the use of pharmaceutical grade water of a low bioburden (purified water or Water for Injection), by keeping areas clean and dry, and through appropriate cleaning and disinfection practices.

The air in most areas contains microorganisms. However, the number of microorganisms will vary according to the cleanroom grade. Air is a

Figure 14.2 Operator loading a flexible film isolator in a laboratory

vector for microorganisms, but it is not a nutritive environment. This means that some bacteria can survive in air streams but they cannot multiply. Bacteria in air are normally found in association with dust particles or skin flakes, rather than as individual microorganisms; the term 'microbial carrying particle' is sometimes used. This makes the microorganisms heavier and more prone to gravitational settling. Therefore, what often matters most is not the numbers of microorganisms in the air but their potential for settling [12].

For preparations to be protected from microbiological contamination during aseptic manufacture, it is essential to filter the air provided to the processing environment [13]. It is also essential that the filtered air is not recontaminated by interaction with contaminated air from the external environment. This, in aseptic manufacture, is achieved by an outward flow of filtered air from cleaner areas to less clean areas, which creates a pressure cascade; this is measured as a pressure differential. Air flow protection is outlined in Chapter 13.

The other contamination source relates to materials and surfaces. Here, the key risks are the transfer of items in and out of a clean area. This can include trolley wheels, which are not correctly sanitised, to cardboard used to hold reagents, to non-sterile items in critical areas. Materials are more at risk if they are of a design that cannot be easily cleaned or disinfected; and from personnel touching surfaces. As mentioned above, another risk is the contamination of surfaces through deposition (i.e. settling from the air) [14]. Control is achieved through minimising the amount of packaging that enters a cleanroom and by using sterilised material where possible, such as gamma irradiated sterile disposable within critical zones, and through effective cleaning and disinfection practices. Equipment should be designed and constructed to be suitable for cleaning and disinfection, such as using robust materials, having smooth finishes, avoidance of difficult to clean nooks and crannies, etc. Those pieces or parts of equipment that come into direct contact with product should be suitable for sterilisation.

14.5 Contamination control

Avoiding contamination control with aseptic processing relates to two key areas:

1. the design of facilities and processes; and
2. the operation of processes.

These are not independent and must combine holistically so that the design process and the facility surrounding it, and the movement of materials and personnel, synergise into an effective integrated system.

14.5.1 Design considerations

Whilst aseptic manufacturing facility design is complex and every facility is unique, careful consideration must be given to the design of aseptic operations, including the class of cleanrooms, areas where the product is transferred into the aseptic processing area, sterilisation devices for closures, depyrogenation ovens or tunnels for vials, and areas for overFsealing. The fundamental aspects of the design are cleanrooms and equipment [15]. A regulatory expectation is that risk assessment has been built into the design process [16].

The fundamental aspect of cleanroom control measures is designed to minimise the introduction, generation and retention of such airborne particles. In relation to cleanroom design, a floor plan of the areas holding the aseptic filling facilities, including preparation and holding areas, filtering and filling areas, and gowning rooms, should be prepared. The air cleanliness class of each area should be identified. The placement of all critical equipment including, but not limited to, unidirectional flow hoods, autoclaves, lyophilisers and filling heads, should be identified. Critical equipment must be housed within barrier or isolation systems and should be recorded [17].

Cleanrooms must be designed and constructed to allow for frequent cleaning and disinfection. Walls and floors should be impervious and smooth, and easy to clean. The junctions between floors and walls and between walls and walls should be coved. Service pipes should be avoided, where possible running within cleanable smooth surfaced conduits. In addition, electrical sockets should be installed with covers.

In terms of cleanrooms and clean zones areas, where the product or vials are exposed, or where connections are undertaken, must be EU GMP Grade A/ISO 14644 class 5, and the surrounding room must be EU GMP Grade B/ISO 14644 class 7. Here the most critical zone is the 'point-of-fill'. This is the location where units of the sterile dosage form are released from the containment system that maintained their sterility in bulk into their final containers, and where these containers are sealed to ensure and maintain the sterility of their contents. Sealing is undertaken either by the insertion of a stopper into a vial or by the sealing of an ampoule by heat. The risk is greatest here, because this is the moment in time when contamination is likely to be of most significance. Furthermore, the sterilisation and depyrogenation processes used for containers, closures, equipment, components and barrier systems should be validated (Figure 14.3).

A further design consideration relates to equipment. Aseptic manufacturing equipment must be designed to facilitate cleaning and disinfection. This means high standards of materials of construction, mainly stainless steel or polymeric materials, and high standards of finish. Equipment should be designed in such a way that personnel interactions are minimised. All filling machines for ampoules, vials and syringes are protected within cabinets provided with Perspex, glass or other such transparent doors or panels. Provided the doors and panels are closed, contamination from personnel is significantly reduced.

The aseptic processing core requires protection by a unidirectional airflow system, which is a standalone clean zone that effectively flushes the work space with clean, HEPA (high efficiency particulate air) filtered air that corresponds to EU GMP Grade A of ISO 14644 class 5 regulatory limits. The unidirectional airflow is either contained within a closed

Published by Woodhead Publishing Limited, 2013

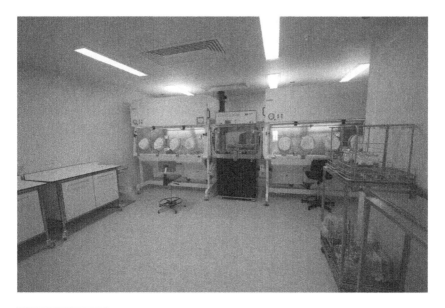

Figure 14.3 An isolator within a cleanroom

cabinet or within a barrier isolator system. It is also necessary to protect the filling machine from contamination. This is achieved by locating the filling machine in a filling room that has been designed and constructed for this purpose (an EU GMP Grade B/ISO 14644 class 7 environment). In addition to filling machines, HEPA-filter unidirectional airflow protection is provided over the doors of autoclaves and ovens entering into aseptic filling rooms.

An isolator is a type of containment device that utilises barrier technology for the enclosure of a controlled work space. With isolators, human intervention is minimised to a far greater extent which results, theoretically, in a significant decrease in the risk of microbial contamination. A second type of barrier system is a restricted access barrier system (RABS), where the filling machine is enclosed and, like an isolator, is accessed from the outside via gloveports. The difference between an isolator and a RABS is that isolators are exposed internally to a gaseous sterilant, usually hydrogen peroxide, whereas RABS devices are cleaned and disinfected by personnel, as with conventional aseptic technology [18].

It is evident from the discussion above that the filling machine equipment design must be carefully considered. After a filling machine is installed (and paid for), there is often little that can be changed in its design without causing other problems. All aseptic process designs should go through the validation system and this must begin with a User Requirement Specification (URS). This is followed by a Design Qualification (DQ), an Operational Qualification (OQ) and a Performance Qualification (PQ). 'In operation' (or 'dynamic') qualification of aseptic filling is achieved under simulated conditions using media fills (Chapter 15).

14.5.2 Aseptic processing

With aseptic processing, the flow (movement) of product and components from formulation to finished dosage form should be identified and mapped (Figure 14.1). This includes the following:

a) *Drug product solution filtration* – The specific bulk drug product solution is filtered through a bacterial retentive filter as the product is passed from the manufacturing area into the aseptic processing area.

   Due to the potential additional risks of the filtration method as compared with other sterilisation processes, a second filtration through a further sterilised microorganism-retaining filter immediately prior to filling is normally undertaken. The final sterile filtration should be carried out as close as possible to the point of fill. The integrity of the sterilised filter should be verified before use and should be confirmed immediately after use by an appropriate method such as a bubble point, diffusive flow or pressure hold test.

b) *Materials* – The containers and seals required for filling and sealing the product are sterilised and must be introduced into the filling room without contaminating them. These are normally sterilised via double-ended autoclaves (for the stoppers and overseals) or through depyrogenation tunnels (for vials). Other materials may be passed into filling rooms via transfer hatches or air locks.

   These materials are prepared and washed in support areas prior to sterilisation or, as with stoppers, can be purchased ready-to-sterilise.

c) *Holding periods* – Time limits for completing each phase of production to ensure the quality of the drug product should be established. Therefore, specifications concerning any holding periods between the compounding of the bulk drug product and its filling into final containers must be set. These specifications should include, for example, holding tanks, times, temperatures and conditions of storage. In addition, procedures used to protect microbiological quality of the bulk drug during these holding periods should be established.

d) *Personnel entry* – Personnel enter the aseptic filling area through changing rooms. Changing rooms should be designed as air locks. This is typically a two-stage process, with the final changing area being of the same cleanroom grade as the area to which it leads (i.e. EU GMP Grade B/ISO class 7). Personnel wear dedicated garments. When personnel undress, they shed microorganisms into the environment; therefore the number of air changes per hour becomes critical to changing rooms.

e) *Personnel operations* – Personnel must follow good aseptic technique, wear the correct gowns, masks and gloves, and adopt cleanroom behaviour disciplines, such as slow careful movements, frequent hand disinfection, and no leaning over exposed product or product-contact components [19].

f) *Filling machine set-up* – Due to reliance upon personnel intervention, the activity of machine set-up is arguably the highest risk activity. It is necessary to sterilise the filling pumps and needles, and stopper bowls, required for the filling of the product in an autoclave, and then to assemble them aseptically and fit them aseptically to the filling machine; this affords the greatest risk to asepsis of any operation in the filling room. Set-up therefore requires good attention to aseptic technique by personnel.

Filling pumps, for example, consist of a stainless steel cylinder and a stainless steel piston, which have to be sterilised separately and then assembled and fitted to the machine, unless a sterile, plastic disposable manifold system is in place. There may be anything from 2 to 8 of these per filling machine.

The key steps involved in set-up include:

- placing settle plates;
- aseptically assembling the pumps;
- aseptically fitting the pumps;
- aseptically fitting the filling needles;
- aseptically installing stopper bowls;
- close settle plates and place for collection;
- disinfecting the machine.

g) *Running the filling line* – Starting the filling machine involves flushing any air out of the pumps and needles and then beginning filling, adjusting and sampling the fill volumes until the process is under control and fully operational. Following this, filling begins.

h) *Cleaning* – At the end of the filling run, the filling line must be disassembled and the machine cleaned. Individual components must be sent back to non-aseptic areas for cleaning and subsequent sterilisation prior to the next filling run.

i) *Oversealing* – After filling, stoppered vials must be crimped and capped in special machines, which are supplied, according to European GMP requirements, with EU GMP Grade A/ISO class 5 cleanliness air.

During filling there are several operations which need to be performed. These are:

- taking samples for periodic volume or weight checks;
- replenishing stoppers in the stopper hoppers or bowls;
- replenishing over-seals in over-seal hoppers or bowls;
- dealing with jammed stoppers or vials, which requires an aseptic intervention by an operator, either directly or through a gloveport.

In relation to the process, the microbiological monitoring programme used during routine production and media fills should be described [20]. The frequency of monitoring, type of monitoring and sites monitored, must be described in procedures [21]. Here there is a requirement for continuous particle monitoring and viable monitoring through the use of settle plates. Active air samples should be taken periodically, along with finger plates of operators' hands, together with end-of-fill surface monitoring [22]. Environmental monitoring is outlined in Chapter 13.

14.6 Types of aseptic filling

Up to this point, this chapter has described aseptic filling in general terms modelled on the filling of a liquid product. There are other types of aseptic fills, which are described below.

14.6.1 Solid dosage forms

Some products are prepared as solid dosage forms, such as antibiotics, particularly β-lactams, which are inherently unstable in solution. For these activities, active ingredients are manufactured aseptically and filled into large cans or plastic containers. These are brought into support areas 'double' or 'triple' bagged. The cans are taken through the hatch into the filling room and filled in a similar way to a liquid parenteral.

14.6.2 Ointments and eye-drops

Plastic tubes for ointments are generally sterilised by irradiation or ethylene oxide and brought into the filling room via the pass-through hatch. The ointment base may be sterilised by dry heat or more commonly by filtration at a temperature sufficiently high to ensure fluidity. Filling then proceeds in a manner similar to a liquid product.

14.6.3 Blow-fill-seal technology

Blow-fill-seal is a process where the containers are formed from plastic granules on-line and then filled and sealed in one operation. Blow-fill-seal units are purpose-built machines in which, in one continuous operation, containers are formed from a thermoplastic granulate, filled and then sealed, all by the one automatic machine. The process is that a pharmaceutical-grade plastic resin is vertically heat extruded through a circular throat, to form a hanging tube called the Parison. This extruded tube is then enclosed within a two-part mould, and the tube is cut above the mould. The mould is transferred to the filling zone, or sterile filling space where filling needle mandrels are lowered, and used to inflate the plastic to form the container within the mould. Following the formation of the container, the mandrel is used to fill the container with liquid. Following filling, the mandrels are retracted and a secondary top mould seals the container. All actions take place inside a sterile shrouded chamber inside the machine. The product is then discharged to a non-sterile area for labelling, packaging and distribution [23].

Blow-fill-seal products are less fragile and lighter to transport than glass containers, but sometimes the active ingredients or preservatives are absorbed by the plastic, which affects product stability. Typical types of blow-fill-seal products include sterile nebulas for deep lung inhalation and opthalmics [24].

One of the advantages of the process is that the equipment is amenable to cleaning and sanitisation using automated steam-in-place systems. The disadvantages are that the operation can suffer many process interruptions arising from burnt containers [25].

14.6.4 Lyophilisation

Lyophilisation or freeze-drying is required for some liquid fill products which are not stable. Preservation is possible because the greatly reduced water content inhibits the action of microorganisms and enzymes that would normally spoil or degrade the substance. Freeze-drying works by freezing the material and then reducing the surrounding pressure to allow the frozen water in the material to sublimate directly from the solid phase to the gas phase [26]. The powder can later be reconstituted using a solvent at the point of administration. Lyophilisation is an additional process step which can present its own process risks.

14.7 Single-use sterile disposable items

A relatively recent advance in biopharmaceutical processing has been the use of single-use disposable technologies. Single-use disposable technologies include tubing, capsule filters, single-use ion exchange membrane chromatography devices, single-use mixers, bioreactors, product holding sterile bags in place of stainless steel vessels (i.e. sterile fluid containment bags), connection devices and sampling receptacles. Single-use disposable technologies are generally manufactured from plastic polymers involving processes of injection moulding, extruding and blow moulding [27].

Single-use disposable items are used in aseptic processing as a contamination control measure, and to reduce equipment recycling times and lower energy costs. The applications include devices for making aseptic connections, sampling devices, mixing devices, product-hold bags and disposable manifold systems [28]. The primary method for the sterilisation of single-use technology is by gamma irradiation. This is because plastics cannot be subjected to heat-based methods of sterilisation without damaging the mould [29].

Of the various applications of single-use devices, the adaption of single-use technology for aseptic connections is arguably the most advantageous. Types of aseptic connections include the connection of a vessel or filter to another item of equipment for the transfer of fluids. Conventional methods of connection involve steps such as clamping or heat welding of tubing. The major risks arise from the external environment and also from microbial contamination that could be transferred from the operator's hands. Innovations in aseptic connection technology have led to the development of single-use connector systems to allow for a totally enclosed and automated process. These are based on the so-called alpha-beta principle, which allows the connection to be performed in an environment that does not require unidirectional airflow cabinets or other equipment to maintain asepsis [30].

A second innovation of importance involves biocontainer bags to hold product. In line with advances with aseptic connections, there is a drive towards the adoption of disposable bag technologies in biopharmaceutical production and away from fixed, stainless-steel equipment, which requires more complex engineering configuration and far more components in terms of separative valves and piping. The common configuration of product holding bags is as single-use assemblies consisting of either two- or three-dimensional bags connected to a manifold of tubing, connectors and filters. The design is such that no part of the equipment will have direct contact with the product unless the component or part of the equipment is also sterile, single-use and maintains the sterile liquid pathway of the closed system assembly [31].

These advantages notwithstanding, the application of single-use sterile disposable technology in the biopharmaceutical industry remains, at the time of writing, in its infancy.

14.8 Conclusion

In an aseptic process, the drug product, container and closure are first subjected to sterilisation methods separately, as appropriate, and then brought together. Therefore it is critical that containers be filled and sealed in an extremely high-quality environment. This chapter has set out the design and operation of aseptic processing and in doing so has emphasised why aseptic processing poses the greatest contamination risk in the preparation of all products intended to be sterile. Careful attention must be placed on cleanroom layout, operations, maintaining environmental control and with validation, of which the key operation is media fills, which is discussed in the next chapter.

14.9 References

1. Halls, N.A. (1994), *Achieving Sterility in Medical and Pharmaceutical Products*, New York: Marcel Dekker, Inc.
2. EMA (2000), 'Decision trees for the selection of sterilisation methods', *European Medicines Agency Committee for Proprietary Medicinal Products*, CPMP/QWP/054/98, London: EMA.
3. Euradlex (2009), *The Rules Governing Medicinal Products in the European Community*, Annex 1, Brussels: European Commission.
4. Food and Drug Administration (2004), *Guideline on Sterile Drug Products Produced by Aseptic Processing*, Rockville, MD: FDA.
5. United States Pharmacopeia (2012), *Microbiological Control and Monitoring of Aseptic Processing Environments*, USP 35–NF 3: Bethesda, MD: United States Pharmacopeia.
6. Aseptic Processing of Health Care Products (1997), 1 – *General Requirements*, ISO 13408-1, Geneva: International Standards Organization.
7. ISO 14698-1 (2003), 'Cleanrooms and associated controlled environments – Biocontamination control,' Part I: *General Principles and Methods*, Geneva: International Standards Organization.
8. IPSE (1999), *Pharmaceutical Engineering Guides for New Renovated Facilities*, vol. 3, *Sterile Manufacturing Facilities*, 1st edition, USA: International Society for Pharmaceutical Engineering.
9. Akers, M. (1999), 'Aseptic processing and the pharmaceutical scientist', *American Pharmaceutical Review*, June: 31–4.
10. Ackers, J. and Agallaco, J. (2001), 'Environmental monitoring: Myths and misapplications', *PDA Journal of Pharmaceutical Science and Technology*, 55(3): 176–84.
11. Sharp, J., Bird, A., Brzozowski, S. and O'Hagan, K. (2010), 'Contamination of cleanrooms by people', *European Journal of Parenteral and Pharmaceutical Sciences*, 15(3): 73–81.
12. Sundström, S., Ljungqvist, B. and Reinmüller B. (2009), 'Some observations on airborne particles in the critical areas of a blow-fill-seal machine', *Journal of Parenteral and Pharmaceutical Sciences and Technology*, 63(1): 71–80.
13. Whyte, W. and Eaton, T. (2004), 'Assessing microbial risk to patients from aseptically manufactured pharmaceuticals', *European Journal of Parenteral and Pharmaceutical Science*, 9(3): 71–9.
14. Sandle, T., Saghee, M.R. and Ramstrop, M. (2010). *Environmental Monitoring and Cleanrooms*, IDMA-APA Guideline, Technical Monograph No. 5, Mumbai: Indian Drug Manufacturers Association.
15. World Health Organization (2002), 'Good manufacturing practices for sterile pharmaceutical products', in: *WHO Expert Committee on Specifications for Pharmaceutical Preparations*, 36th report, Geneva: World Health Organization, 2002 (WHO Technical Report Series, No. 902), Annex

6; and in *Quality Assurance of Pharmaceuticals*, A compendium of guidelines and related materials, vol. 2, 2nd updated edition, Good manufacturing practices and inspection, Geneva: World Health Organization, 2007; and in *Quality Assurance of Pharmaceuticals*, A compendium of guidelines and related materials, Geneva: World Health Organization, 2010 (CD-ROM).

16. Gapp, G. and Holzknecht, P. (2011), 'Risk analysis of sterile production plants: a new and simple, workable approach', *PDA Journal of Parenteral and Pharmaceutical Sciences and Technology*, 65(3): 217–26.

17. Akers, J.E. (1988), 'A review of current technology in parenteral manufacturing (as per Erratum 42(2):141)', *PDA Journal of Parenteral and Pharmaceutical Sciences and Technology*, 42: 53–6.

18. Chiarello, K. (2004), 'Pharma industry drives innovation in barrier/isolation design', *Pharmaceutical Technology*, March: 44–53.

19. Whyte, W. and Hejab, M. (2007), 'Particle and microbial airborne dispersal from people', *European Journal of Parenteral and Pharmaceutical Sciences*, 12(2): 39–46.

20. Roganti, F. and Boeh, R.J. (2004), 'Design of an aseptic process simulation', *Pharmaceutical Technology*, September: 76–84.

21. Cundell, A.M. (2004), 'Microbial testing in support of aseptic processing', *Pharmaceutical Technology*, June: 58–66.

22. Ginsbury, K. (2007), 'Continuous microbiological air monitoring for aseptic filling lines', *PDA Journal of Parenteral and Pharmaceutical Sciences and Technology*, 61(4): 225.

23. Lee, N. (2006), *Practical Guide to Blow Moulding*, Shropshire, UK: Smithers Rapra Technology.

24. Yam, K.L. (2009), *Encyclopaedia of Packaging Technology*, London: John Wiley & Sons.

25. Price, J. (1998), 'Blow-fill-seal technology, Part I: A design for particulate control,' *Pharmaceutical Technology*, February.

26. Harris, E.L.V. and Angal, S. (1989), *Protein Purification Methods*, Oxford: Oxford University Press.

27. Sandle, T. and Saghee, M. (2011), 'Some considerations for the implementation of disposable technology and single-use systems in biopharmaceuticals', *Journal of Commercial Biotechnology*, 17(4): 319–29.

28. Rao, G., Moreira, A. and Brorso, K. (2008), 'Disposable bioprocessing: The future has arrived', *Biotechnology and Bioengineering*, 102(2): 348–56.

29. Chmielewskia, A.G., Haji-Saeida, M. and Ahmedb, S. (2005), 'Progress in radiation processing of polymer', *Nuclear Instruments and Methods in Physics Research*, 236(1–4): 44–54.

30. Mach, C.J. and Riedman, D. (2008), 'Reducing microbial contamination risk in biotherapeutic manufacturing', *BioProcess International*, 6(8): 20–6.

31. DeFife, K. and Pierce, L. (2009), 'Versatility of a single-use bioreactor platform for culture of diverse cell types', *BioPharm International*, 22(2): 30–7.

Media simulation trials

DOI: 10.1533/9781908818638.227

Abstract: This chapter examines the primary qualification test for aseptic processing: media simulation trials. Media trials are undertaken once an aseptic process has been qualified and are designed to provide assurance that the process of filling products aseptically is done with a minimal likelihood of contamination. Media trials use a microbiological growth medium in place of product and subject the aseptic process to 'worst case' conditions, including practising personnel interventions. Filled vials are then incubated and later inspected for microbial growth. However, there are many variables to consider when establishing media trials. The chapter outlines the requirements for a media trial policy, explores acceptance criteria, outlines the steps involved in the media trial process, and concludes by outlining the important considerations for a failure investigation.

Key words: media simulation, aseptic filling, validation, interventions, growth promotion, process simulation, filling lines, pharmaceutical manufacturing, microbiological contamination.

15.1 Introduction

The sterilisation methods described in the first part of this book relate to methods of terminal sterilisation. With terminal sterilisation, each unit treated in a properly validated autoclave cycle is, at the end of the process, in all likelihood sterile. The same probability of non-sterility applies to each unit. Aseptic manufacturing is a far more risky process than terminal sterilisation. In contrast to terminal sterilisation, with aseptic manufacturing all units start off sterile and most of them remain uncontaminated as the product is dispensed into each unit. Whilst aseptic manufacturing is designed and operated in a way to prevent contamination, during the course of filling some units may be exposed to greater risks of contamination than others due to certain events [1]. The unpredictability relates to both technological limitations and the occasional need for personnel interventions during the course of an aseptic fill. Therefore it can never be said with absolute certainty that every single unit was manufactured under the same controlled circumstances.

It is due to the combination of variables and the inability to construct a process where each unit can uniformly be said to have the same chance of being sterile or non-sterile, that regulatory agencies require that aseptic processes be validated through simulation, as described in both EU GMP and FDA guidelines. This simulation is the media trial and other synonyms in common use are 'broth trial' and 'media placebo' [2]. To be representative, media fill studies should simulate aseptic manufacturing operations as closely as possible. Media filling trials are used to validate established procedures and are carried out when all relevant procedures have been established, equipment qualified and the personnel involved have been appropriately trained.

By simulating the product fill process and using a microbiological growth medium, a media simulation provides information to the extent that the process does or, as intended, does not compromise the sterility of individual components and finished product. In order to provide a robust test, a media fill programme should incorporate the contamination risk factors that occur on a production line and accurately assess the state of process control [3].

Regulators also require that the simulation is repeated regularly and that the microbiological challenge in the environment around the process is monitored to detect any excessive challenges or trends.

This chapter presents an overview of the common requirements for media simulation trials and outlines the practices which must be assessed, including repeated personnel interventions, and discusses the criteria upon which a media simulation trial can be said to be a success or a failure.

15.2 Defining a media simulation trial

In media simulation trials, a placebo is substituted for the product, and the media processed in a manner identical to that in which the product is processed. In its simplest form, an aqueous liquid microbiological growth medium is substituted for an aqueous liquid product. For solid products and ointments, either liquids are used or more complex simulations are run using substitute products, placebos which need to be reconstituted in growth media. This chapter focuses on liquid media fills, given that these are the most common types of simulations.

The media used is microbiological culture media. The most commonly used medium for aqueous liquid media fills is Tryptone Soya Broth (TSB). TSB is a general purpose microbiological growth medium containing casein, soy bean meal and dextrose, it has a near neutral pH and is expected to recover a broad spectrum of different types of microorganisms. Due to concerns with prions, some manufacturers have substituted TSB for vegetable peptone broth, formulated using a pea peptone, digested using fungal enzymes. The only exception is with β-lactam antibiotics, where TSB should not be used. Instead, liquid placebo should be used for liquid handling stages (water, saline, buffered saline, 0.1% peptone, etc.) and solids for powder handling stages.

There is no similarity in the composition of this or any other microbiological medium, with aqueous pharmaceutical products; there is no pharmaceutical product which has been formulated with the deliberate intention of encouraging microbial survival and growth. The media is processed as if it was a product. At the end of the fill, the filled media units are incubated. After incubation, the numbers of contaminated units are scored versus the number of uncontaminated units.

The purpose of the media fill is to provide an index of the probability of microbiological contamination arising in particular aseptic processes. Media fill results do not provide an index of the probability of there being non-sterile product units in product populations, unlike with the Sterility Assurance Level concept. The results of media fills are used in comparison with predetermined acceptance criteria for validation purposes, and at three- or six-monthly intervals against the same criteria to determine if the validated condition is still maintained [4].

15.3 Objectives of a media simulation trial

The media trial is designed to evaluate the following points in manufacturing of parenteral dosage forms:

- facility and room design;
- design of filling machine;

- flow of the manufacturing process;
- heating, ventilation, and air conditioning (HVAC) design and validation;
- utility design and validation;
- response to any deviation;
- trends in environmental monitoring data;
- decontamination programme in relation to cleaning and sensitisation;
- process simulation;
- personnel training and qualification.

Media fills are conducted regularly to verify established aseptic filling processes (typically every 6 months). In addition, media fills are also used in validation of aseptic processes as one of the final stages of a Performance Qualification.

Outside of scheduled media fills for established processes, media fills are undertaken for the reasons set out below.

- all completely new aseptic processes require validation by media fill;
- any process, irrespective of the equipment being old or new, beginning in a new cleanroom requires media fills as part of validation;
- a new filling machine in an established cleanroom requires validation media fills;
- an established filling line, which has undergone significant modification;
- media fills should also be repeated after significant modification to the HVAC system that affects filling machines, equipment, process and changes to the shift system. Such significant changes should be identified through a change control system;
- An upward shift in environmental monitoring data could also lead to media trials being undertaken.

Furthermore, where a production shutdown has occurred or where a filling line has not been used for a period exceeding four weeks, a media trial should be considered prior to commencing filling operations.

15.4 The media trial protocol

Before undertaking a media simulation trial, the key steps that require assessment during the simulation should be outlined and justified in a policy or rationale. Once detailed, the requirements should be captured within a standard operating procedure for production staff to follow. The protocol will need to note the following [5]:

- identification of the cleanroom;
- identification of the filling line and equipment;
- type of container/closure to be used;
- line speed;
- number of units to be filled;
- number and type of interventions;
- number of personnel to participate;
- type of media to be used;
- volume of medium to be filled into the containers;
- incubator identification;
- incubation time and temperature;
- batch record details;
- acceptance criteria.

The following key points should be considered for exact simulation of media fill run [6].

15.4.1 Type of product being filled

It is normally taken that the type of product filled, unless it requires special manipulation, is not significant. The important variables to consider with media fills are the types and sizes of the vials and the speed at which they are filled.

15.4.2 Batch size of product

Either the maximum product batch size is filled or a representative number of units are filled. This choice is discussed below in relation to run duration.

15.4.3 Containers and closures

There is a choice to be made over how many vial combinations to include in different media trials. It may be that the widest neck diameter presents

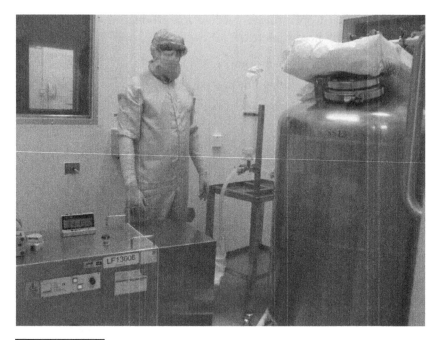

Figure 15.1 Liquid media being filtered in for a media trial

the 'worst case', as it allows more opportunity for contamination ingress, but this may not be the case (e.g. small vials may be less stable at the point of filling). In the long run, the decision over what and how many sizes to include in a media fill validation protocol is decisional, and for regulatory purposes the reasons for taking the particular decisions must be justified and documented (Figure 15.1).

15.4.4 Fill volume

In terms of fill volume, there should always be sufficient liquid in each container to 'wet' all the surfaces during incubation. However, in relation to the volume of growth medium filled into each container this is either reduced, in relation to the volume of product typically filled or, alternatively, the exact volumes are replicated. Some manufacturers use identical volumes for small fills but with larger fills the exact volume is not replicated and instead the filling speed is adjusted to leave the containers open under the filling heads for the same time as they would be in routine filling.

Published by Woodhead Publishing Limited, 2013

15.4.5 Filling line speed

The filling line should be run at the same speed as per product fills, unless the fill volume is altered for the reasons set out above.

15.4.6 Personnel (operators, working shifts)

All personnel involved with aseptic filling must qualify at least once per year in a media fill. This includes aseptic filling operators, engineers and microbiology personnel. The number of staff within a filling room during the media trial must equal the maximum number of staff permitted in a filling room during a product fill. Normal staff activities, such as shift handovers, must be included in the simulation.

15.4.7 Filling line configuration

The filling line must be set up as per a product fill.

15.4.8 Product hold time

The hold time for the media must equal the maximum permitted hold time for product, prior to filling.

15.4.9 Number of units being filled

The number of units filled is, according to regulations, never less than 3000. This is an expression of the minimum number of units for which a contamination rate of no more than one contaminated unit in 1000 units (0.1%) can be demonstrated with 95% confidence [7]. FDA regulatory guidance requires that a minimum of either 5000 or 10000 units are filled, as outlined in the acceptance criteria discussion below [8]. In terms of the maximum number, refer to Section 15.4.11 on Run duration below.

15.4.10 Acceptance criteria

The acceptance criteria must be predetermined. In the case of media fills, a maximum number of contaminated units must be specified for the aseptic process to be acceptable.

ISO 13408 'Aseptic processing of health care products' contains tables based on how many units need to be filled for one, two, three, four, etc. contaminated units to represent a 0.1% contamination rate with 95% confidence [9]. However, for validation media fills, the realistic target for contaminated units, irrespective of the number of units filled, must be zero. A zero rate is increasingly the expectation of regulators.

However, one container growing, although requiring an investigation, will occur at some time and this should not necessarily lead to closing down a filling line. In relation to this, the Pharmaceutical Inspection Convention and Pharmaceutical Inspection Co-operation Scheme (PIC/S) guidance is useful [10]. It notes that the target should be zero growth and the following should apply:

a) when filling fewer than 5000 units, no contaminated units should be detected.

b) when filling 5000 to 10 000 units:

- one (1) contaminated unit should result in an investigation, including consideration of a repeat media fill;

- two (2) contaminated units are considered cause for revalidation, following investigation.

When filling more than 10 000 units:

- one (1) contaminated unit should result in an investigation;

- two (2) contaminated units are considered cause for revalidation, following investigation.

15.4.11 Run duration

Media fills must be run for long enough to fill a statistically significant minimum number of units. The fill must last for long enough to be able to simulate all of the potentially contaminating events that might occur; and it needs to be run in order to address the potential for contamination to build up over time. Many manufacturers elect to run media fills to replicate the actual product fill. This is achieved by either filling the maximum number of containers that is allowed for a product fill, or by filling intermittently, with fill periods punctuated by periods of inactivity or by filling at the end of a product fill. Of these choices, the former provides a stricter challenge, as it also tests staff fatigue. This approach also ensures that all staff shift changes are captured and will detect for

Published by Woodhead Publishing Limited, 2013

the, theoretical, possibility of the concentration of contaminants increasing in a cleanroom over the time it is occupied and operational.

15.4.12 Interventions

Given that the primary source of contamination in aseptic processes is personnel, the inclusion of interventions in the media fill is arguably the most important component. An intervention is a personnel activity, whereby a task is carried out within the ISO class 5 critical zone, either within the unidirectional airflow device protecting the filling machine or through a gloveport as part of a RABS or isolator. Representative personnel interventions, which are typically undertaken during product fills, should be simulated during the media trial. These are discussed in the section below.

15.4.13 Elements which affect assurance of sterility

Most, if not every, aseptic process is unique. Even in the same factory, two lines set up for the simplest process such as filling liquid products into ampoules could differ significantly from each other. Therefore, the protocol should specify the requirements for each filling line and product combination.

One of the difficulties with devising a protocol is that a tension exists between the concept of using worst-case conditions in a media fill and not attempting to validate unacceptable aseptic practices. For this, a review of incidents during product filling over the past year should be considered and things that could reasonably happen should be included in the media simulation.

15.5 Conducting media simulation trials

The general principle of media fills is that the process should be simulated in a way that addresses every risk of microbiological contamination that could occur in practice. Thus the media fill must be conducted exactly as if the process were being run in the worst possible way that would still be acceptable.

When conducting media simulation trials, the following steps are undertaken.

15.5.1 Preparation of the culture media

Most manufacturers simulate aseptic processes by taking dehydrated culture medium as their starting point. The media should be irradiated prior to entering the plant. The media is dissolved in the manufacturing area and then passed through a process sterilising filter and into a receiving vessel. The media is then used to fill the ampoules, vials or syringes. The process begins with media preparation, because the media fill emulates the regular product fill situation in terms of equipment, processes, personnel involved and time taken for pre-fill, product holding and filling.

Not all manufacturers simulate the filtration step. However, some regulatory agencies request that the simulation of sterile filtration is included as part of the media fill.

15.5.2 Deactivation of gas on the filling line

Some processes use inert gas (i.e. CO_2 or nitrogen) to fill the container headspace. Such gas lines should be disconnected, or compressed air should be substituted for the gas. This is because such gases will prevent the growth of many microorganisms, which runs counter to the objectives of the media fill.

15.5.3 Process simulation

All of the events that occur in relation to a specific process must be simulated in the time that the media fill is running. This is the case, even though some of the events may be infrequently undertaken in practice. Typical contaminating events include [11]:

- filling machine set-up;
- aseptic assembly of equipment and filling equipment preparation;
- aseptic sample connections and disconnections;
- representative numbers of personnel undertaking normal duties;
- microbiological environmental monitoring;

- equipment change-out;
- off-loading of stoppers from autoclaves;
- replenishment of stoppers in the hoppers (if applicable);
- replenishment of containers in the container-feed (i.e. from a depyrogenation tunnel);
- machine breakdowns;
- spillages;
- glove change (for gloveports or isolators);
- adjustments of fill head assemblies;
- filling machine adjustments (e.g. weight checks);
- personnel shift changes and other occasions where personnel may leave or enter the filling room;
- traceability of vials (e.g. through laser etching).

In addition, representative process interventions must be replicated; it is essential to include in a simulation test the various interventions that are known to occur during normal production runs. For example [12]:

- removal of containers that have fallen over;
- repair or replacement of needles/tubes;
- replacement of on-line filters;
- invasive microbial sampling (e.g. changing settle plates in the filling zone);
- simulating the duration of stoppages on the line;
- the filling and handling of stoppers;
- removal of containers with missing stoppers;
- unblocking vial jams.

A look back at the main interventions undertaken during product fills across the intervening period between media trials provides important information about the most common types of interventions and the frequency at which they are conducted. Frequency is important, for if an intervention is carried out several times during a product fill, it should be undertaken at a similar rate during the media fill.

15.5.4 Environmental monitoring

During the media trial, the level of environmental monitoring conducted should be at least equal to that undertaken during a product fill.

Environmental monitoring should be captured in a formal programme. The programme is designed to describe the routine particulate and microbiological monitoring of processing and manufacturing areas [13].

The purpose of environmental monitoring, particularly microbiological environmental monitoring, is to discover the unexpected, unpredicted vulnerability of facility or process to microbiological contamination. The monitoring levels should be the same as for product fills and comply with regulatory guidance.

15.5.5 Simulation of lyophilisation

Some types of products, which are stable only for a short time in solution, undergo lyophilisation to preserve them (Chapter 11). It is important to partly simulate this process as part of the media trial [14].

For the simulation, the filled, partially stoppered vials are put into trays and taken and loaded into a lyophiliser (Figure 15.2). There is some vulnerability of the contents of the vials to contamination at this stage, because the vials are only partially stoppered. However, the lyophilisation

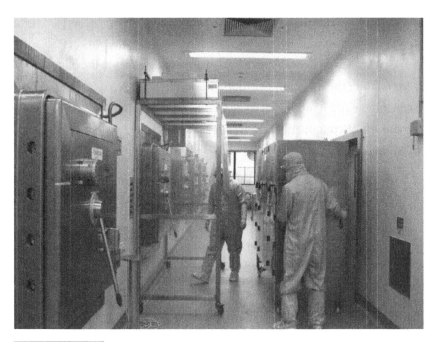

Figure 15.2 Loading a lyophiliser

process itself must not be simulated exactly. This is because the freezing of vials and consequent formation of ice crystals kills microorganisms. Thus, the freezing should not be simulated.

15.5.6 Batch record

As with a product fill, a media filled batch record must be prepared and reviewed by Quality Assurance.

15.5.7 Incubation of filled units

During product fills, some vials of product may be rejected on the filling line (i.e. a cracked vial). With media simulation trials, either this practice is documented and followed or all media-filled closed containers should be incubated irrespective of whether they belong in the population that would normally be released as 'good' product. However, these 'reject' containers are not included in the decision-making criteria of the media fill, but they can provide important information about filling activities.

Filled units must be incubated as soon as possible after filling, normally within 24 hours. Incubation should be declared to have begun when the vials have reached the required temperature. The incubation of media fills is typically for 14 days. There is no written regulatory requirement in terms of incubation time or temperature. However, a common regime is to incubate the containers for 7 days at 20–25°C, followed by 7 days at 30–35°C. The first temperature range encourages the growth of fungi and the second encourages the growth of bacteria.

It is customary to incubate containers the right way up for one half of the incubation period and inverted for the other half. For this, it is important that the fill volume of the containers was sufficient to enable contact of all the container-closure seal surfaces when the container is inverted and also sufficient to allow the detection of microbial growth.

15.5.8 Inspection

At the end of the incubation period, each vial must be inspected by the staff normally employed to inspect product vials. Each vial is examined using an artificial light source, for visible turbidity which will indicate the possibility of microbial growth.

Any turbid vials must be sent to a microbiology laboratory. A contaminated container should be carefully examined for any breach in the integrity of the container system. Any microorganisms from every contaminated unit obtained in any media fill should be sub-cultured and identified to species level, ideally using genotypic techniques. The identity of any microbial contaminants is a major part of the information content of the media fill, and where possible the identified microorganisms should be related to the events that were happening when the contaminated unit was filled.

15.5.9 Laboratory confirmation of media

At the end of incubation, after each vial has been inspected for microbial growth, representative vials must be tested for microbial growth promotion. This is to ensure that the medium was capable of supporting growth.

Although the media will have been tested by a microbiology laboratory prior to use, it is important to verify it post use, because the media may have come into contact with traces of product, antibiotic, detergent, disinfectant and so forth during the filling run.

The microorganisms used for growth promotion typically mirror the set used for the sterility test. These include *Bacillus subtilis* (ATCC 6633), *Staphylococcus aureus* (ATCC 6538), *Pseudomonas aeruginosa* (ATCC 9027), *Candida albicans* (ATCC 10231) and *Aspergillus niger* (ATCC 16404). Sometimes environmental isolates (or 'wild types') are included with the test set.

15.6 Frequency of media simulation trials

Media fills are generally done on every filling line at least twice a year. Within this programme, it is sensible to ensure that on multi-container filling lines every container size has been filled at least once in a reasonable time frame, say over 2 years; for this a matrix approach is often adopted. Otherwise the possibility of unexpected contamination as it relates to a particular size may never be addressed.

15.7 Media fill failures

The major practical issue of periodic media fills is what to do in response to data containing contaminated units. Typically, if a media fill fails, the media fill detects only one positive vial, a marginal fail in the context of the PIC/S acceptance criteria discussed above. If several containers grow, something is clearly wrong with the process and aseptic conditions have failed.

All incidences of growth must be investigated, although different actions will be taken in relation to the continuation of product filling, depending on whether the failure is considered to be marginal or consequential. The FDA guidance on aseptic filling notes [15]:

> For any size, intermittent incidents of microbial contamination in media filled lines can be indicative of a persistent low-level contamination problem that should be investigated. Accordingly, re-occurring incidents of contaminated units in media fills for an individual line, regardless of acceptance criteria, would be a signal of an adverse trend on the aseptic processing line that should lead to problem identification, correction and revalidation.

Investigation considerations could include [16]:

- microbiological environmental monitoring data;
- particulate monitoring data;
- personnel monitoring data;
- sterilisation cycles for media, equipment, components and filters;
- HEPA filter evaluation;
- area air flow patterns and pressures;
- operator training and technique;
- unusual events during the fill;
- storage conditions of sterile items;
- identification of contaminants;
- housekeeping procedures and training;
- calibration and validation of sterilising equipment;
- pre- and post-filter/housing integrity testing;
- product/process defects and limitations of inspection process.

The outcome of the investigation of most marginal media fill failures is often inconclusive, and contamination is typically the result of a human commensal microorganism shed by an operator. Actions from marginal failures are generally along the lines of counselling, retraining and improved supervision of operators. The media fill should be repeated as soon as possible and a further media fill on the container size implicated should be scheduled into the next periodic media fill, in addition to those sizes defined by the predetermined matrix.

With consequential failures (more than one vial), product manufactured on the filling line after the date of the media fill, and product still in the company's warehouse(s), should be quarantined until the failure investigation is completed.

15.8 Media fill invalidation

Media fills may be invalidated under exceptional circumstances. These circumstances should be limited to:

- failure of growth promotion test;
- failure of physical conditions of the Aseptic Filling Suite area (e.g. HVAC);
- failure to follow procedure that would lead to stopping a production batch;
- other reasons that would lead to stopping a production batch.

15.9 Conclusion

This chapter has outlined the requirements for media simulation trials and in doing so has shown that such trials are an indispensible part of aseptic filling, as well as being a regulatory requirement. It has also shown that there are several key choices to be made in how to approach media fills and for this a policy or rationale is required. Whichever approaches are taken, it is important to note that media fills should never be used to justify an unacceptable practice.

A successful media simulation trial (one with zero growth detected in any unit) should not, in itself, signal that the process to make 'sterile' product has been validated, due to the insensitivity of the growth media and the impossibility of a media trial covering every nuance of every type of product fill and event which has occurred or is likely to occur. It is important that environmental controls remain in place in relation to good cleanroom operations and that personnel continue to adhere to good aseptic practises [17].

15.10 References

1. Agalloco, J.P. and Akers, J.E. (2002), 'A critical look at sterility assurance', *European Journal of Parenteral Science*, 7(4): 97–103.
2. Cundell, A.M. (2004), 'Microbial testing in support of aseptic processing', *Pharmaceutical Technology*, June: 56–66.
3. Friedman, R. and Mahoney, S. (2003), 'Risk factors in aseptic processing', *American Pharmaceutical Review*, 6(1): 44–6, 92.
4. Vincent, D.W. (2006), 'Regulatory and validation considerations for aseptic processes', *Journal of Validation Technology*, 12(2), 107–33.
5. Dixon, A.M. (2006), 'Process simulations (media fills)', in Dixon, A.M. (ed.), *Environmental Monitoring for Cleanrooms and Controlled Environments*, New York: Informa Healthcare, pp. 93–112.
6. Halls, N.A. (2002), *Microbiological Media Fills Explained*, West Sussex: Sue Horwood Publishing Ltd.
7. Bernuzzi, M., Halls, N.A. and Raggi, P. (1997), 'Application of statistical models to action limits for media fill trials', *European Journal of Parenteral Sciences*, 2: 3–11.
8. Kawamura, K. and Abe, H. (2004). 'A novel approach to the statistical evaluation of media fill test by the different from no contamination data', *PDA Journal of Pharmaceutical Science and Technology*, 58(6): 309–20.
9. International Standards Organization (ISO) (2008), ISO 13408-1 *Aseptic Processing of Health Care Products – Part 1: General Requirements*, Geneva: International Standards Organisation.
10. PIC/S (2011), PIC/S Guide: Validation of Aseptic Processes PI 007-5, *Pharmaceutical Inspection Convention (PIC) and the Pharmaceutical Inspection Co-operation Scheme*, Brussels.
11. Budini, M. and Boschi, F. (2011), 'Aseptic process simulations/media fills', in: Saghee, M.R., Sandle, T. and Tidswell, E.C. (eds), *Microbiology and Sterility Assurance in Pharmaceuticals and Medical Devices*, New Delhi: Business Horizons, pp. 701–32.
12. Agalloco, J. (2005), 'Managing aseptic interventions', *Pharmaceutical Technology*, March: 56–66.
13. Halls, N.A. (2002), *Microbiological Environmental Monitoring Explained*, West Sussex: Sue Horwood Publishing Ltd.
14. Roganti, F. and Boeh, R.J. (2004), 'Design of an aseptic process simulation', *Pharmaceutical Technology*, September: 76–84.
15. US Food & Drug Administration (2004), *Guidance for Industry Sterile Drug Products Produced by Aseptic Processing – Current Good Manufacturing Guide*, Bethesda, MD: US Department of Health and Human Services, Food and Drug Administration, Center for Drug Evaluation and Research, Center for Biologics Evaluation and Research, Office of Regulatory Affairs.
16. Snyder, J.E. (2002), 'Corrective and preventive action planning to achieve sustainable GMP compliance', *Journal of GXP Compliance*, 6(3): 29–39.
17. Ljungqvist, B. and Reinmuller, B. (1997), *Cleanroom Design: Minimizing Contamination Through Proper Design*, Buffalo Grove, IL: Interpharm Press.

Cleaning and disinfection of sterile processing facilities

DOI: 10.1533/9781908818638.245

Abstract: This chapter examines the cleaning and disinfection of cleanrooms used for the processing of products intended to be sterile. The differences between detergents (which clean) and disinfectants (which inactivate or destroy microorganisms) are outlined. The key criteria for the selection of disinfectants and the factors which influence their efficacy are described. Particular emphasis is given to the requirements of GMP regulated cleanrooms. The chapter proceeds to describe the important aspects of a cleaning and disinfection protocol and then the steps involved for cleaning and disinfection, and in doing so outlines important areas for consideration, such as disinfectant rotation. The conclusion is an overview of the requirements for the validation of disinfectants.

Key words: cleaning, detergent, disinfection, disinfectant, biocide, sporicide, microbiology, chemical agent, microbial cell, cleanroom, contamination control.

16.1 Introduction

As Chapter 13 described, cleanrooms require a series of physical parameters to be met in order for them to continue to function efficiently and to meet the cleanliness level required in terms of airborne particulates. This chapter also described the microbiological levels that must be met in relation to different grades or classes of cleanroom, which are assessed through an environmental monitoring programme. One important means to achieve microbiological control is through an established and effective cleaning and disinfection regime. Such a programme should apply to all grades of cleanroom and to other controlled environments, although the frequency of application and the choice of and preparation of reagents will vary. The highest standards will apply to cleanrooms dedicated to the processing of products intended to be sterile; and even higher standards are required for aseptic processing facilities [1].

The use of detergents and disinfectants, and the need to keep cleanrooms clean, is a regulatory requirement within the pharmaceutical sector. The main regulatory documents relating to the use of disinfectants in pharmaceutical manufacturing are:

- US Code of Federal Regulations: 21 CFR 211.56b and 21 CFR 211.56c (which refer to sanitation); CFR 211.67 (which refers to equipment and maintenance); CFR 211.182 (which describes the need for a cleaning programme); and CFR 211.113b.
- FDA Aseptic Processing Guide, revised 2004.
- USP (General Chapter: Disinfectants and Antiseptics).
- Annex 1 to the EU Guide to Good Manufacturing Practice.

The act of cleaning and disinfection may seem straightforward. However, there are several variables which can affect the performance of cleaning and disinfection agents. This chapter examines the differences between cleaning (with the use of detergents) and disinfection (using biocides), discusses the selection of the appropriate chemicals and materials, looks at cleaning techniques, and outlines the requirements for the validation of disinfectants.

16.2 Cleaning

Cleaning is the process of removing residues and soil (dirt, dust, protein, skin cells, etc.) from surfaces to the extent that they are visually clean. To support validation studies, cleanliness can be supported through the use of swabs to detect levels of Total Organic Carbon (TOC) or water rinses to enumerate microorganisms. Cleaning validation of pharmaceutical equipment is a specialist area.

Cleaning involves defined methods of application together with the use of a detergent. Cleaning steps are additionally necessary prior to the application of a disinfectant. It is essential that a surface or item of equipment has been properly cleaned before the application of a disinfectant, in order for the disinfectant to work efficiently. The activity of cleaning can remove or dilute microbial populations and many detergents contain chemical additives that can 'disinfect' [2].

16.2.1 Detergents

A detergent is a chemical used to clean equipment or surfaces by removing unwanted matter (referred to as 'soil'). Detergents generally work by penetrating soiling and reducing the surface tension, which fixes the soil to the surface, to allow its removal (detergents are 'Surface Active Agents' or surfactants) [3]. This is an important action, because microorganisms on solid surfaces can be resilient to removal and resistant to disinfection. Detergents contain differently charged ions that cause microorganisms to repel each other. This repulsion causes the microorganisms to disassociate from the surface and become suspended. Suspended microorganisms can then be removed from the surface by the rinsing effect of the detergent (or a subsequent water rinse) or be destroyed by application of a disinfectant; microorganisms in the planktonic state are easier to kill than those in the sessile state. With particularly dirty areas, material may require removal using a vacuum cleaner of appropriate design. Care must be taken with this step, so as not to spread dirt around the facility.

There are various types of natural and synthetic detergents available, each with different modes of cleansing action. In addition to cleaning properties, some detergents have anti-microbial properties due to their ionic nature (either anionic or cationic). Generally, for the cleaning and disinfection of pharmaceutical facilities, non-foaming and non-ionic detergents are preferred, since these are the most compatible with the types of disinfectants commonly used. The vast majority of all non-ionic detergents are condensation products or ethylene oxide with a hydrophobe.

16.2.2 Selection of detergents

The selected detergent must be compatible with the disinfectants used, in that it must not neutralise disinfectant activity. The type of surface material to which the intended detergent is to be applied is important. If the detergent damages the surface, such as the effect of acids on steel or alkalis on aluminium, then pockets can be created that harbour microorganisms and where cleaning and disinfectant agents may not penetrate. To minimise this effect, the detergent should be used at a concentration that is effective for cleaning but which does not corrode the surface to which it is applied. The detergent must also be effective against the type of soiling likely to be present in the pharmaceutical environment.

16.3 Disinfection

Disinfection refers to either the inactivation or destruction of microorganisms. International standards, to which disinfectants used in pharmaceutical facilities must be validated, have criteria for the quantitative assessment of a disinfectant where a known population of microorganisms must be reduced by a certain value. Importantly, in the context of this book, disinfection is not the same as sterilisation and no certified disinfectant will be capable of achieving the theoretical levels of microbial destruction achieved by sterilisation processes. The reader should note, however, that certain disinfectants may also be classified as sterilants when used in a certain way, an example here is hydrogen peroxide [4]. The process of disinfection is performed using manual or automated methods, such as a Clean-in-Place (CIP) system.

16.3.1 Disinfectants

A disinfectant is one of a diverse group of chemicals which reduces the number of microorganisms present in solution. They form part of a wider group of anti-microbial agents called biocides. To be classed as a disinfectant, a chemical agent must inactivate or destroy *vegetative* microorganisms; an important emphasis here is the word 'vegetative', for a disinfectant will not necessarily inactivate or destroy bacterial or fungal spores. Those disinfectants that do so are conventionally described as sporicidal disinfectants to distinguish them from other types of disinfectants.

Hand sanitisation is also important in relation to personnel working in cleanrooms. Personnel carry many types of microorganisms on their hands and such microorganisms can be readily transferred from person to person, from person to equipment or onto critical surfaces. Microorganisms (including *Staphylococcus*, *Micrococcus* and *Propionibacterium*) are either present on the skin but not multiplying (transient flora) or are multiplying microorganisms released from the skin (residential flora) through the shedding of skin cells [5].

16.3.2 Types of disinfectants

Disinfectants vary in their spectrum of activity, modes of action and efficacy [6]. Some are bacteristatic and cause a metabolic injury that halts the growth of the bacterial population. Here the disinfectant can cause selective and reversible changes to cells by interacting with nucleic acids, inhibiting enzymes or permeating into the cell wall. Once the disinfectant is removed, or neutralised, from contact with the cells, the surviving bacterial population could, theoretically, regrow. Other disinfectants are bactericidal in that they destroy bacterial cells through different, irreversible physiochemical mechanisms including structural damage to the cell, leakage or coagulation of cytoplasm and cell lysis. Some disinfectant types have specific targets within the bacterial cell [7].

The two principle categories of disinfectants are non-oxidizing and oxidizing.

■ *Non-Oxidizing Disinfectants* – The majority of disinfectants in this group have a specific mode of action against microorganisms and generally have a lower spectrum of activity compared to oxidizing disinfectants. Disinfectants classified here include:

– *Alcohols* – Alcohols have an antibacterial action against vegetative cells. The effectiveness of alcohols against vegetative bacteria increases with their molecular weight (i.e. ethanol is more effective than methanol and in turn isopropyl alcohols are more effective than ethanol). Alcohols, where efficacy is increased with the presence of water, act on the bacterial cell wall by making it permeable. This can result in cytoplasm leakage, denaturation of protein and eventual cell lysis. Alcohols are one of the so-called 'membrane disrupters'.

– *Aldehydes* – This group includes formaldehyde and gluteraldehyde. Gluteraldehyde is a very effective disinfectant (and sterilant) and has a wide spectrum of activity, effective against bacterial and fungal spores. However, gluteraldehyde is rarely used today due to personnel health and safety concerns.

– *Amphoterics* – Amphoterics are acidic and have a relative wide spectrum of activity, but are limited by their ability to damage bacterial endospores. An example is alkyl di(aminoethyl) glycine or its derivatives.

- *Acid Anionics* – Acid anionics are weak acids with a relatively limited spectrum of activity and are very pH dependent. An example of this group is carboxylic acid.

- *Biguanides* – Biguanides are polymers supplied in salt form, such as chlorhexidine, alexidine and hydrochloride. Biguanides have a relatively wide spectrum of activity, with the exception of killing bacterial endospores.

- *Phenolics* – The most commonly used phenolic is basic phenol (carbolic acid), although synthetic variants are widely used. Phenol can be made more complex by the addition of halogens such as chlorine (the bis-phenols and halophenols) to make compounds such as triclosan and chloroxylenol. Phenols are bactericidal and antifungal, but are not effective against bacterial spores.

- *Quaternary Ammonium Compounds (QACs)* – QACs are cationic salts of organically substituted ammonium compounds and have a fairly broad range of activity against microorganisms, although more effective against Gram-positive bacteria at lower concentrations than Gram-negative bacteria. They are considerably less effective against bacterial spores. QACs are sometimes classified as surfactants. An example is benzalkonium chloride.

■ *Oxidizing Disinfectants* – This group of disinfectants generally has non-specific modes of action against microorganisms. They have a wider spectrum of activity than non-oxidizing disinfectants, with most types able to damage bacterial endospores. The disinfectants in this group pose greater risks to human health. This group includes:

- *Halogens* – Halogens can be divided into chlorine-releasing agents and iodophors. Both types have a broad spectrum of activity against a range of microorganisms and are normally effective sporicides. Examples of chlorine releasing chemicals are sodium trichloroisocyanurate, sodium hypochlorite and chlorinated trisodium phosphonate.

- *Oxidizing Agents* – This group includes oxygen-releasing compounds such as peracetic acid and hydrogen peroxide. They are often used in the gaseous phase as surface sterilants for equipment. These peroxygens function by disrupting the cell wall causing cytoplasm leakage and can denature bacterial cell enzymes through oxidation.

16.3.3 Factors affecting disinfectant efficacy

Different species of microorganisms vary in their resistance to different disinfectants. These can be affected by the population of microorganisms present, their species, and the community to which they are bound.

In relation to numbers, an antimicrobial agent is considerably more effective against a low number of microorganisms than a higher number or a population with a greater cell density. Similarly, a disinfectant is more effective against a pure population than mixed population of microorganisms. Different types of microorganisms have varying levels of resistance to broad spectrum disinfectants (Figure 16.1). The increased resistance is primarily due to the cell membrane composition or type of protein coat.

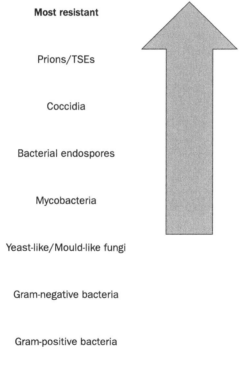

Most resistant

Prions/TSEs

Coccidia

Bacterial endospores

Mycobacteria

Yeast-like/Mould-like fungi

Gram-negative bacteria

Gram-positive bacteria

Least resistant

Figure 16.1 Diagram depicting spectrum of microbial resistance to disinfectants

Published by Woodhead Publishing Limited, 2013

The location of microorganisms can influence the effectiveness of a disinfectant. Microorganisms in suspension are easier to kill than those fixed to surfaces. This is due to the mechanisms of microorganism attachment, such as bacteria fixing themselves using fimbriae or when a biofilm (slime layer) community develops. Such positioning impacts the contact time required for the disinfectant to bind to the microorganism, cross the cell wall and act at the target site.

Other factors affecting disinfectant efficacy are concentration and time. Disinfectants are manufactured or validated to be most effective at a set concentration range. The setting of this concentration range involves establishing the minimum inhibitory concentration (MIC). The MIC is the lowest concentration of the disinfectant that is shown to be bacteriostatic or bactericidal. The MIC is measured through kinetic studies of the dilution coefficient.

Time is an important factor in the application of disinfectants. Contact time is the time taken for the disinfectant to bind to the microorganism, pass through the cell wall and reach the specific target site for the disinfectant's particular mode of action. Contact time is expressed generally for each disinfectant type at its optimal concentration range. The killing affect, for a constant concentration of a disinfectant, increases over time until the optimal contact time is established. However, in practical situations, many variables enter the equation such as the type, concentration and volume of the disinfectant, the nature of the microorganisms, the amount and type of material present (which may interfere), and the temperature of the disinfectant and the surface it is applied to.

One final factor, in relation to the use of detergents (above), is the presence of interfering substances. Soil on the surface or in the equipment requiring disinfection, can influence the efficacy of the disinfectant in a variety of ways and may increase the time required to complete inactivation. In order for a disinfectant to be effective, it must come into contact with and be absorbed by the microbial cell (Figure 16.2). If substances, such as oil, dirt, paper or grease, act as a spatial barrier between the microbial cell and the disinfectant, the efficacy of the disinfectant will be adversely affected.

16.3.4 Selecting disinfectants

It is clear from the above discussion that the effectiveness of a disinfectant is dependent upon several factors. In addition, certain regulatory or

Figure 16.2 A disinfectant efficacy study

health and safety standards may apply. This section outlines the most important criteria for disinfectant selection [8].

1. *Wide spectrum of activity* – A disinfectant must have a wide spectrum of activity. This refers to the ability of the disinfectant to kill different types of microorganisms and those that are in different physiological states.

2. *Sporicidal activity* – Periodically, for disinfecting surfaces, a sporicidal disinfectant should be used (e.g. on a monthly or quarterly basis) [9]. This is to avoid the development of resistant microorganisms.

3. *Rapid action* – The disinfectant must have a rapid action, with an ideal contact time of less than 10 minutes. The contact time is the time taken for the disinfectant to bind to the microorganism, traverse the cell wall and membrane and reach its specific target site. The longer the contact time, then the longer the surface needs to be left before use. A relatively short contact time meets the demands of pharmaceutical manufacturing where cleanrooms are cleaned before and after use, and where periods of downtime need to be minimised.

Published by Woodhead Publishing Limited, 2013

4. *Requirement to rotate disinfectants* – Often two disinfectants are used for regular disinfection, and are commonly used in rotation, for premises that are inspected by the European Medicines Agency, i.e. a Good Manufacturing Practice (GMP) requirement. When two disinfectants are used, the disinfectants selected must have different modes of action [10]. The argument for rotating two disinfectants is to reduce the possibility of resistant strains of microorganisms developing. Although the phenomenon of microbial resistance is an issue of major concern for antibiotics, there are few data to support development of resistance to disinfectants [11]. Nonetheless, many regulatory agencies require rotation to be in place.

5. *Correct temperature and pH for activity* – Some disinfectants require certain temperature and pH ranges in order to function correctly.

6. *Compatibility between detergent and disinfectant* – For effective disinfection, surfaces must first be cleaned with detergents. Some disinfectants are not compatible with certain detergents. In such circumstances, detergent residues could neutralise the active ingredient in the disinfectant. Before selection, a check should be made that the disinfectant is compatible with the detergent used.

7. *Residues* – Some disinfectants leave residues on surfaces. Whilst this can mean a continuation of an antimicrobial activity, residues can also lead to sticky surfaces and/or the inactivation of other disinfectants. Where this is the case, a water rinse should be applied to the surface after the application of the disinfectant.

8. *Surface compatibility* – Different disinfectants are not compatible with all types of surfaces. The disinfectants can damage the material to which they are applied, causing corrosion and discolouration. For more aggressive disinfectants, a wipe down using water or a less aggressive disinfectant such as an alcohol, is sometimes necessary to remove the residues [12].

9. *Safety* – The disinfectants selected must be relatively safe for operator use. A related concern is the impact upon the environment, especially in the way that waste disinfectant solutions are disposed of.

10. *Sterility* – Certain high-grade cleanroom activities (i.e. aseptic filling areas) require disinfectants to be sterile (e.g. aseptic preparation areas). For these purposes, disinfectants are either sterile filtered (through a 0.2 μm filter) or they are provided in gamma irradiated containers with outer wrappings.

16.3.5 *Hand sanitisers*

It is important that operators working in cleanrooms regularly sanitise their hands and, for sterile processing, this must be done prior to the commencement of each critical activity. Hand sanitisers fall into two groups: alcohol-based, which are more common; and non-alcohol-based. The most commonly used alcohol-based hand sanitisers are isopropyl alcohol or a form of denatured ethanol (i.e. industrial methylated spirits), normally at a 70% concentration. Sanitisers are applied to either bare skin (on entering a cleanroom) or to gloved hands (within the cleanroom).

The more common non-alcohol-based sanitisers contain either chlorhexidine or hexachlorophene. Hand sanitisers must not cause excessive drying and must be non-irritating (Figure 16.3). Carrying out such a review, based on the above factors, prior to purchasing a disinfectant, does not guard against the incorrect use of that disinfectant within the cleanroom. Any disinfectant will only be effective if it is used at the correct concentration and by wiping the disinfectant onto the surface [13].

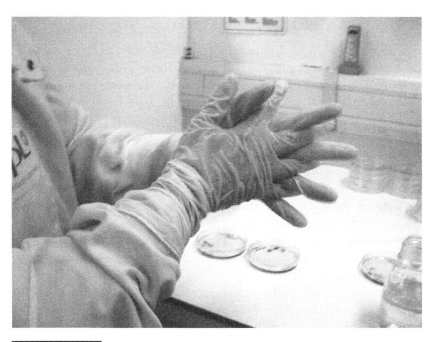

Figure 16.3 A hand disinfection sanitisation study

16.4 Cleaning and disinfection in practice

No matter how carefully detergents and disinfectants are selected, if they are not used correctly then they will not perform to their intended purpose: the reduction of a microbial population. For this, cleaning and disinfection methods should be outlined in a protocol for personnel to follow [14].

The following information should be outlined within the protocol:

- Details of the cleaning frequencies, methods, equipment and materials should be in written procedures. Cleaning of equipment and materials should take place at regular intervals.

- Disinfectants and detergents must be prepared in a manner that does not introduce adventitious contamination.

- Where the disinfectant or detergent is provided as a concentrate, the appropriate pharmaceutical grade water should be used as diluent and the solution prepared at the optimal temperature.

- Disinfectants and detergents used in EU GMP Grade A and B (ISO 14644 class 5 and 7) cleanrooms should be sterile before use.

- A cleaning log should be kept. The purpose is to keep a record of the areas cleaned, agents used and the identity of the operator.

An area to which a disinfectant is applied must first be properly cleaned with an appropriate detergent using 'mechanical action' (wiping or mopping). It is important that the cleaning and application of the detergent is performed correctly, because improperly cleaned areas where organic matter remains or areas which have a detergent residue, could potentially confer some protection to microbial populations and impair the efficacy of the subsequently applied disinfectant.

For surfaces in sterile processing area cleanrooms, the solutions should be applied using certified cleanroom mop heads, cloths and wipes (Figure 16.4). Such cleanroom certified items are for single applications and are non-particle shedding, non-woven and lint free (typically a hydro-entangled polyester/cellulose blend), ideally with a large liquid holding capacity.

When using mops and buckets for applications like floor cleaning, the double or triple bucket system is an effective way to avoid cross-contamination and minimise the re-deposition of soil. An example of a typical application is:

Published by Woodhead Publishing Limited, 2013

- Make up detergent or disinfectant in front bucket according to instructions.
- Fit a sterile disposable or autoclavable mop-head to mop frame.
- Soak the mop in the front bucket and apply to ceiling, wall or floor.
- The first application of disinfectant or detergent is from bucket 'A'.
- After the first application, the mop head or cloth is wrung out into a discard bucket 'B'. Wring out contaminants from the mop into empty bucket below wringer.

Figure 16.4   Operator cleaning a cleanroom

- The mop head or cloth is then placed into a second bucket of detergent or disinfectant (bucket 'C').

- After the second application of detergent or disinfectant, the mop head or cloth is wrung out into the discard bucket 'B'.

- The mop head or cloth may then be dipped into the bucket 'A' and the sequence continued as required.

When applying a disinfectant, as previously discussed, the critical aspect is the contact time. The disinfectant is only effective when left in contact with the surface for the validated time. This can be achieved more easily when the disinfectant is applied in overlapping strokes.

16.5 Environmental monitoring

To ensure the effectiveness of a cleaning and disinfection programme, microbiological environmental monitoring of surfaces and equipment is necessary. The primary methods for conducting these tests involve the use of cotton swabs, with a recovery diluent and later plating onto agar or dissolving prior to membrane filtration, and contact plates. The agars used should contain appropriate neutralising agents in order to eliminate any disinfectant residues and thus allow any recovered microorganisms to grow [15]. Environmental monitoring is discussed in further detail in Chapter 13.

16.6 Validation of disinfectants

All disinfectants used in GMP cleanrooms must be validated in order to demonstrate their efficacy [16]. This is demonstrated through performance testing to show that the disinfectant is capable of reducing the microbial bioburden found on manufacturing area surfaces to an acceptable level.

With disinfectant validation there are various standards. The main bodies issuing disinfectant validation guidances are:

- ASTM (American Society for Testing Materials);
- AOAC (Association of Official Analytical Chemists International);
- BSI (British Standards Institution);
- TGA (Australian Therapeutic Goods Administration);
- USP (United States Pharmacopeia).

Since standards often conflict, the reader should consider the most appropriate standard in relation to a particular regulatory agency.

The standard European approach for disinfectant validation consists of a basic suspension test and a two-part simulated-use surface test. Suspension testing is not typically performed in North American pharmaceutical manufacturing facilities; in contrast, it is the common European method. Instead, validation testing proceeds directly to the surface test. Both US and European approaches discuss, but do not clearly define, the need for a final field trial where the performance of the disinfectant is assessed in practical use through environmental monitoring [17].

The purpose of the quantitative suspension test is to evaluate the activity of a disinfectant against a range of microorganisms under conditions that more closely simulate practical use. The test consists of inoculating a prepared sample of the disinfectant under test in simulated 'clean' and 'dirty' conditions, using a challenge suspension of bacteria or fungi. After a specified contact time, an aliquot is removed and the bactericidal/fungicidal action is immediately neutralised by the addition of a proven neutraliser. Following this, the number of surviving microorganisms in each sample is determined and the reduction in viable microorganisms is calculated.

The surface test is arguably more relevant than the suspension test. It may arise that the disinfectant concentration shown to be optimal for the suspension test needs to be increased to meet the requirements of the surface test [18]. With the surface test, representative manufacturing surface samples are inoculated with a selection of microbial challenge organisms. A disinfectant is applied to the inoculated surfaces and exposed for a predetermined contact time, after which the surviving organisms are recovered using a qualified disinfectant-neutralising broth and test method (surface rinse, contact plate or swab). The number of challenge organisms recovered from the test samples (exposed to a disinfectant) is compared to the number of challenge organisms recovered from the corresponding control sample (not exposed to a disinfectant), to determine the ability of the disinfectant to reduce the microbial bioburden [19]. Successful completion of the validation qualifies the disinfectant evaluated for use. An important choice involves the selection of test surfaces [20].

16.7 Conclusion

For cleanrooms to be maintained in a compliant state, the correct use of detergents and disinfectants, supported by the use of defined cleaning and disinfection practises, is of great importance. This is not a straightforward task, for there is a complicated choice to be made in relation to different types of disinfectants. In addition, an understanding is required of the various factors that affect disinfectant efficacy. This chapter has outlined some of these key criteria in relation to both the properties of the chemicals used to prepare disinfectants and with the variations which arise in their application in the practical setting.

16.8 References

1. Sandle, T. (2012), 'Application of disinfectants and detergents in the pharmaceutical sector', in: Sandle, T., *The CDC Handbook: A Guide to Cleaning and Disinfecting Cleanrooms*, Surrey, UK: Grosvenor House Publishing, pp. 168–97.
2. Sandle, T. (2012), 'Cleaning and disinfection', in Sandle, T., *The CDC Handbook: A Guide to Cleaning and Disinfecting Cleanrooms*, Surrey, UK: Grosvenor House Publishing, pp. 1–31.
3. Farn, R.J. (2006), *Chemistry and Technology of Surfactants*, London: John Wiley & Sons.
4. Block, S.S. (1977), *Disinfection, Sterilisation and Preservation*, 3rd edition, Philadelphia, PA: Lea and Febiger.
5. Larson, E. (1988), 'A causal link between handwashing and risk of infection? Examination of the evidence', *Control Hospital Epidemiology*, 9: 28–36.
6. Denyer, S.P. and Stewart, G.S.A.B. (1998), 'Mechanisms of action of disinfectants', *International Biodeterioration and Biodegradation*; 41: 261–8.
7. Vina, P., Rubio, S. and Sandle, T. (2011), 'Selection and validation of disinfectants', in: Saghee, M.R., Sandle, T. and Tidswell, E.C. (eds), *Microbiology and Sterility Assurance in Pharmaceuticals and Medical Devices*, New Delhi: Business Horizons, pp. 219–36.
8. Sandle, T. (2003), 'Selection and use of cleaning and disinfection agents in pharmaceutical manufacturing', in: Hodges, N. and Hanlon, G. (eds), *Industrial Pharmaceutical Microbiology Standards and Controls*, Basingstoke, UK: Euromed Communications.
9. Pharmig (2006), *A Guide to Disinfectants and Their Use in the Pharmaceutical Industry*, Standstead Abbots, UK: Pharmaceutical Microbiology Interest Group.
10. Connor, D.E. and Eckman, M.K. (1992), 'Rotation of phenolic disinfectants', *Pharmaceutical Technology*, September: 148–62.
11. McDonnell, G. and Russell, A. (1998), 'Antiseptics and disinfectants: Activity, action and resistance', *Clinical Microbiology Reviews*, January: 147–79.
12. Sandle, T. (2012), 'Practical selection of cleanroom disinfectants', *Hospital Pharmacy Europe*, 62: 39–41.
13. Kramer, A. (2002), 'Limited efficacy of alcohol-based hand gels', *Lancet*, 359: 1489–90.

14. Montalvo, M. and Hewing, A. (2003), 'How to develop an effective and successful cleaning validation program', *Journal of Validation Technology*, 10(1): 62–82.
15. Sandle, T. (2012), 'Environmental monitoring: A practical approach', in: Moldenhauer, J., *Environmental Monitoring: A Comprehensive Handbook*, vol. 6, River Grove, US: PDA/DHI, pp. 29–54.
16. United States Pharmacopeia (2009), 'Disinfectants and antiseptics', Rockville, MD: United States Pharmacopeia.
17. Sandle, T. (2012), 'Validation of disinfectants', in: Sandle, T., *The CDC Handbook: A Guide to Cleaning and Disinfecting Cleanrooms*, Surrey, UK: Grosvenor House Publishing, pp. 241–61.
18. Bloomfield, S. F., Arthur, M., Begun, K. and Patel, H. (1993), 'Comparative testing of disinfectants using proposed European surface test methods', *Letters in Applied Microbiology*, 17: 119–12.
19. van Kilgeren, B., Koller, W., Bloomfield, S.F., Bohm, R., Cremieux, A., *et al.* (1998), 'Assessment of the efficacy of disinfectants on surfaces', *International Biodeterioration and Biodegradation*, 41: 289–96.
20. Bessems, E. (1998), 'The effect of practical conditions on the efficacy of disinfectants', *International Biodeterioration and Biodegradation*, 41: 177–83.

17

Biological indicators

DOI: 10.1533/9781908818638.263

Abstract: This chapter examines biological indicators, which are specially prepared populations of microorganisms with a defined population and resistance to a specific sterilisation process. Biological indicators are used to measure the effectiveness of a sterilisation cycle and can provide a probabilistic estimation of sterility. This chapter examines the application of biological indicators for different sterilisation processes, provides detail on the types of biological indicators available, outlines the characteristics of biological indicators and describes their use. Some of the common errors that can occur when biological indicators are used are also addressed.

Key words: biological indicator, sterilisation, D-value; population, resistance, spores.

17.1 Introduction

There are different ways in which to verify the effectiveness of sterilisation. These methods include physical measurements and biological challenges [1]. This chapter is concerned with biological challenges through the use of biological indicators. With filtration, specific challenges of microorganisms can be used in solution to test the bacteria retentive nature of the filter. This falls outside the scope of what an accepted biological indicator is. The application of biological indicators, and the concern of this chapter, is in relation to gaseous sterilisation, vapour sterilisation, radiation sterilisation and sterilisation by heat. With these different methods, the use of biological indicators to verify steam sterilisation cycles arguably accounts for the greatest use of biological indicators. For this reason, and as by way of illustration, this chapter focuses upon examples applicable to this type of process, although much of what is discussed within the chapter applies to all uses of biological indicators.

Both the *European Pharmacopoeia* (section 5) and the *United States Pharmacopoeia* require the use of biological indicators in order to validate sterilisation processes. In terms of routine operations and revalidation, practices vary so it is recommended that at least an annual revalidation takes place to verify the worst case sterilisation cycle using biological indicators.

The term 'biological indicator' has wide usage outside the pharmaceutical industry. The term 'biological indicator' (or 'bio-indicator') also applies generally to the application of plants or animals to various conditions where the reaction of the biological material is examined. In one sense, the use of a canary in a cage by a miner to detect pockets of natural gas was arguably one of the first biological indicators. Today, to assess sterility, biological indicators are commonly used in both the food and pharmaceutical industries [2].

Biological indicators (or bio-indicators) are preparations of a specific microorganism, with high resistance towards particular sterilisation methods. Biological indicators are used by medical device manufacturers, pharmaceutical manufacturers and healthcare institutions to provide measured response of the efficacy of sterilisation processes. Since sterilisation can only be considered as the probability of there being an absence of microorganisms, where true sterility can only be demonstrated through infinite exposure [3], then greater assurance for sterilisation can be measured through physical (thermometric) data and from biological indicators to provide confidence that a sterilisation process has been successful.

There is a recurrent debate as to whether physical data or biological data is the most important when examining a sterilisation processes, as well as considering if both measures are needed simultaneously. This chapter does not set out to discuss the respective merits of these two approaches, although the importance of biological indicators is well established, and this author considers that biological monitoring is the most effective method [4]. Given that biological indicators are as much as one million times more resistant than typical bioburden, they also challenge the system at enormously higher population numbers than would be present in any normal environment. Thus it follows that successful destruction of the microbial population on the biological indicator provides a high level of assurance that the product is, in all probability, sterile [5].

Biological indicators are 'standardised' preparations of specific microorganisms with known characteristics (a defined population, purity and resistance characteristic). The microorganisms used to prepare biological indicators are those capable of forming endospores and the microorganism is used in the 'spore state'. A biological indicator is prepared by depositing bacterial spores from a spore crop onto a carrier, such as filter paper or a medium contained within an ampoule. Destruction of the spores is indicative of the probability of sterility.

This chapter discusses the important requirements for biological indicators and discusses their application in specific types of sterilisation processes.

17.2 Application of biological indicators

Different biological indicators are used for different sterilisation processes [6]. Biological indicators are designed for use with:

- ethylene oxide gas;
- hydrogen peroxide vapour;
- dry heat;
- steam;
- radiation.

With each of these:

- Ethylene oxide gas is used to kill bacteria, mould and fungi in medical supplies such as bandages.
- Dry-heat sterilisation uses an oven to raise the temperature of items that are wrapped in foil or fabric.
- Steam sterilisation uses an autoclave, a self-locking machine that sterilises its contents with steam under pressure.
- Irradiation is used to sterilise materials that may be damaged by moist heat, such as plastics.

These major types of sterilisation are covered in different chapters of this book.

The microorganism used will vary, depending upon the means of sterilisation which requires testing. Microorganisms are selected based on the criteria that they are non-pathogenic, are easy to culture, and in relation to how resistant they are to the chosen method of sterilisation.

Different microorganisms are more resistant than others to different types of sterilisation [7]. For example, with steam sterilisation, spore bearing microorganisms are more resistant than non-spore bearing microorganisms. A microorganism like Staphylococcus (commonly carried on human skin) would have a typical D-value at 121°C for a 15-minute autoclave cycle of only 15 seconds, whereas an endospore forming thermophilic Bacillus would have a D-value of at least 1.5 minutes. The D-value is a measure of resistance to the sterilisation process and is discussed below.

With steam sterilisation, for example, *Geobacillus stearothermophilus* (formerly described as *Bacillus stearothermophilus*) is the most commonly used organism to prepare a biological indicator (as required by the pharmacopoeias). This microorganism is used due to its theoretical resistance to particular types of sterilisation, including heat [8]. The principle is that if these spores are destroyed, then it can be assumed that any contaminating microorganisms in the sterilisation load would also have been killed, as these microorganisms will, in all probability, have a lower resistance than any spores that might be present, and such environmental microorganisms will probably have been present in far lower numbers [9].

In terms of different sterilisation processes, the biological indicator types and sterilisation combinations used are shown in Table 17.1.

Table 17.1	**Sterilisation methods and recommended biological indicators**

Sterilisation method	Biological indicator	Reference culture
Steam sterilisation	*Geobacillus stearothermophilus*	ATCC 7953, NCTC 10007, NCIMB 8157 or CIP 52.81
Dry heat sterilisation	*Bacillus atrophaeus*	ATCC 9372, NCIMB 8058 or CIP 77.18
Ionising radiation	*Bacillus pumilus*[1]	ATCC 27142, NCTC 10327, NCIMB 10692 or CIP 77.25
Gas sterilisation	*Bacillus atrophaeus*	ATCC 9372, NCIMB 8058 or CIP 77.18

Note:
[1]The *European Pharmacopeia* states that, for radiation, other strains of microorganisms, having demonstrated equivalent performance, may be used.

Reference culture refers to the culture collection from which the microorganism used to prepare the biological indicator was sourced. The use of reference cultures is in accordance with the European, United States and Japanese pharmacopoeia. This allows for standardisation and conformance with ISO standards or with the pharmacopeia.

Published by Woodhead Publishing Limited, 2013

17.2.1 Types of biological indicators

Biological indicators are available in many different forms. Examples include strips (the classic 'spore strip'), discs, suspensions, test tubes and ampoules. With these:

- Spore strips are biological indicators that are packaged in a pouch made of glassine, a paper that is resistant to moisture and air at ambient temperatures and pressures. The spore strip requires transfer to a culture medium post-sterilisation.

- Spore discs are usually made of borosilicate paper or stainless steel. Spore suspensions are diluted aliquots that are derived from a primary batch of spores. The spore disc requires transfer to a culture medium post-sterilisation.

- Other spore suspensions which are inoculated directly onto surfaces, such as rubber closures. These require transfer to a culture medium post-sterilisation.

- Test tubes that are available in a variety of sizes and are usually made of expansion-resistant glass. Ampoules are small, self-contained, vials hermetically sealed with a flame. They have a score mark around the neck so that the sealed top can be snapped off by hand. Typically, ampoules are used to contain hypodermic injection solutions. These are self-contained systems that comprise the microorganism and growth medium required for recovery in a primary pack ready for use. Microbial growth is indicated by a change in pH (with a colour indicator), which measures the production of acid metabolites in the growth medium by outgrowing spores and replicating microbial cells.

In general, spore strips are used to test solid items, within a porous load cycle, and ampoules to test liquids, where the biological indicator is placed inside a bottle or vial.

17.3 Characteristics of biological indicators

A biological indicator is defined in the International Organization for Standardization (ISO) 11139 terminology document as: 'a test system containing viable microorganisms providing a defined resistance to a specified sterilisation process' [10]. Biological indicators are prepared in such a way that they can be stored under defined conditions within a defined expiry date. In the United States, biological indicators must be registered and approved by the US Food and Drug Administration as a class 2 medical device.

A biological indicator is characterised by the name of the species of bacterium used as the reference microorganism, and the originating culture collection, the number of viable spores per carrier and the D-value. The most important characteristic of a biological indicator is that sporulation must readily occur on a defined medium and, if there are any survivors, spore germination will occur [11]. The characteristics are examined below. These characteristics relate to tests that must be undertaken by the manufacturer of the biological indicator. Some users elect to perform confirmatory testing of biological indicator lots using independent test facilities. One reason for this would be to assess if the transportation conditions have affected the biological indicators.

17.3.1 Purity

Biological indicators must be verified for purity by at least a phenotypic identification of the microorganism. The required microorganism, according to the biological indicator label, must be the only microorganism recovered.

17.3.2 Population

The target population for biological indicators is typically more than 1×10^6, although for some applications, biological indicators with different populations can be used (Table 17.2). The reason why this population is commonly used is because it is generally accepted that 'devices purporting to be sterile', such as an autoclave, are designed to achieve a 10^{-6} microbial survival probability (i.e. there is less than one chance in a million that a microorganism would survive the sterilisation process) [12].

Biological indicators must have a minimum population, as defined by the pharmacopoeiae. To verify this, a population verification, as per USP total viable spore count, is normally performed. The acceptance criteria state that the results should be not be less than 50% or more than 300% of the labelled certified population.

Published by Woodhead Publishing Limited, 2013

Table 17.2	Characteristics of different biological indicators

Sterilisation method	Biological indicator	Population	D-value
Steam sterilisation	*Geobacillus stearothermophilus*	$\geq 5 \times 10^5$ per carrier	Not less than 1.5 minutes at 121 °C[1]
Dry heat sterilisation	*Bacillus atrophaeus*	$\geq 1 \times 10^6$ per carrier	Not less than 2.5 minutes at 160 °C[2]
Ionising radiation	*Bacillus pumilus*	$\geq 1 \times 10^7$ per carrier	Not less than 1.9 kGy[3]
Gas sterilisation	*Bacillus atrophaeus*	$\geq 1 \times 10^6$ per carrier	Not less than 2.5 minutes for a test cycle involving 600 mg/L of ethylene oxide, at 54 °C and at 60% relative humidity[4]

Notes:

[1] It is verified that exposing the biological indicators to steam at 121 ± 1°C for 6 minutes leaves revivable spores, and that there is no growth of the reference microorganisms after the biological indicators have been exposed to steam at 121 ± 1°C for 15 minutes.

[2] Dry heat at temperatures greater than 220°C is frequently used for sterilisation and depyrogenation of glassware. In this case, demonstration of a 3-$\log_{10}$ reduction in heat-resistant bacterial endotoxin can be used as a replacement for biological indicators.

[3] It is verified that there is no growth of the reference microorganisms after the biological indicators have been exposed to 25 kGy (minimum absorbed dose).

[4] It is verified that there is no growth of the reference microorganisms after the biological indicators have been exposed to the test cycle described above for 25 minutes and that exposing the indicators to a reduced temperature cycle (600 mg/L, 30°C and 60% relative humidity) for 50 minutes leaves revivable spores.

17.3.3 D-value

Arguably the most important characteristic of biological indicators is the level of resistance. This is defined by the decimal reduction value (or D-value). It is of significance only under precisely defined experimental conditions.

The D-value is the value of a parameter of sterilisation (duration or absorbed dose) required to reduce the population of a known microorganism by 1-log (or 90% of the population). Thus, after an organism is reduced by 1 D, only 10% of the original microbial population remains (i.e. the population number has been reduced by one decimal place in the counting scheme). When referring to D values, it is normal to give the temperature or dose as a subscript to the letter D. For example, with steam sterilisation, a hypothetical organism is reduced by 90% after exposure to temperatures of 121°C for 1.5 minutes, thus the D-value would be written as $D_{121°C} = 1.5$ minutes. D-values will vary according to the resistance of the microorganism and the population challenge. Generally, the longer the exposure time or lower the dose, and the more resistant the microorganism, then the higher the D-value.

The acceptance criteria for the D-value are defined by the USP, which states:

> The requirements of the test are met if the determined D-value is within 20% of the labelled D-value for the selected sterilising temperature and if the confidence limits of the estimate are within 10% of the determined D-value.

In order to verify the D-Value, the USP and ISO 11138–14 allows for the use of three methods. These are:

1. the Most Probable Number method by direct enumeration;

2. a Fraction Negative method (i.e. Spearman/Karber); or

3. to assess the D-value accuracy by using the USP Survive/Kill calculated cycles.

Regardless of which of the three methods is used, a specialised item of equipment will be needed to calculate the D-value. For example, with steam sterilisation this is a Resistometer, also known as a BIER (Biological Indicator-Evaluator Resistometer) Vessel, which is an item of test equipment that can very quickly and accurately deliver and control precise sterilisation process parameters. The standard ANSI/AAMI ST44:20025 states that with a Steam BIER Vessel, the equipment must be capable of reaching the target temperature set point within 10 seconds or less from the time 'steam charge' occurs. In addition, it must maintain that set temperature to within ±0.5°C and then at cycle end, the post-vacuum time to reach atmospheric pressure must be within 10 seconds or less [13].

Direct enumeration is the process of determining the lethality of the sterilisation process by construction of a survivor curve using direct enumeration (physical counts through serial dilutions) of surviving organisms. At least five points employing graded exposure times, with all other parameters (except time) remaining constant, are utilised. The data generated will enable the calculation of the time of exposure needed to achieve sterility of the biological indicator.

The most common method deployed to calculate D-values is the Fractional Negative Method. This method also requires graded exposure times to assure survivors, but the post-processing testing methods are different. For this method, a minimum of five exposure times are required and multiple groups of biological indicators (typically 10 or 20) are exposed to varying cycle exposure times. The examination is for partial kill, looking for that fraction which is negative. This is normally running one exposure designed for all test biological indicators to survive; one exposure designed for all test biological indicators to be killed, and several exposures in between, set at equidistant time intervals.

After exposure to the process, the samples are assayed by direct immersion into the appropriate culture medium (pass/fail) in lieu of the physical count performed. Using the data generated and statistical models provided in the standard (Holcomb-Spearman Karber or Stumbo Murphy Cochran), the death kinetics or D-value may be calculated. Using the D-value data, an exposure time needed to achieve the desired sterility assurance level can be determined. For example, to verify the resistance of a particular biological indicator in a steam vessel at 121°C using the Limited Spearman-Karber Fraction Negative Method, 20 biological indicators would be exposed per group to various exposure times at 121°C. After each exposure, each group of biological indicators would be aseptically transferred to a growth medium and incubated at the appropriate temperature.

D-values vary with different carriers, even where the same spore crop is used. Thus, the same spore crop used to inoculate a paper strip and a rubber closure will give a different D-value, and there is the probability that the rubber closure will give a higher D-value. This variation explains why, for instance, the D-value for a self-contained biological indicator in a glass ampoule has a higher D-value than spores inoculated onto a cotton thread. A similar phenomenon occurs with different fluids. Spores suspended in water will have a lower D-value than spores suspended in a saline solution.

17.3.4 Z-value

A Z-value is defined as the number of degrees Celsius required to change a D-value by one factor of ten. In the practical sense, it is a measure of how susceptible a spore population is to changes in temperature. For example, if the Z-value of a population is 10 degrees, then increasing the sterilisation temperature by 10 degrees will result in a log reduction of the D-value.

To work out a Z-value, at least three D-value/temperature pairs are required. Z-values can be estimated graphically (using line of best fit) or calculated mathematically. Z-values are useful for calculating F values (in conjunction with D-values), especially to show the relationship between lethalities.

17.3.5 Incubation times and media

The ISO 14161 standard, which provides guidance for users of BIs, recommends an incubation period of 7 days for established sterilisation processes, such as ethylene oxide and moist heat, and 14 days for non-standard or new sterilisation processes [14]. Due to concerns about the recovery of sub-lethally damaged microorganisms, some users elect to increase the incubation times beyond 7 days.

17.3.6 Other factors

Other factors need to be considered when using biological indicators. These include the shelf life (where temperature and humidity are important), strip size and package size of the biological indicator.

17.3.7 Certification and verification

All biological indicators must come with a certificate of conformity. The certificate should indicate the population, D-value and purity of the microorganism. Due to the variability in the preparation of biological indicators, some users elect to have biological indicators verified. For example, this would be the case with spores inoculated onto a paper carrier to create a spore strip. With biological indicators prepared by the user (i.e. inoculating a spore suspension onto a rubber closure), these must always be verified, as there is no other comparative data available.

Without possession of these characteristics, the biological indicator is of little value. Due to the importance of these parameters, it is recommended that a positive control be run alongside each test set of biological indicators.

With the different sterilisation methods and biological indicator types presented in Table 17.1 above, the following is recommended by the *European Pharmacopeia* (monograph 5.1.2):

Table 17.3 Biological indicators with vapour sterilisation methods

Sterilisation method	Biological indicator	Population	D-value
Steam sterilisation	*Geobacillus stearothermophilus* (alternatively *Clostridium sporogenes*, *Bacillus subtilus* or *Bacillus coagulans* may be used, if justified)	Between 1×10^5 and 5×10^6	D-value$_{121°C}$ of between 1.5 and 3.0 minutes
Dry heat sterilisation	*Bacillus atrophaeus*	Between $\leq 10^4$ to $\geq 10^9$ per carrier	Between 1 and 3 minutes at 160°C
Ionising radiation	*Bacillus pumilus* (alternatively a more resistant microorganism may be used if detected from product bioburden)	Not specified	Not specified. The pharmacopeia notes that physical measurements are often used in place of biological indicators.
Gas sterilisation	*Bacillus atrophaeus*	Between $\leq 10^4$ to $\geq 10^9$ per carrier	Between 2.5 and 5.8 minutes for a test cycle involving 600 mg/L of ethylene oxide, at 54°C and at 60% elative humidity
Vapour sterilisation	*Geobacillus stearothermophilus* (alternatively *Clostridium sporogens* or *Bacillus subtilus* may be used, if justified)	Not specified	Not specified

Although not recommended by the *European Pharmacopeia*, it is typical to use biological indicators of *Geobacillus stearothermophilus* with vapour sterilisation methods as recommended by the *United States Pharmacopeia* (Table 17.3) (15).

In relation to gas and radiation methods, the product to be sterilised should be assessed using a method whereby resistance determinations are demonstrated for the biological indicators used for the initial qualification compared to the natural product bioburden; as outlined in Annex A of ISO 11135 'Determination of lethal rate of the sterilisation process – Biological indicator/bioburden approach' [16]. The knowledge of this rate and the population and relative resistance of the bioburden allows the exposure time required to achieve a Sterility Assurance Level (SAL) of 1×10^6 or greater to be established.

17.4 Use of biological indicators

Biological indicators are used either to validate a sterilisation cycle or to routinely confirm the effectiveness of the cycle, either as part of revalidation or to periodically assess standard cycles.

When placing biological indicators with the product to be sterilised, a rationale must be drawn up to indicate how many biological indicators are to be used and where they are to be located. It is recommended that the biological indicators are placed at the locations presumed, or wherever possible, found by previous physical measurement to be least accessible to the sterilising agent. Thus, with a steam sterilisation cycle, which would include points where the lowest temperature has been recorded, and where items more difficult to sterilise are being challenged, the biological indicators should be placed in areas that are theoretically less accessible, such as inside a piece of tubing.

After the sterilisation cycle has been completed, the biological indicators should be processed by a microbiology laboratory. With spore strips, aseptic technique is used to transfer carriers of spores to the culture media, so that no contamination is present at the time of examination. With biological indicators that include an ampoule of culture medium, these are placed directly into an incubator. The incubation temperature should relate to the type of microorganism used to prepare the biological indicator so that, for example, *Geobacillus stearothermophilus*, which is used to assess super heat, is incubated in a temperature range of 55–60°C. After incubation, growth of the reference microorganisms subjected to a sterilisation procedure indicates that the procedure has been unsatisfactory.

17.4.1 Overkill method

Once a D-value has been established, many sterilisation cycles have 'overkill' built in. This is either simply doubling the cycle time (or sterilisation dose), or is taken from a mathematically calculated SAL.

Typically, the SAL is developed to give a sterilisation cycle designed to achieve a 12-log reduction of the challenge population.

The overkill method requires a total of three consecutive (half standard exposure time) cycles to be performed, which result in total inactivation of the biological indicators, of which the initial population was not less than 10^6. By demonstrating the inactivation of the 10^6 biological indicator using one half of the exposure time, a SAL of 10^6 is assured when the exposure time is doubled for the routine full cycle. In addition to the three successful half cycles, the standard requires a cycle of short duration (fractional), from which survivors can be recovered, to be performed to demonstrate (validate) the adequacy of the recovery technique. Also, it is during this fractional cycle that the resistance of the bioburden is proven to be equal to or less than the resistance of the biological indicator.

17.5 Areas of concern and testing errors

As with any biological test there are aspects of biological indicator testing which can cause testing difficulties. Some of these issues are next examined.

(a) *The bioburden of the product being sterilised* – This can affect the results of the study, such as leading to an increase in the D-value or promoting survival of spores through a clumping effect by one microorganism covering another. Therefore, the following should be considered:

■ total numbers of organisms present, as the item to be sterilised, just prior to sterilisation must be known;

■ types of organisms present;

■ number of resistant spore formers present;

■ resistance of this bioburden;

■ sampling frequency and statistical analysis.

(b) *Variability between different lots of biological indicators* – Each lot of biological indicators will vary slightly in its population, resistance and kill time. This variability can arise from heterogeneity within a spore population, which can be caused by genotypic and phenotypic variations within the spore crop. This is one of the reasons why the USP recommends that supplier audits take the place of biological indicator manufacturers. In addition, it is good practice to audit any contract test laboratories who may undertake biological indicator testing.

(c) *Shipping conditions* – Biological indicators may be affected by the transport from the manufacturer. Any available transport and stability data from manufacturer should be reviewed [17].

(d) *Storage conditions* – Most biological indicators will have prescribed storage conditions. These may be strictly defined, or 'controlled temperatures' will be referred to. Controlled room temperature is defined in the USP as:

> A temperature maintained thermostatically that encompasses the usual and customary working environment of 20°C to 25°C (68–77°F) that results in a mean kinetic temperature calculated to be not more than 25°C; and that allows for excursions between 15°C and 30°C (59–86°F) that are experienced in pharmacies, hospitals and warehouses . . .

Humidity, if it is not defined by the manufacturer, is typically 20% to 70% relative humidity.

Storage conditions and times should be assessed by a stability trial. This is of great importance as, theoretically, the D-value of a biological indicator will decrease over time.

(e) *Delay in transferring the biological indicator to storage medium* – Theoretically, the ability to recover spores, especially those which are sub-lethally damaged, may be affected by the time taken to transfer a biological indicator, which has undergone steam sterilisation to the required culture medium. For this purpose, the USP states in the Guide to General Chapters Microbiological tests: Biological Indicators, that:

> . . . after completion of the sterilising procedure . . . and within a noted time not greater than 4 hours, aseptically remove and add each strip to 10 to 30 ml of Soybean Casein Digest medium . . .

(f) *Test method used by contract test laboratory to determine the D-value* – Variation can arise when biological indicators are evaluated by contract manufacturers for population and D-value by contract manufacturers. Variables can include techniques, utensils and equipment. The main source of variation is if the contract test laboratory uses a different technique for D-value determination from the manufacturer. A related variation can arise from the culture medium, and incubation conditions for different brands and different lots of culture media may not have the same degree of 'ability to promote growth of injured spores'.

(g) *Preparation of biological indicators* – Variation can occur with the preparation of biological indicators. This is of particular concern when users prepare their own biological indicators, such as inoculating spores onto stoppers. Areas of concern here include:

- how spores are put onto carriers;
- places where the inoculation is too thick, and irregular clumps occur;
- how often the spore suspension is re-suspended;
- pipetting technique;
- drying times;
- the fluid in which the spore suspension is held (typically water or ethanol);
- problems from media residues;
- excessive damage to the surface.

17.6 Conclusion

This chapter has examined some of the key characteristics of biological indicators that are of great importance in assessing sterilisation in the pharmaceutical industry. Thermometric data provides abundant information as to what might theoretically happen; however, it is only through biological material that the question: 'what if the material to be sterilised has a high bioburden?' can be answered.

The emphasis of the chapter has been upon some of the factors that might cause variation and testing problems. An element of variation will always be present when biological material is used; however, attempts should be made to reduce this variation to a minimal level.

17.7 References

1. Sandle, T. (2011), 'The use of biological indicators for steam sterilization', *Global BioPharmaceutical Resources Inc.*, Newsletter July: 1–12.
2. Sharp, J. (1995), 'What do we mean by "sterility"?' *PDA Journal of Pharmaceutical Science and Technology*, 49(2): 90–2.

3. Tidswell, E. (2011), 'Sterility', in: Saghee, M.R., Sandle, T. and Tidswell, E.C. (eds), *Microbiology and Sterility Assurance in Pharmaceuticals and Medical Devices*, New Delhi: Business Horizons, pp. 589–614.

4. Pflug, I.J. and Odlaug, T.E. (1986), 'Biological indicators in the pharmaceutical and medical device industry', *Journal of Parenteral Science and Technology*, 40: 242–8.

5. van Doorne, H. (2000), 'A basic primer on pharmaceutical microbiology', in: Prince, R. (ed.), *Microbiology in Pharmaceutical Manufacturing*, Bethesda, MD: Parenteral Drug Association; Godalming, UK: Davis Horwood International Publishing, pp. 71–123.

6. American Society for Healthcare Central Service Personnel of the American Hospital Association (1989), *Recommended Practices for Central Service, Sterilisation*. Chicago, IL: American Hospital Association.

7. Halls, N.A. (1998), 'Resistance "creep" of biological indicators', in: Morrissey, R.F. and Kowalski, J.B. (eds), *Sterilisation of Medical Products*, Champlain, NY: Polysciences Publications, Inc.

8. Joslyn, L.J. (1991), 'Sterilisation by heat', in: Block, S.S. (ed.), *Disinfection, Sterilisation, and Preservation*, 4th edition, Philadelphia, PA: Lea and Febiger, pp. 495–526.

9. Agalloco, J.P., Akers, J.E. and Madsen, R.E. (1988), 'Moist heat sterilisation – myths and realities', *PDA Journal of Pharmaceutical Science and Technology*, 52(6): 346–50.

10. ISO 11139 (2006), *Sterilisation of Health Care Products – Vocabulary*, Geneva: International Standards Organisation.

11. Foster, S.J. and Johnstone, K. (1989), 'The trigger mechanism of bacterial spore germination', in: Smith, I., Slepecky, R.A and Setlow, P. (eds), *Regulation of Prokaryotic Development*, New York: Plenum Publishing Corporation, pp. 89–108.

12. ISO 11138–3:2006 – *Sterilisation of Health Care Products – Biological Indicators* – Part 3: Biological indicators for moist heat sterilisation processes, Geneva: International Standards Organisation.

13. ANSI/AAMI ST44:2002 – 'Performance requirements for resistometers', USA: Advancing Safety in Medical Technology.

14. ISO 14161 (2009), Sterilisation of Health Care Products – Biological Indicators – Guidance for the selection, use and interpretation of results, Geneva: International Standards Organisation.

15. PDA (2011), PDA Technical Report No. 51, 'Biological indicators for gas and vapor-phase decontamination processes: Specification, manufacture, control and SSE', Rockville, MD: Parenteral Drug Association.

16. ISO 11135 – Part 1 (2007), *Sterilisation of Health Care Products – Ethylene Oxide* – Part 1: Requirements for development, validation, and routine control of a sterilisation process for medical devices, Geneva: International Standards Organisation.

17. SGM Biotech Report #000401RA, 3 May 2001: *The Effects of Transient Conditions using Shipping on SGM Strip Biological Indicators Containing* Bacillus stearothermophilus *Spores*, US: SGM.

18

The Sterility Test

DOI: 10.1533/9781908818638.279

Abstract: This chapter addresses the Sterility Test, a mandatory release test for aseptically filled pharmaceutical drug products and also undertaken for some terminally sterilised products and medical devices, where parametric release does not apply. The most common method is the cultural based method described in the pharmacopoeia. However, there are new and emerging rapid microbiological methods that are gaining acceptance. This chapter describes the Sterility Test and discusses approaches to method validation and difficulties that some products present. It concludes with a summary of rapid methods.

Key words: Sterility Test, culture media, sterility, rapid microbiological methods, growth promotion, quality control, batch release, validation.

18.1 Introduction

This chapter examines one of the most important tests required for products purportedly to be sterile: the Sterility Test, sometimes called the 'test for sterility'. The sterility of pharmaceutical products is either assessed parametrically, through a review of physical data, or by testing a representative number of items from a batch. For aseptically filled products, the parametric release is not permitted and the only way that a batch can be released is through the Sterility Test [1]. For this purpose, it has been a mainstream microbiological test on final products, and some intermediates, since it was first published in the *British Pharmacopoeia* in

1932. This published test was a direct inoculation test of seven days duration, the membrane filtration being introduced in 1957. Due to not all of the items from a batch being tested, since the Sterility Test is a destructive process and in doing so would leave no items remaining, it means that the term 'sterility' cannot be proved by simply performing the test, but can only be quoted in terms of probability.

The 'classic' Sterility Test only examines for those bacteria and fungi that can grow under the particular cultural conditions of the test. Since 2012, the FDA has allowed rapid methods to be used as alternatives to the methods described in the pharmacopoeia [2]. This chapter describes the Sterility Test, the culture media and testing requirements. It also considers the method limitations, including reference to the probability that a batch is or is not sterile. It also includes an overview of some of the rapid microbiological methods which may, in time, replace the Sterility Test method described in the pharmacopeia.

18.2 Sterility Test methods

The most widely practiced method of Sterility Testing is that described in the three main pharmacopeiae (European, United States and Japan, which were harmonised in 2009). These are cultural-based methods used for the assessment of pharmaceutical drug products. Since 2012, the US Food and Drug Administration have permitted the use of alternative rapid microbiological methods. These are not yet in widespread use, although they are discussed briefly within this chapter. For medical devices, the Sterility Test undertaken post-sterilisation is a modification of the pharmacopoeia Sterility Test, normally a variant of the direct inoculation method, where the device is immersed in a culture medium.

18.3 Pharmacopeia Sterility Test

There are two principle methods of Sterility Testing, as defined in the pharmacopoeiae [3], membrane filtration and direct inoculation. Of these methods, membrane filtration is the method of choice, because a larger size can be tested. The pharmacopoeia require that the entire contents of a small volume product are filtered and at least half the contents of a large volume product pass through a membrane filter. With the direct inoculation method, only a few millilitres of a liquid product

Published by Woodhead Publishing Limited, 2013

are transferred into the test media. Furthermore, any microorganisms present are far more likely to be separated from potentially inhibitory substances in the product through the act of filtration or can be eliminated by rinsing the filter. It is also common for membrane filtration systems to be enclosed, such as the Steritest™ system (introduced in 1975), which minimises risk of contamination by reducing transfer steps [4].

Membrane filtration is the appropriate method for all aqueous, alcoholic, oily and solvent products that can pass through a sterile filter with a porosity of 0.45 μm (Figure 18.1). The standard filter is manufactured from cellulose esters or other similar plastics. The filter acts to separate the product from any microorganisms, so that the product passes through the filter and any microorganisms present in the product are trapped within the filter matrix. A rinse solution (i.e. phosphate buffered saline, saline or Ringer's solution) is used to remove any product residues. This washing process is normally performed three or four times and the filter should remain wet throughout.

The filter is divided into two portions, or more than one filter is used, as in the widely used Steritest™ polycarbonate filtration system. To each filter, culture media is added, so that any microorganisms trapped in the filter membrane, following incubation at a suitable temperature, will

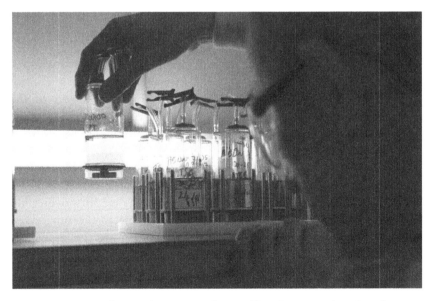

Figure 18.1 Inspecting a membrane filtration test chamber (image courtesy of Tim Sandle)

Published by Woodhead Publishing Limited, 2013

replicate. Two culture media are used. The pharmacopoeias recommend fluid thioglycollate medium (FTM), incubated at 30–35°C to isolate bacteria (aerobic and anaerobic) and soya bean casein digest medium (tryptone soya broth, TSB), incubated at 20–25°C to isolate aerobic bacteria and fungi. FTM has resazurin, an oxidation-reduction indicator, added to create a chemical layer (indicated by a pink colouration) to allow the growth of both aerobic and anaerobic microorganisms.

However, many products will not readily filter (i.e. protein-based products that will block the filter pores), as they are so inherently anti-microbial that the direct inoculation method is used. Direct inoculation may also be preferred over membrane filtration if the membrane filtration method simply cannot be validated. When the direct inoculation method is selected, the laboratory should be able to justify why it has selected this method over the membrane filtration technique. The direct inoculation technique involves the addition of a portion of the product to two different culture media, FTM and TSB, as per the membrane filtration technique. This is half the contents of the product vial to each culture medium – for product between 50 mg and 300 mg – or the entire contents for product of less than 50 mg. For large volumes of product, a concentrate of the culture medium is sometimes added to the product.

For the direct inoculation technique, products which have anti-microbial activity must be neutralised before a portion of the product is added to the culture medium. This is performed either by the addition of a neutraliser or by dilution of the product.

Each Sterility Testing session should have a negative control consisting of the test media and test consumables. Such a control is designed to indicate if the culture media, or some aspect of the test environment, could result or increase the risk of a false positive developing in the Sterility Test. All test consumables should be recorded for each test.

The incubation time for both test methods is 14 days. The previous incubation, which stood for 50 years, was 7 days. This was increased to 14 days in 1997. This was because it was estimated that 30% of Sterility Test failures occurred between 7 and 14 days, due to the time taken for sub-lethally damaged or stressed microorganisms to grow [5]. Microorganisms isolated from a Sterility Test are more likely to be stressed due to the transfer from their environment into a more hostile environment (the product) and then into a completely different nutrient-rich environment (the culture media). These microorganisms are also likely to be low in number, as little as one cell. These factors contribute

Figure 18.2 A technician preparing direct inoculation test bottles (image courtesy of Tim Sandle)

to a relatively long lag phase at the start of the microbial cell growth cycle in the culture medium (Figure 18.2) [6].

For products which produce suspension, flocculation, turbidity or deposits, so that the presence or absence of microbial growth cannot be readily seen, a subculture step is required. To subculture a suitable portion of the culture, media is transferred to a container of the same media type and incubated for a further time period (as discussed below).

The items incubated must be clearly labelled with the identity of the product, the medium used, the temperature of incubation and the date of testing. Throughout the incubation of the Sterility Test, the articles must be examined regularly for growth, which is often every day or every other day. When inspecting the items being tested, care must be taken to prevent undue agitation, especially of the thioglycollate medium. If anaerobic conditions are not maintained, this will be indicated by the resazurin indicator. At the end of the incubation period, the articles must be inspected, by gentle swirling, for visible turbidity against an artificial light source.

If turbidity is seen, an investigation must be performed (this is examined in Chapter 19). For the test to be valid, certain conditions must be met:

- The culture media used is sterile, often shown by incubating articles of culture media alongside the Sterility Test.

- The culture media can support microbial growth, from growth promotion testing.

- The product does not have a microstatic or microbicidal effect, or can be eliminated – as indicated by Sterility Test validation.

- Contamination is not introduced into the test by external sources.

18.4 Test environment

The Sterility Test must be undertaken in an environment that does not introduce contamination and lead to the potential of a false positive occurring. A suitable environment is either a unidirectional airflow device held within a cleanroom or, preferably, an isolator, which will provide a greater level of security. Environmental monitoring should be undertaken during each test session, to demonstrate that the environment is within control [7].

18.5 Sterility Test media

All media used for the Sterility Test must have passed a growth promotion test for nutritive properties and must not have exceeded its nutritive properties expiry time. The pharmacopoeia requires microorganisms to be used as shown in Table 18.1.

18.6 Sterility Test method validation

Each product type must be validated to show that in the presence of the culture media it does not possess any anti-microbial activity, sometimes referred to as bacteriostasis and fungistasis. For validation, three different batches of product must be examined [8]. Validation is also performed if there is a substantial change to a previously validated product or to the culture media.

Table 18.1	Culture media, incubation temperatures and microorganisms for growth promotion

Medium	Temperature	Microorganisms for *European Pharmacopeia*	Microorganisms for *United States Pharmacopeia*
FTB	30–35°C	*Clostridium sporogenes* (ATCC 11437) and *Staphylococcus aureus subsp. aureus* (ATCC 6538) and one of the following aerobic bacteria: *Bacillus subtilis subsp. spizizenii* (ATCC 6633) or *Pseudomonas aeruginosa* (ATCC 9027).	Anaerobic microorganism: *Clostridium sporogenes* (ATCC 11437 or ATCC 19404) or *Bacteroides vulgatus* (ATCC 8482) One of either *Staphylococcus aureus subsp. aureus* (ATCC 6538) or *Bacillus subtilis subsp. spizizenii* (ATCC 6633) One of either *Pseudomonas aeruginosa* (ATCC 9027) or *Micrococcus luteus* (*Kocuria rhizophila*) (ATCC 9431)
TSB	20–25°C	Inoculate with a minimum of one of the following fungi: *Candida albicans* (ATCC 10231) or *Aspergillus brasilensis* (ATCC 16404) and with a minimum of one of the following aerobic bacteria: *Staphylococcus aureus subsp. aureus* (ATCC 6538), *Bacillus subtilis subsp. spizizenii* (ATCC 6633) or *Pseudomonas aeruginosa* (ATCC 9027)	*Candida albicans* (ATCC 10231) and *Aspergillus brasilensis* (ATCC 16404)

The Sterility Test validation involves, for each type of microorganism listed below:

■ *Membrane filtration method* – after transferring the contents of each final product vial/bottle through the membrane, less than 100 cfu is added to the final portion of the saline rinse.

■ *Direct inoculation method* – after transferring the contents of each final product vial/bottle into the culture medium, less than 100 cfu is added to the test culture media bottle.

Published by Woodhead Publishing Limited, 2013

Table 18.2 Microorganisms required for Sterility Test validation

Microorganism	Culture medium
Staphylococcus aureus subsp. *aureus* (ATCC 6538)	FTB, TSB
Bacillus subtilis subsp. *spizizenii* (ATCC 6633)	FTB, TSB
Pseudomonas aeruginosa (ATCC 9027)	FTB, TSB
Clostridium sporogenes (ATCC 19404)	FTB
Candida albicans (ATCC 10231)	TSB
Aspergillus brasilensis (ATCC 16404)	TSB

Table 18.2 lists Ph. Eur. recommendations. It is also in keeping with USP. The USP requirements are the same as those for the validation of culture media, which are described above.

Each microorganism is added singularly to a test bottle or chamber. Therefore for the membrane filtration test, several replicate tests are required in order to include all the required microorganisms, making it an expensive test method, depending upon the market value of the product.

For the validation, positive controls of media in the absence of product must be used. Bacteria must grow in not more than three days and fungi in not more than five days. 'Growth' is defined as 'clearly visible growth' in comparison to the positive controls.

This approach is relatively straightforward, for standard products. However, many pharmaceuticals are not readily testable using the method as described in the pharmacopoeias, without some form of test modification or product neutralisation.

Examples of potentially difficult products are:

■ mercurial compounds;

■ antibiotics;

■ turbid samples;

■ medical devices;

■ oily samples;

■ catgut;

■ radiopharmaceuticals;

■ cell lines.

Such products can be overcome by:

- *Changing the membrane filter* – the two main filter types are cellulose nitrate and cellulose acetate. Sometimes successful validation can be as simple as selecting the correct filter type. Cellulose nitrate filters are used for testing aqueous, oily and weakly alcoholic solutions, whereas cellulose acetate filters are used for the testing of strongly alcoholic solutions.

- *Varying the number of membrane filter rinses* – anti-microbial effects can be overcome by varying the number of rinse solutions. Variations can be made to the rinse solution itself through the addition of neutralisers. Common general additives include polysorbate-80 or the surfactant Triton X-100. For antibiotics, the main neutraliser is penicillinase [9].

Table 18.3 shows some examples of neutralising agents appropriate for different anti-microbial agents [10]:

- The dilution of some products prior to direct inoculation can overcome

Table 18.3 Neutralising agents for different products in relation to the Sterility Test

Anti-microbial agent/product	Neutralising agent
Benzalkonium chloride 0.01%	0.5% lecithin and 3% polysorbate-80
Chlorohexine	Lecithin and polysorbate-80
Parabenz	5% polysorbate-80 or 0.07% lecithin and 0.5% polysorbate-80
Mercurial compounds	Thioglycollate/sodium thiosulphate/thioglycollate with cysteine
Azide	Azolectin
Sorbic acid	Dilution and polysorbate-80
Collagen implant	3% polysorbate-80
Organic acids	Polysorbate-80
Penicillin/cephalosporins	Penicillinase (β-lactamase – volume determined from antibiotic assay). Considered less effective for cephalosporins – membrane filtration recommended
Chloraphenicol	Chloramphenicol acetyltransferase
Sulphonamide	P-aminobenzoic acid

anti-microbial properties, as can varying the volume of the culture media used.

■ Turbid samples present a problem, especially when the direct inoculation method is used. For normal Sterility Testing, turbid samples require sub-culturing at 3–7 days after the initial test and then re-incubating the sub-cultured product for an additional 7 days alongside the original Sterility Test, therefore total test time becomes 14 + 7 days.

■ Some products, particularly solids or articles, require manipulation prior to filtration or direct inoculation. Typically this involves either dissolving the product in water, if it is water soluble or has been freeze-dried, or dissolving with a solvent (i.e. creams or water insoluble substances). Direct inoculation is either dissolving or adding the solid (or disassembling the article) directly into the culture media. The addition of a heating step can either facilitate or speed up the dissolution. Variation to these approaches can influence the success or otherwise of the validation. However, such approaches can often be variable and it is important to cover all possible differences in product volumes and consistency in the validation exercise.

■ Some products are not testable using the culture media described in the pharmacopoeias, therefore alternative or modified media may be used. An example of modified media is for the testing of penicillins where the addition of penicillinase to media is required. Furthermore, the testing of medical devices, according to the USP, is performed using alternative thioglycollate medium, which is not listed in the EP because the pharmacopoeia does not cover medical devices.

18.7 Stasis Test

The final aspect of Sterility Test validation is the stasis test (or inhibition test), which is not a mandatory test according to the pharmacopoeias, but is generally included as part of best practise. The stasis test is a form of Sterility Test validation that is performed at the end of the incubation period, that is, after 14 days has elapsed and the product has been examined for growth. The stasis test involves challenging the product with a low level (often <100 cfu) of different bacteria (bacteriostasis) and fungi (fungistasis). For products that are membrane filtered, only two microorganisms can be tested at any one time, therefore tests on several batches may be required to complete the test on a given product.

The stasis test is particularly important for Sterility Testing of antibiotics, slow release products, products which are inherently anti-microbial or for tests where the methodology is marginal, such as a test on an antibiotic cream where there is method variability, such as in the amount of cream tested for each test. The test is important for such products, because they could potentially pass the traditional Sterility Test at time zero but then slowly release antibiotics or other anti-microbial substances over the duration of the incubation, which would inhibit the growth of any slow growing, stressed or damaged microorganisms.

18.8 GMP requirements

When conducting Sterility Tests, a number of Good Manufacturing Practice (GMP) requirements must be adhered to. Many of these relate to record-keeping. During Sterility Testing, detailed records must be kept, which should include:

■ description of method;

■ details of the method of transfer into clean room or isolator;

■ number of product units tested;

■ batch/lot number;

■ stage of manufacturing (e.g. finished product/intermediate/final bulk);

■ personnel performing the tests;

■ dates of testing;

■ test method;

■ volume tested;

■ diluents/solvents used;

■ media batch numbers;

■ temperature and incubation time;

■ date of reading the test and who by;

■ the result (pass or fail);

■ environmental monitoring results;

■ negative control results.

18.9 Can the Sterility Test really confirm product sterility?

Based on statistical probability, the Sterility Test is one of the most meaningless microbiological tests performed. This is because very little of the batch is tested; the EP and USP allow a maximum of 20 units to be tested from a batch size of 500 or more. For batches of a size in the several thousands, the chance of detecting a contaminated unit is very small. For example, if 5% of a batch is contaminated and only 10 samples are tested for sterility, then 84/100 Sterility Tests would pass each time [11]. Therefore, the Sterility Test can only detect gross contamination. There is no value in increasing the numbers of samples presented for Sterility Testing by doubling, as some companies have done, in response to something like a series of poor environmental monitoring results. Statistically there is no greater chance of detecting a failure, coupled with the lack of any conclusive link between the amount of contamination detected through environmental monitoring and Sterility Test failures [12]. This sampling issue has been only partially addressed by the FDA's 2012 revision to CFR 610.12. The clause notes that more samples would be expected to be tested from a batch of 100 000 units than from a batch of 5000 units, but does not offer any guidance as to what a suitable number of articles should be.

Even under conditions of heavy contamination, the Sterility Test will only show the presence of those microorganisms that will grow under the test conditions. These conditions relate to the particular culture media and incubation conditions; recovery methods and diluents, and the assumption that microorganisms will not pass through a filter of 0.45 µm porosity when the membrane filtration method is employed. Therefore, the test can only detect gross contamination of those microorganisms that will produce visible turbidity in the culture media under the conditions applied.

Data that is far more meaningful to give a probability if sterility is derived from the quality systems; sterility assurance and the microbiological and physical environmental monitoring employed during the production process. Furthermore, more accurate results can be derived from new technology, such as real-time epi-fluorescence counting theoretically detecting any microbial genetic material in a product (see below).

However, these limitations accepted, the Sterility Test is a regulatory requirement for the release of products that cannot be terminally sterilised (i.e. aseptically filled or heat-liable products). Sterility 'pass' remains a criterion for product release using the relatively unchanged pharmacopoeial methods. Parametric release remains some way off in the future. The FDA 'Sterile Products Produced by Aseptic Processing' (issued in 2004) only cites the compendial Sterility Test.

18.10 Rapid microbiological methods

The Sterility Test – as a cultural medium growth test – has remained relatively unchanged since the 1960s. As discussed above, its established weaknesses are that only a small proportion of the batch is tested and that the test will only grow those microorganisms capable of growing under the test conditions, in the presence of particular culture media at particular incubation temperatures and for given incubation times. This situation is further complicated by the fact that most microorganisms likely to be present are in a stressed or sub-lethally damaged state [13].

With the 2012 revision to the Code of Federal Regulations (CFR) 610.12, the FDA eliminated any reference to specified Sterility Test methods, culture media formulae (or formulations) and culture media test requirements. This permitted the use of rapid microbiological methods in territories under the FDA's jurisdiction, the change from pharmacopoeial methods, whilst possibly remaining more difficult within Europe.

There are several emerging rapid method technologies for the Sterility Test. These are summarised in the Table 18.4 [14–18].

In describing rapid methods, the FDA makes reference to the USP chapter for rapid methods: USP General Chapter 1223 'Validation of Alternative Microbiological Methods' and to The International Conference on Harmonisation (ICH) Q2 (R1) 'Validation of Analytical Procedures: Text and Methodology', for the establishment of validation test parameters. Such parameters may include limit of detection (the lowest number of microorganisms that can be detected by the method), specificity (ability of the test method to detect a range of organisms), ruggedness (degree of reproducibility of results obtained by analysis of the same sample under a variety of normal test conditions, i.e. different analysts, different instruments and different reagent lots) and robustness (capacity of the test method to remain unaffected by small, but deliberate variations in method parameters, i.e. changes in reagent concentration or incubation temperatures).

| **Table 18.4** | Summary of rapid microbiological Sterility Test methods |

Method	Description
Growth-based (CO_2 detection)	During microbial growth, CO_2 in the closed container accumulates and is detected by a fluorometric sensor. The generation of CO_2 indicates the presence of growing microorganisms.
ATP bioluminescence	Luciferin/luciferase enzyme reagent catalyses the conversion of microbial adenosine triphosphate (ATP) into ADP and light.
Adenylate Kinase based enzyme-amplification combined with ATP bioluminescence	The presence of microbial adenylate kinase catalyses the conversion of an ADP-containing reagent into ATP at significantly higher levels than microbial ATP alone. Amplified-ATP is then detected by a luciferin/luciferase-based bioluminescence assay.
Viability staining and solid phase cytometry	Any microorganisms retained on a filter are labelled with a non-fluorescent substrate. Within the cytoplasm of metabolically active cells, the substrate is enzymatically cleaved (by esterase) to release a fluorochrome. Cells with intact membranes will retain the fluorescent label. An argon laser scans the surface of the membrane and viable cells are detected. Viable cells may be subsequently observed using a phase-contrast microscope and an automated stage.

18.11 Conclusion

This chapter has examined the Sterility Test. In doing so, the two primary pharmacopeial methods have been outlined, together with some of the practical aspects of these methods, including method validation requirements. It has also discussed the statistical limitations of the test and has emphasised the need for focusing on sterility assurance, including environmental controls during batch manufacture, in order to increase confidence in the probability that the product is sterile. This focus on sterility assurance is one of the key overarching themes running throughout this book.

The chapter has concluded by considering rapid microbiological methods in light of the FDA CFR 610.12, which indicate a change to the standard approach for Sterility Testing.

18.12 References

1. Gilbert, P. and Allison, D.G. (1996), 'Redefining the "sterility" of sterile products', *European Journal of Parenteral Sciences*, 1: 19–23.
2. Kux, L. (2011), 'Amendments to sterility test requirements for biological products', 21 CFR Parts 600, 610, and 680, *Federal Register*, 76(119): 36019–27. Available from: *http://www.gpo.gov/fdsys/pkg/FR-2011-06-21/ pdf/2011-15346.pdf* (accessed 1 August 2012).
3. Baird, R. (1990), 'Monitoring microbiological quality: conventional testing methods', in: Denyer, S. and Baird, R. (eds), *Guide to Microbiological Control in Pharmaceuticals*, West Sussex: Ellis Horwood, pp. 125–45.
4. Van Doorne, H., Van Kampen, B.J., Van der Lee, R.W., Rummenie, L., Van der Veen, A.J. and De Vries, W.J. (1998), 'Manufacture of parenteral products in the Netherlands. A survey of eight years of media fills and sterility testing', *PDA Journal of Pharmaceutical Science and Technology*, 52(4): 159–64.
5. Bugno, A. and Pinto, T. (2003), 'The influence of incubation conditions in sterility tests', *PDA Journal of Pharmaceutical Science and Technology*, 57(6): 399–403.
6. Sandle, T. (2011), 'Practical approaches to sterility testing', in Saghee, M.R., Sandle, T. and Tidswell, E.C. (eds), *Microbiology and Sterility Assurance in Pharmaceuticals and Medical Devices*, New Delhi: Business Horizons, pp. 173–92.
7. Bill, A. (2000), 'Microbiology laboratory methods in support of the sterility assurance system', in: Baird, R., Hodges, N. and Denyer, S. (eds), *Handbook of Microbiological Quality Control*, London: Taylor & Francis.
8. Deeks, T. (2001), 'Microbiological validation master plan', in: Prince, R. (ed.), *Microbiology in Pharmaceutical Manufacturing*, Boca Raton, FL: PDA.
9. Hodges, N.A., Denyer, S.P., Hanlon, G.W. and Reynolds, J.R. (1996), 'Preservative efficacy tests in formulated nasal products: Reproducibility and factors affecting preservative efficacy', *Pharmaceutical Microbiology Interest Group News*, 48: 1237–42.
10. Russell, A.D., Ahonkhai, I. and Rogers, D.T. (1978), 'A review: Microbiological applications of the inactivation of antibiotics and other antimicrobial agents', *Journal of Applied Bacteriology*, 46: 207–45.
11. Therapeutic Goods Administration Guidelines for Sterility Testing of Therapeutic Goods (2002), Australia.
12. Sandle, T. (2000), 'Environmental monitoring in a sterility testing isolator', *Pharmaceutical Microbiology Interest Group News*, 1: 3–5.
13. Miller, M.J. (2011), 'The implementation of rapid microbiological methods', in: Saghee, M.R., Sandle, T. and Tidswell, E.C. (eds), *Microbiology and Sterility Assurance in Pharmaceuticals and Medical Devices*, New Delhi: Business Horizons.
14. Jimenez, L., Rana, N., Amalraj, J., Walker, K. and Travers, K. (2012), 'Validation of the BacT/ALERT-3D system for rapid sterility testing of biopharmaceutical samples', *PDA Journal of Pharmaceutical Science and Technology*, 66(1): 38–54.

15. Gray, J.C., Morandell, D., Gapp, G., Le Goff, N., Neuhaus, G. and Staerk, A. (2011), 'Identification of microorganisms after milliflex rapid detection – A possibility to identify non-sterile findings in the milliflex rapid sterility test', *PDA Journal of Pharmaceutical Science and Technology*, 65(1): 42–54.

16. Gray, J.C., Staerk, A., Berchtold, M., Mercier, M., Neuhaus, G. and Wirth, A. (2010), 'Introduction of a rapid microbiological method as an alternative to the pharmacopoeial method for the sterility test', *American Pharmaceutical Review*, 13(6): 88–94.

17. Gressett, G., Vanhaecke, E. and Moldenhauer, J. (2008), 'Why and how to implement a rapid Sterility Test', *PDA Journal of Pharmaceutical Science and Technology*, 62(6): 429–44.

18. Moldenhauer, J. (2006), 'Viability-based rapid microbiological methods for Sterility Testing and the need for identification of contamination', *PDA Journal of Pharmaceutical Science and Technology*, 60(2): 81–8.

19

Investigating sterility test failures

DOI: 10.1533/9781908818638.295

Abstract: This chapter presents the key considerations for investigating Sterility Test failures. The emphasis is upon the conventional Sterility Test method in relation to invalid test results; with the investigation into process issues applicable to all types of Sterility Testing. The chapter focuses on the likely occurrences of false positives and the areas for consideration including the Sterility Test environment, operator technique, consumables and reagents. Reference is made to genotypic microbiological identification and current FDA recommendations in relation to the number of permitted repeat Sterility Tests.

Key words: Sterility Test, microbiological, false positive, cleanroom, contamination control.

19.1 Introduction

The Sterility Test is a key microbiological test for the examination of products purportedly to be sterile (Chapter 18). The test is used as a product release test, where the sterility of a product is defined by the absence of viable and actively multiplying microorganisms when the product is tested in specified culture media (compendial test) or using an alternative rapid microbiological method. A failure with product sterility leads to an adulterated product [1].

   The method for conducting the Sterility Test is clearly documented in the European and United States pharmacopoeias. Occasionally, the Sterility Test will produce a positive result [2]. This demands both examination of the laboratory test and of the production process, to determine why the Sterility Test failure could have occurred. The conclusion of such an investigation will be either that the Sterility Test was invalid due to some type of 'laboratory error', a position for which a great deal of caution is required given that regulatory agencies require a robust rationale to be in place where a test is to be invalidated, or that the product was contaminated due to some event or incident in the manufacturing or filling of the product. This chapter examines some of the areas to consider when looking at Sterility Test failures.

19.2 Failure investigations

For aseptically filled products, the Sterility Test is a mandatory product release test, and over a period of time Sterility Test failures may occur. When such failures occur, as with any so-called microbiological data deviation, a documented investigation is required. The object of such investigations is to establish the root cause, to undertake corrective and preventative actions (CAPA) and to demonstrate that the action taken is effective [3].

19.2.1 Investigation procedure

An investigation into a Sterility Test failure should be conducted based on an SOP, which should be one written for microbiological data deviations rather than a generic investigation procedure designed for, say, chemical analysis. The investigation must be conducted by appropriately trained and competent personnel, with an expectation that such an investigation is led by a microbiologist. The investigation, once completed, must be properly documented and reviewed by an independent person [4].

19.2.2 Immediate actions

Once a Sterility Test failure has been detected, there are some actions which should be taken immediately [5]. The batch must be placed in quarantine and a decision taken about the status of the filling line on which the batch was filled. A documented decision should be made as to whether the line should continue to be used to fill product. At the same time, a decision should also be taken regarding other filling lines based about the question: is the Sterility Test failure based around something specific to a certain product or line, or is there a common breakdown with the sterility assurance system? This is something that can only be assessed based on a limited amount of initial information. These decisions may need to be re-examined as the investigation proceeds (Figure 19.1).

19.2.3 Conducting investigations

When conducting the investigation, a number of areas must be considered, covering both the test and test environment and the production process (manufacturing and filling activities).

The examination of the manufacturing process should be based on a line of inquiry which asks: Was something different about the manufacture

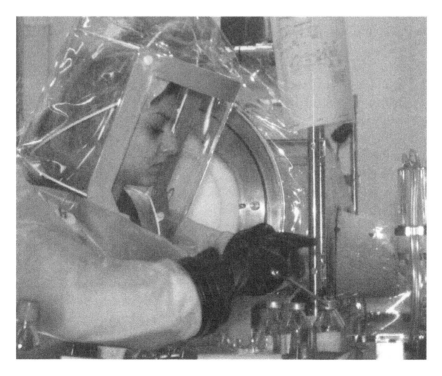

Figure 19.1 Operator undertaking the Sterility Test inside an isolator

Published by Woodhead Publishing Limited, 2013

of the product which failed compared with other batches? To answer this, a review of the manufacturing and batch processing records, together with discussions with manufacturing staff, is required.

Considering the Sterility Test operation first, those areas which should be examined include [6, 7]:

1. *Culture media* – The culture media used in the Sterility Test should be examined. This will include an assessment of the type of media, consideration of who prepared the media, and the growth promotion test results, sometimes described as the fertility or nutritive properties test. These are quality control tests that are performed on the media used during the Sterility Test, to demonstrate that it is capable of supporting the growth of microorganisms, and the sterilisation records relating to the manufacture of the media. If the media was externally purchased, the supplier should be contacted to see if there have been any customer complaints.

   Where the media was used in the Sterility Test, the negative control test result should be carefully assessed. Negative controls are undertaken during the same test session as the product test samples and include the media used within the Sterility Test. If the negative controls recorded growth, this may indicate a problem with the test environment or with the technique of the operator who conducted the Sterility Test. Where growth occurred in the negative controls, the contaminating microorganisms from the negative control and the failed Sterility Test should be carefully compared for microbial identification. This will need to take place using genotypic identification methods with technology based on 16S RNA.

2. *The relative difficulty of the Sterility Test procedure should be considered* – Some freeze-dried products or small volume products require more manipulations and could account for contamination occurring during the Sterility Test due to operator manipulations [8].

3. *The history of the Sterility Test should be reviewed* – especially the frequency of Sterility Test failures and instances where tests have been abandoned through complications. This will provide information about the reliability of the test and the testing environment, and there may be patterns which emerge for certain operators.

   The examination should consider the results of other tests conducted that day, as well as the record for the number of failures and the number of retests conducted.

4. *Environmental monitoring data* – the examination of environmental monitoring data will be of great importance in making any connection of the contaminating microorganism in the Sterility Test to either the Sterility Testing environment or operator, or to the manufacturing or filling environment. Environmental monitoring should be undertaken in the dynamic state and consist of a combination of techniques, including active air sampling, settle (exposure) plates, surface contact (RODAC) plates, swabs or flexible films, and operators' gloved hand plates [9]. The assessment should include a review of the recent environmental monitoring trends in addition to the test session under examination, for whilst the actual test session may appear satisfactory, the recent trend may be indicative of a contamination problem that an individual Sterility Testing session may not, given the relative imprecision of environmental monitoring methods.

    Environmental monitoring data should include both the test room and the testing environment (UDAF or isolator). In addition, the assessment should include the disinfection and cleaning records for the room.

5. *Sterility Test operator* – the history of the technician who conducted the Sterility Test should be carefully examined. If the technician has a good or bad recent history, this may provide an indication of the possibility of contamination occurring during the Sterility Test. The experience of the technician is also a factor to weigh up, as is the technician's training record (e.g. was the technician trained to carry out the test for the particular product?).

6. *Testing environment* – the testing environment, be it a UDAF unit with a classified cleanroom or an isolator, should be considered. The recent maintenance records should be checked in conjunction with ongoing physical test data such as pressure differentials, leak rates and sanitisation cycles. The examination of the sanitisation cycle should include an assessment of the gassing agent, including the chemical properties.

    In addition, the cleaning and maintenance records of the Sterility Test room and UDAF or isolator must form part of the investigation. A further factor to consider is whether any of the materials or equipment used in the Sterility Test required an additional sterilisation step, such as autoclaving test tubing. If so, the scope of the investigation should be extended to include the function of the steriliser and the load preparation (Figure 19.2).

Published by Woodhead Publishing Limited, 2013

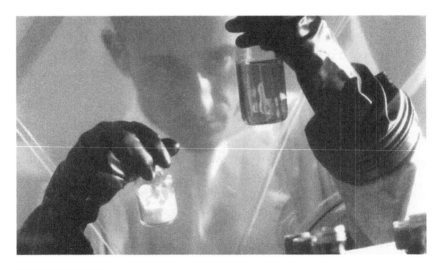

Figure 19.2 Inspecting Sterility Test media for turbidity

A number of steps in the manufacturing process require examination. These include:

- *Incoming raw materials* – were the materials received as satisfactory in terms of their container integrity and, most importantly, did they pass the microbial enumeration test and test for specified pathogens satisfactorily?

- *Process* – the manufacturing process should be examined for any unusual events or occurrences. For example, were hold times extended? In addition, were sterilisation records satisfactory? These types of questions should form the basis of the analysis.

- *Intermediate process bioburden* – the test results from the intermediate process bioburden (total viable count) should be examined to determine if the microbial trend was increasing or decreasing through the process and if such variations offer a reason for an unusual build-up in microbial contamination which might, in turn, relate to the Sterility Test failure.

- *Pre-final filtration bioburden* – the most important in-process sample is the one of the bulk solution prior to final filtration near the point of use (the filling operation). Both the level of the microbial challenge, against the validated parameters for the filter, and the microbial identification of any contaminants should be considered in relation to any possibility of contamination carry through.

- *Endotoxin results* – in-process endotoxin results should be examined as part of the review. Sometimes high level endotoxin values can be recorded where total viable count results are satisfactory, indicating the presence of bacteria. The endotoxin final product test result should also be considered. A failure or high level or endoxin, in conjunction with the Sterility Test failure, may be indicative of gross contamination and will offer a pointer towards the possible origin, i.e. water-borne contamination through the presence of Gram-negative rods.

- *Filling room and line* – were the filling room and line operating to standard in terms of physical parameters and microbiological controls? Had the room passed the 6-monthly HVAC tests, including particle cleanliness classification? Utility maintenance records should be examined as part of this review. Account should also be taken of any recent change controls that might impact upon the operation of the filling line.

- *Filling room operations* – the filling room operations must be carefully studied, including a review of all interventions into the ISO Class 5/ Grade A zone.

- *Operators* – the operators involved in the filling of the product should be interviewed and ideally they should play a role in the investigation team.

  When considering the activities of operators within the filling room, the investigation should consider the number of personnel present in the room together with the names of the personnel; certain individuals may, for example, be trainees or may be associated with adverse trends. One factor to consider is whether the operators were fatigued at the time of filling, since tiredness can lead to mistakes happening. When looking at each individual, an assessment should be made of the personnel related environmental monitoring for the filling operation in question and for the recent trends in association with the staff. This will include finger dabs and gowning assessments. The survey should also account for the recent media filling trial results, especially if any of the operators were associated with a media fill failure.

- *Media fills* – Data from the most recent media fill should be analysed. This will be doubly important if the most recent media fill recorded any turbid vials. If the investigation into the fill indicates that any interventions may have been the cause, consideration should be made as to whether the interventions were included and simulated during the media fill or if there were any concerns when the intervention was simulated. In some instances, it may be appropriate to schedule a media filling trial if the filling activity is considered to be a probable cause of the Sterility Test failure.

■ *Environmental monitoring* – the viable and non-viable particulate data in relation to the product fill and data relating to the background environment should be examined. This will include identification results of all microorganisms recovered. Where similar species have been recovered, these should be characterised to determine if the microorganisms are related at the genetic level using genotypic testing. The results of such analysis should be related back to the microorganism(s) recovered from the Sterility Test failure.

The review of environmental monitoring data should include both critical and non-critical areas, with a consideration of recent trends for the filling room and the process. Trend data may indicate a gradual deterioration in operational conditions.

■ *Cleaning and disinfection* – cleaning and disinfection records pertaining to the filling room and filling zone should be examined. Inadequate cleaning may explain why microbial contamination occurred. Such a review should consider the effectiveness of cleaning techniques and the expiry time of the detergents and disinfectants used for the cleaning on the day of the product fill.

The microorganism isolated from the Sterility Test failure should be considered in terms of disinfectant efficacy, particularly whether the microorganism would be killed by the disinfectant. If there are doubts, as in the case of isolation of a Gram-positive sporing rod, a decision should be made whether or not a disinfectant challenge test (using the suspension test method) should be undertaken to demonstrate if the microorganism is resistant to the in-use concentration of the disinfectant.

19.3 Sterility Test and process area link

The key piece of information, which draws together the investigation between the Sterility Test and the process area, is the microorganism detected within the Sterility Test failure. The assessment as to where else the microorganism is found, in either the Sterility Test environment or the process area, provides important information as to the origin of the contamination. Any suggested link must be made at the genetic level. If the microorganism can be linked to the process area, then the Sterility Test can be confirmed. If the microorganism is linked to the Sterility Test area, a link cannot be automatically confirmed. Although it is a possibility, a reason for the contamination occurring during the Sterility Test must be made together with a robust case for making the connection. Where this occurs, the response must be to undertake a re-test [10].

If no link can be made, then the only acceptable response is to confirm the Sterility Test as a genuine failure and to reject the batch.

19.4 Re-testing

The pharmacopoeias allow for a re-test of the product if persuasive evidence exists to show that the cause of the initial sterility failure was induced by the laboratory. Identification and speciation of the isolate(s) is a significant contributing factor to the final decision. Such identification must be carried out at the genotypic level, for it must be unequivocally demonstrated that the microorganism isolated from the product is identical to an isolate from the Sterility Test materials and/or the testing environment. Justifying a repeat Sterility Test based only on morphological or biochemical characterisation of microorganisms should not be permitted, because it is probable that the same types of contaminants in the test environment would be similar to any which might have contaminated the product. For example, it is likely that Gram-positive bacteria transient or residential to human skin, such as Micrococci or Staphylococci, could contaminate a product during aseptic filling and would also be found in the test environment, given that such organisms are the predominant cleanroom microflora.

If the Sterility Test can be invalidated by the laboratory, then the pharmacopoeias allow for a repeat Sterility Test to be conducted, which requires double the original number of samples to be tested. The repeat Sterility Test should not be conducted until the investigation has been concluded and Quality Assurance authorise a repeat test to be carried out. In terms of the number of permitted repeat Sterility Tests, the FDA CFR 610.12 (2012 update) allows for only one repeat Sterility Test, provided that the original Sterility Test can be invalidated due to laboratory error. Repeat testing is undertaken with the same number of test samples as used in the original test, with negative product controls tested concurrently. If the repeat Sterility Test fails, even if this is attributed to testing error, no further repeat Sterility Tests can be undertaken and the product cannot be released.

19.5 Concluding Sterility Test failure investigations

When concluding Sterility Test failure investigations, the investigation should lead to the establishment of a root cause or most probable root cause. This will centre upon deciding how the contamination got into the product: was this the result of something relating to the process or to the filling of the final product, or was this a so-called 'false positive' and the result of a contaminant transferred during the Sterility Test operations? Care must be taken and a robust case constructed if the investigation concludes laboratory error. Such a conclusion must be unequivocal and be based on genetic microbial identification testing at the DNA or RNA levels.

It is possible that the investigation will conclude with more than one root cause. This may lead to a thorough review of processing or filling operations, together with appropriate preventative actions to prevent re-occurrence. Where the root cause is established, the pharmaceutical organisation must make decisions about batches of product already on the market, as well as release considerations for batches under quarantine. This will be based around whether the root causes relate to a specific batch incident or to a wider process problem.

The documentation for the Sterility Test failure investigation should be detailed and cover most of the points raised in this chapter, as well as other considerations specific to the product line. Regulatory authorities will expect a logical, detailed and well-presented investigation report.

19.6 Conclusion

This chapter has emphasised the seriousness of a Sterility Test failure and has outlined the importance of conducting a logical investigation into the failure. This has centred on two strands, consideration of laboratory error and the investigation into an accepted failure in relation to the production process. When concluding Sterility Test failure investigations, the investigation should lead to the establishment of a root cause or most probable root cause. This will centre upon deciding how the contamination got into the product: was this the result of something relating to the process or to the filling of the final product, or was this a so-called 'false positive' and the result of a contaminant transferred during the Sterility Test operations? It is possible that the investigation will conclude with more than one probable root cause. This may lead to a thorough review of processing or filling operations, together with appropriate preventative actions to prevent re-occurrence. Where the root cause is established, the pharmaceutical organisation must make decisions about batches of product already on the market, as well as release considerations for batches under quarantine. This will be based around whether the root causes relate to a specific batch incident or to a wider process problem.

The aim of the chapter was to provide the reader with guidance for failure investigations and to demonstrate why some areas are worthy of greater consideration than others.

19.7 References

1. Tidswell, E. (2011), 'Sterility', in: Saghee, M.R., Sandle, T. and Tidswell, E.C. (eds), *Microbiology and Sterility Assurance in Pharmaceuticals and Medical Devices*, New Delhi: Business Horizons, pp. 589–614.
2. Sykes, G. (1956), 'The technique of Sterility Testing', *Journal of Pharmacy and Pharmacology*, 8: 573–88.
3. Lagomarsino, M. (2011), 'Investigation of microbiological data deviations', in: Saghee, M.R., Sandle, T. and Tidswell, E.C. (eds), *Microbiology and Sterility Assurance in Pharmaceuticals and Medical Devices*, New Delhi: Business Horizons, pp. 477–92.
4. Lee, J.Y. (1990) 'Investigation sterility test failures', *Pharmaceutical Technology*, 14(2): 38–43.
5. Sutton, S. (2007), 'Investigations', in: *Pharmaceutical Quality Control Microbiology: A Guidebook to the Basics*, Bethesda, MD: PDA/DHI Publishing, Inc.
6. Schroeder, H.G. (2005), 'Sterility failure analysis', *PDA Journal of Pharmaceutical Science and Technology*, 59(2): 89–95.
7. Sandle, T. (2012), 'Sterility test failure investigations', *Journal of GXP Compliance*, 16(1): 66–73.
8. Sandle, T. (2004), 'Practical approaches to sterility testing', *Journal of Validation Technology*, 10(2): 131–41.
9. Sandle, T. (2000), 'Environmental monitoring in a sterility testing isolator', *Pharmaceutical Microbiology Interest Group Newsletter*, 1: 3–5.
10. Ernst, R.R., West, K.L. and Hoyle, J.E. (1969), 'Problem areas in Sterility Testing', *Bulletin of the Parenteral Drug Association*, 23(1): 29–39.

20

Auditing sterilisation processes and facilities

DOI: 10.1533/9781908818638.307

Abstract: This chapter outlines the auditing sterile processing facilities and contains information of interest to both the auditor (in relation to preparing for and carrying out audits) and the auditee (in preparing to receive an audit). In doing so, reference is made to regulatory guidance, including those issued by the FDA and from the European Medicines Agency. The chapter provides a framework for conducting audits, including systems based and risk centric audits. The core part consists of an overview of the key focal points in relation to sterile products manufacture, such as utilities, cleanrooms, sterilisation and testing.

Key words: auditing, inspections, regulatory, standards, sterile processing, cleanrooms, contamination control, quality assurance, quality control, pharmaceutical.

20.1 Introduction

Pharmaceutical preparations are expected to be safe and efficacious [1]. Safety relates to the effectiveness of the medicine, and to the avoidance of chemical and microbiological contamination [2]. As with any other type of pharmaceutical manufacturing, sterile manufacturing is subject to inspections by regulatory authorities and to audits. Due to the importance of maintaining sterility, sterile manufacturing is often subject to the highest level of regulatory assessment [3]. As section III of the FDA Guidance on Sterile Products notes [4]:

Nearly all drugs recalled due to non-sterility or lack of sterility assurance in the period spanning 1980–2000 were produced via aseptic processing.

Some years on, that trend remains unchanged.

Sterility, as this book has explained, is achieved through protective controls and good practices during processing and by the presentation of the final dosage form. 'Sterile products' encompasses the preparation of terminally sterilised products and the aseptic preparation of products through sterile filling.

The preparation and operation of audits represents an important part of the biannual or annual cycle for pharmaceutical organisations. There are various definitions of quality audits. One definition that fits well with this book is that an audit is a systematic and independent examination, undertaken to determine whether quality activities and related results comply with planned arrangements, and whether these arrangements are implemented effectively and are suitable to achieve the objectives. The objectives are centred on compliance with quality systems and maintaining sterility.

Within the context of sterile operations, the primary concern is with microbiological contamination. Here the main risk concerns are with viable microorganisms, particulate matter and pyrogens.

This chapter presents an overview of the general audit topics relating to the manufacture of sterile products and presents some of the more important aspects that the manufacturer should review on a regular basis. Audits are performed either internally, such as with one department evaluating the work of another, or externally by clients or customers. Regulatory bodies recommend that sterile products manufacturers undertake regular self-inspections, in order to monitor Good Manufacturing Practice (GMP) principles and to propose necessary corrective measures where deficiencies are noted.

The principles of audits apply equally well to regulatory inspections. A regulatory inspection is, in essence, a thorough audit undertaken by an external regulatory body, such as the Federal Drug Administration (FDA), a European inspector (as required by the European Medicines Agency), by the World Health Organisation (WHO), or by a national agency.

This chapter outlines the audit process and the scope of audits. The substantial topics featured are the 'focal points' and reflect the deficiencies most commonly cited by regulators. The overriding focal point is the one unifying feature common to all manufacturers of sterile products. That is to produce a product that is sterile. Although sterility is defined as 'the absence of all viable microorganisms', as this book has emphasised, sterility can only be expressed in terms of probability for each item of product produced, which cannot be tested for sterility without destroying each item. Therefore, there is a great deal of importance placed upon control systems and standards, which provide the consistency required to produce sterile products.

20.2 The audit process

As emphasised above, there is no significant distinction between the terms 'inspection' and 'audit', other than providing an indication of who is performing it. Each audit differs in terms of what is looked at and this can range from the entire facility to one laboratory test. The scope also varies according to the agency, the inspector, as standards become revised through the changing list of current GMP topics, and how the facility performs during the inspection. One commonality is that all audits will be against a standard or guideline. In relation to regulatory standards, the reader is referred to Chapter 3.

In terms of the audit process, audits should be conducted in an independent and detailed way by designated competent person(s) with reference to appropriate standards. Audits should focus on looking for conformance requirements and aim to be factual and objective. Whilst the auditor should be knowledgeable with the subject area, a good audit technique also requires effective listening and observation.

Before an audit begins there should be pre-written plan or programme, which is then followed. It is important that all audits are recorded. Audit reports should contain all the observations made during the inspections and, where non-conformances (or non-compliances) have been found, proposals for corrective and preventative actions (CAPA). CAPA should be accompanied by timelines, agreed between the auditor and auditee. At the end of the process there should be a follow-up review to determine if the required actions have been completed satisfactorily.

With non-conformances, there are three components:

1. description of the non-conformance and the reason for the failure(s) to meet the requirements;

2. objective evidence which can be proved;

3. record of the specific details of what has been examined and found.

Published by Woodhead Publishing Limited, 2013

Although each audit process will differ to a degree, many follow the pattern:

- *An opening meeting* – At the opening meeting the audit plan will be reviewed. This will include audit schedule, products or operations to be examined, and the procedures and records to be reviewed;
- A *facility tour* – including manufacturing areas and quality control laboratories;
- *An assessment phase* – will consist of a review of procedures, operations, records and interviews with personnel to assess compliance with requirements;
- A *closing meeting* – at which the deficiencies or failures to comply with appropriate standards are presented formally;
- some type of follow-up or review of the actions.

Audits are either structured in a way that follows the manufacturing flow, for example a forward trace audit involving following production flow from receipt of components or materials through to dispatch of finished products, or an audit looking at different aspects of the quality system (so-called 'system audits').

Whichever approach is adopted, the auditor will review documents and inspect the process, often to determine if what is written down is actually being undertaken. The auditor will also examine documents to determine if they follow standards and will request data to demonstrate if statements can be supported by information, such as the test data relating to air changes per hour in a particular cleanroom.

20.3 Scope of audits

The scope of audits varies according to the objectives of the audit plan. There are areas which are covered when an entire facility is inspected. There are personnel matters (including training), premises (including environmental control and associated environmental monitoring), equipment, documentation, production, distribution of the medicinal products, and arrangements for dealing with complaints and recalls. Such examinations should be based on the principles of Quality Assurance [5]. Audits should focus on the key 'quality systems' relating to pharmaceutical and medical device manufacture. A quality system is made up of a number of components, with each part relating to the overall quality system and the aim of producing a quality product, one

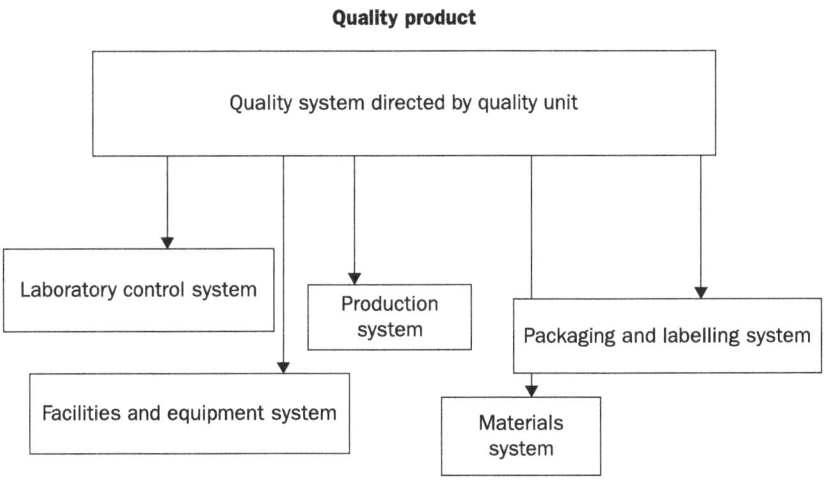

Quality product

```
┌─────────────────────────────────────────────────────┐
│        Quality system directed by quality unit        │
└─────────────────────────────────────────────────────┘
```

```
┌──────────────────────────┐   ┌──────────────┐
│ Laboratory control system │   │  Production  │
└──────────────────────────┘   │    system    │   ┌──────────────────────────────┐
                               └──────────────┘   │ Packaging and labelling system │
                                                   └──────────────────────────────┘
┌──────────────────────────────┐   ┌──────────────┐
│ Facilities and equipment system │   │  Materials   │
└──────────────────────────────┘   │    system    │
                                    └──────────────┘
```

Figure 20.1 An illustration of the key 'quality systems'

that is both efficacious and contamination free [6]. This relationship is illustrated in Figure 20.1.

In the context of the larger scope of the company-wide audit, this chapter addresses the pertinent points of the audit process that relate to sterility and sterilisation only.

20.4 Key focal points for auditing sterile manufacturing facilities

20.4.1 General appearance of the facility

The overall design and appearance of the facility should give the auditor confidence that the site is suitable for the manufacture of sterile products. This includes such areas as security, cleanliness, the physical measures taken to avoid cross-contamination and mix-up, the availability of written procedures, and whether or not these are being followed.

20.4.2 Quality documentation

The auditor should examine the quality policy for the site and the documents which stem from it, including site policies and standard operating procedures. The auditor should review important documents, including:

- organisational charts;
- change control procedure;
- training procedures;
- complaints procedure;
- CAPA procedure.

20.4.3 Facility design

The design and layout of the facilities in which pharmaceutical manufacturing and laboratory testing take place are critical to the manufacture of sterile products. Of direct applicability to sterile manufacturing are cleanrooms. With the premises used for the manufacturing of sterile pharmaceuticals, there should be separate and defined areas of operation to prevent contamination, with controlled access and different grades of cleanrooms appropriate to the activities being undertaken [7]. The cleanroom class should be appropriate to the activities undertaken within it and the auditor will examine whether cleanrooms are constructed in a way to make them easy to clean and disinfect [8].

An auditor will wish to seek assurance that there is proper directional flow of air, controlled material transfer and people movement (the most important aspects of cleanroom design). The auditor will also request data to demonstrate that the cleanroom classification is met in terms of air cleanliness, particulate levels and microbial contamination levels.

In relation to cleanrooms, data should be available to present during an inspection relating to [9]:

(a) Heating Ventilation and Air Conditioning (HVAC) system operations. Reports for the recent commissioning, as well as the initial qualification, should be available.

(b) Types of HEPA (high efficiency particulate air filters) in place, relating to the appropriate grades of filters along with Certificates of Conformance. The policy for HEPA filter repair and replacement should be available.

(c) The results from the annual or 6-monthly recertification of the cleanroom. This will include data relating to particle classification (which should be to ISO 14644 unless justified otherwise), pressure differentials (ΔP) and room air change rates (air volume replacement and pressure differential data is reciprocal) [10].

(d) Evidence should be available to demonstrate that pressure differentials are monitored continuously throughout processing and that data is recorded. Where any deviations have occurred, a record of the action taken should also be available.

(e) In addition, engineering records for HEPA filter leak testing should be available. Depending upon the design of the HEPA filters, leak testing should provide assurance that there are no integrity breaches relating to sealing gaskets, frames or the filter media.

(f) For UDAF (unidirectional airflow devices), additional data must be supplied about the air velocity, together with a justification as to where the air velocity is measured in terms of filter face locations and working height.

(g) For UDAF devices used for aseptic filling, the organisation should have available airflow visualisation (or 'smoke') studies of the activities that take place under the UDAF and the relationship between the UDAF and the room housing the UDAF.

Other areas of interest will be:

(h) *Storage areas* – these areas should be clean and tidy, with appropriate controlled access. An inspector will probably seek to verify that storage areas for products and raw materials are maintained at an appropriate temperature and that records are kept.

20.4.4 Facility operations

There are a number of parts of the facility operation that an auditor will wish to inspect. These will include:

(a) *Material transfer and flow* – materials and products have to be stored and handled so that the potential for mix-ups of different products or of their ingredients is minimal and that cross-contamination is avoided. If a product is filled at the facility, the auditor should, as minimum, study the process flow and observe some parts of the filling activity through an observation window. The auditor should note how items of equipment are transferred from sterilisation devices to filling machines and how the product is connected.

(b) Sterilisation devices, such as depyrogenation ovens and autoclaves will be examined. Due to the criticality of the sterilisation process, an auditor will check validation cycles and records relating to these items. Furthermore, with sterilisation devices, it is a good idea to prepare inspection packs, which should contain the protocol, report, and data relating to the validation, including [11]:

(i) Justification of locations and the results of biological indicator studies, where evidence should be available to show that the points deemed to be the greatest risk have been monitored;

(ii) Justification of locations and the results of temperature probes and sensors.

Furthermore, in relation to sterilisation devices, each should have gone through a defined qualification route (as set out below). This will no doubt be reviewed by the auditor. An example of what is required is provided by a review of an autoclave [12]:

- Installation Qualification (IQ) results must be available, particularly utility connections and instrument specifications.

- With the Operational Qualification (OQ) records, it is important to provide evidence showing that thermocouples were positioned throughout the chamber within hot and cold regions.

- With the Performance Qualification (PQ), the results of the thermocouples and biological indicator studies will be scrutinised in order to prove that the device can be operated consistently and achieve the required lethality levels.

(c) *Vessels and equipment* – all items of equipment should be maintained in a clean and sanitised state (and sterile where appropriate), with appropriate status labels visible (indicating if the equipment is 'clean' or 'dirty'). For sterile vessels, these are held under positive pressure.

In terms of the process itself, an auditor will probably inquire:

- whether time limits are established and justified for each phase of processing period. This is particularly important for the period between the start of bulk product compounding and its sterilisation, for the filtration processes, and the time of product exposure while on the processing line;

- whether contamination or mix-up is likely or unlikely;

- the policy prescribing how many personnel are allowed within any cleanroom;

- the methods and validation of cycles for automated equipment;

- whether equipment and items which have been sterilised are appropriately covered or held under clean airflows to prevent recontamination.

During manufacture, a number of in-process tests will be conducted as part of quality control. The data relating to these samples and the test results should be made available, with evidence that any out-of-specification results have been investigated.

Examples of in-process tests include:

- pH of buffers;
- in-process viable counts;
- bacterial endotoxin tests of process rinses;
- bioburden assessment of the prefiltration bulk;
- specific tests relating to the product, often for biochemical or inorganic chemical quality.

20.4.5 Material and equipment control

In relation to materials and equipment, the auditor will undoubtedly look at:

(a) Incoming materials include sterile supplies and starting materials and should be of an appropriate cleanroom grade and the supplier should be identified through an approved supplier list.

(b) An auditor will note whether there is adequate cleaning, drying and storage of equipment. Equipment cleaning validation studies, using chemical (total organic carbon) and microbial (either swabs or water rinse tests), should be available to present at the audit.

(c) For aseptic processing, all equipment entering the critical zone must be sterilised (or purchased sterile). With such sterilised equipment, the time period between the sterilisation of the equipment and its time of use should be established. For this, validation is normally undertaken by holding equipment and using it in media simulation trials.

20.4.6 Quality control

Quality Control (QC) laboratories, particularly microbiology laboratories, are likely to be included in the facility tour. An inspector will expect that laboratories are housed in a dedicated area, separate from Production. The microbiology laboratory should be designed appropriately with different activities segregated, such as microbial identification located in a separate area to the processing and reading of environmental monitoring plates.

In the microbiology laboratory, an auditor will probably wish to see locations for and test results relating to:

- sterility testing;
- endotoxin testing;
- incubators for environmental monitoring samples;
- areas where environmental monitoring samples are read;
- water testing.

In addition to such batch release testing, if the facility undertakes parametric release, this process will be scrutinised in relation to the procedure and data used to make batch release decisions.

20.4.7 Utilities

The utilities, which input into pharmaceutical manufacturing, will be subject to regulatory inspection. These include:

(a) *Water (purified water or Water for Injections) (WFI)* – with water systems, the validation results should be presented as a package, including [13]:

- *Design Qualification* – including detailed diagrams;
- *Construction Validation* – i.e. material certification;
- *Installation Qualification* – including verification of instruments, valves, heat exchangers, distillation units, etc. In addition, data relating to cleaning and passivation may be viewed;
- *Operational Qualification* – data relating to flow and pressure rates, temperature, sensitisation, alarms, pumps and filter integrity should be available;
- *Performance Qualification* – involves monitoring the water systems for microbial and chemical quality for a period of a minimum of 4 weeks (phase I) and for a period of 1 year (phase II). Trend data should be made available to the auditor.

The routine test data most likely to be required for water systems is:

- pH;
- total organic carbon;
- conductivity;
- microbial bioburden (total viable aerobic counts):
  - When used in bulk for manufacturing purposes, the pharmacopoeiae also apply a microbiological limit to WFI; this is not more than 10 cfu per 100 mL.
- Bacterial endotoxins:
  - The level across the pharmacopoeias is 0.25 EU/mL (for WFI and highly purified water).

  When examining the water system one of the key concerns of auditors will be the frequency and method system sanitisation and the presence of any 'dead legs' in relation to the water system piping.

(b) *Steam* – with steam (or 'clean steam') used to supply steam sterilisation devices, an auditor is likely to review test records to look at the frequency of testing (which is typically 5-monthly or more frequent), the sampling ports (to confirm if they are representative) and test results (relating to bacterial endotoxin, non-condensable gases and dryness) [14].

(c) *Compressed air* – it is important that where such gases are used in relation to product filling, that they are certified as sterile at point-of-use, (which is normally through a 0.2 μm sterilising grade filter), and that the point-of-use filters have been integrity tested.

Air is also classed as a utility in relation to HVAC systems. HVAC has been examined above in relation to cleanroom operations.

20.4.8 Support activities

In order to achieve microbial control in cleanrooms, the use of defined cleaning techniques, together with the application of detergents and disinfectants, is important [15]. As such, this subject is likely to come under regulatory scrutiny.

A related area is environmental monitoring data, which describes the microbiological testing undertaken in order to detect changing trends of microbial count and microflora within cleanroom environments. Trend data will be asked for during most audits.

20.4.9 Personnel

The training of personnel to work in cleanrooms, and their practices and behaviours are of the utmost importance and the qualification of personnel will feature in any audit. An auditor will be aware that personnel are the primary source of contamination within cleanrooms, due to the continuous shedding of epidermal cells, many of which contain microorganisms, and will be conscious for any signs of improper gowning, breaches of procedure or behaviours which indicate hygiene concerns.

20.4.10 Batch review and release

The system for the review and release of sterilised products will be examined during the audit and example batch records will be requested, then the auditor will compare these against procedures.

20.5 Conclusion

Sterile manufacturing and the sterilisation of products and materials represents the most complex part of pharmaceutical production. The importance of maintaining control throughout all parts of the process rests on the seriousness of the risk that contaminated medicines or devices could have on patient health, as well as the loss of expensive products. This is why audits of sterile facilities need to be thorough and undertaken regularly.

This chapter has presented an overview of the key focal points for the audit of sterile manufacturing facilities. In doing so, it has also provided some guidance on preparing for inspections, considering both the human aspect in terms of behaviours and the practical in terms of a documentation overview.

20.6 References

1. Halls, N.A. (1994), *Achieving Sterility in Medical and Pharmaceutical Products*, New York: Marcel Dekker, Inc.
2. Sharp, J. (1995), 'What do we mean by sterility?', *PDA Journal of Pharmaceutical Science and Technology*, 49, 90–92.

3. Sharp, J. (1991), *Good Manufacturing Practice: Philosophy and Applications*, Buffalo Grove, IL: Interpharm Press.

4. Food and Drug Administration (2004), *Guideline on Sterile Drug Products Produced by Aseptic Processing*, Rockville, MD: Food and Drug Administration.

5. Sharp, J. (2005), *Good Manufacturing Practice: Rationale and Compliance*, Boca Raton, FL: CRC Press.

6. Hargreaves, P. (2007), 'Good manufacturing practice in the control of contamination', in: Deyner, S.P. and Baird, R.M. (eds), *Guide to Microbiological Control in Pharmaceuticals and Medical Devices*, 2nd edition, Boca Raton, FL: CRC Press, pp. 121–42.

7. Ljungqvist, B. and Reinmüller, B. (1997), *Clean Room Design – Minimizing Contamination through Proper Design*, Buffalo Grove IL: Interpharm Press.

8. Ramstorp, M. (2011), 'Microbial contamination control in pharmaceutical manufacturing', in: Saghee, M.R., Sandle, T. and Tidswell, E.C. (eds), *Microbiology and Sterility Assurance in Pharmaceuticals and Medical Devices*, New Delhi: Business Horizons, 615–700.

9. Whyte, W. (2001), *Cleanroom Technology: Fundamentals of Design, Testing and Operation*, London: John Wiley & Co.

10. Schicht, H.H. (2003), 'The ISO contamination control standards – a tool for implementing regulatory requirements', *European Journal of Parenteral and Pharmaceutical Sciences*, 8(2): 37–42.

11. Pflug, I.J. and Odlaug, T.E. (1986), 'Biological indicators in the pharmaceutical and medical device industry', *Journal of Parenteral Science and Technology*, 40: 242–8.

12. Amer, G. and Beane, R.G. (2000), 'Autoclave qualification: Some practical advice', *Journal of Validation Technology*, 7(1): 90–4.

13. Vincent, D.W. (2003), 'Qualification of purified water systems', *Journal of Validation Technology*, 10(1): 50–61.

14. Latham, T. (1995), 'Clean steam systems', *Pharmaceutical Engineering*, 15(2):

15. Sandle, T. (2003), 'Selection and use of cleaning and disinfection agents in pharmaceutical manufacturing', in: Hodges, N. and Hanlon, G., *Industrial Pharmaceutical Microbiology Standards and Controls*, Basingstoke, UK: Euromed Communications.

Conclusion

Abstract: This chapter presents an overview of the main themes that occur throughout this book. The chapter emphasises the importance of sterility in relation to pharmaceutical products and medical devices and reviews the essential process and environmental controls that become in-built into a system to maintain sterility. The chapter also considers the most widely used sterilisation methods in relation to terminally sterilised products and the areas of concern in relation to aseptic filling. In joining these various elements together, the chapter re-considers the key focal points.

Key words: sterilisation, sterility, sterile products, terminal sterilisation, aseptic filling, medicinal products, medical devices, Good Manufacturing Practice, pharmaceutical technology, microbiology.

A common goal of many pharmaceutical manufacturers, biotechnology researchers and producers of medical devices, is to produce safe products. One fundamental aspect of 'safety' is freedom from microbial contamination. This book has been concerned with sterility and products and articles, used within the pharmaceutical, healthcare and medical device sectors that are intended to be sterile. Sterility, a term subject to differing, and sometimes competing definitions, can be taken to be the absence of any microorganism capable of reproduction. The importance of sterility is because the products and materials that this book is concerned with, whether subject to a terminal sterilisation process or produced aseptically, could cause patient harm or even death.

It is additionally important that products produced for administration by injection are free from pyrogenic substances, of which bacterial endotoxins pose the greatest concern.

Sterility can be achieved through the destruction of all viable life forms by applying a lethal agent to the item that must be sterilised. Several sterilisation methods exist, each method destroying microorganisms in a different way and with a different degree of effectiveness. Sterilisation, as this book has emphasised, is an absolute concept: either something is sterile or it is not.

Two broad categories for the sterilisation of pharmaceutical products have been outlined. Either the product is prepared in its final container and then subject to a terminal sterilisation cycle or a sterile product (often sterilised by filtration) is brought together with sterile bottles, caps and overseals (or through plastic moulding) and the product is filled aseptically. Of these two processes, aseptic filling presents the greatest contamination risk. With medical devices, these are terminally sterilised, most often by ethylene oxide gas, gamma irradiation or electron beam radiation.

In relation to the method of terminal sterilisation, this book has considered established methods, emerging methods and potential methods. Of immediate concern and of practical importance to the pharmaceutical sector are the established methods. These are summarised in Figure C.1 below, where the methods are subdivided into physical and chemical categories, with physico-chemical being where both categories are combined, such as using a chemical and then subjecting it to heat.

Of the methods of sterilisation considered, the most common method remains sterilisation by heat. This book considered the differences between dry heat and moist heat processes where, in general, moist heat is the most effective method, provided that the item to be sterilised can be subjected to this method without degradation.

With the different methods of sterilisation examined, the efficacy of the sterilisation process is dependent upon different variables. With heat, for example, the key variables are temperature and time. Here, as the book outlined, temperature and time are inversely proportional. This means that as temperature increases, the time taken to achieve sterilisation decreases. This is known as the thermal death time, the minimum time required to kill a suspension of organisms at a predetermined temperature in a specified environment.

A further variable, common to all sterilisation methods, is the number of microorganisms. Here, the higher the number of microorganisms, then the higher the temperature required to achieve sterilisation becomes, or the longer the required duration is. In relation to microbial destruction, the killing of microorganisms occurs exponentially, whereby some fraction of the living population dies per unit time.

Other factors which affect the success or otherwise of sterilisation include the nature of the microorganisms present. Provided that the

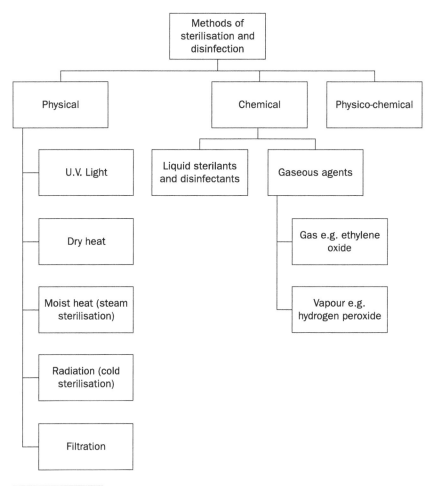

Figure C.1   Established methods of sterilisation

microorganisms are of a lower resistance than the microorganisms used during the validation cycle, be that as biological indicators or from an assessment of the product bioburden, then the possibility of a sterilisation cycle failure is low. However, to know this, the user must understand the types and numbers of microorganisms present on or in the product, as well as the risk from environmental contamination present in the processing environment, where the strict operation of controlled environments or cleanrooms is of importance.

Further factors influencing sterilisation include the type of material to be subjected to the sterilisation process, which relates to the ease at which sterilisation can be achieved and whether the material or product will suffer any damage following sterilisation. A related factor is whether any organic material or dirt is present on the material, which may hamper the efficacy of the sterilisation process.

With each process, the most important activities are centred on the validation and verification of the sterilisation process, where the process is subject to physical and biological validation, and for the implementation of controls during routine processing runs. Such validation and controls are essential in order to demonstrate that any biological challenge, or intrinsic bioburden on product or item, can be effectively and reliably killed.

Aseptic processing, which formed the second part of this book in relation to discussions on cleanroom, disinfection, aseptic filling, and the Sterility Test, presents greater challenges and risks to those tasked with producing a sterile product for injection into people. Aseptic processing is the placing of a sterilised product (often sterilised by filtration) into a sterilised package that is then sealed under aseptic conditions. Regarding this subject, the book has placed considerable emphasis upon controls, facility design, operator behaviour, and cleaning and disinfection regimes.

As a concluding comment, sterilisation is a complex and challenging arena. If designed well, using validated processes and with an exacting adherence to Good Manufacturing Practices, then the risks of patient harm stand as relatively low. Hopefully this book has gone some way towards presenting this complex and challenging topic in a straightforward way, to be of use to those new to the subject, or those with a passing interest, and as a reliable aide-mémoire to the more experienced practitioner.

Index

Published by Woodhead Publishing Limited, 2013

Published by Woodhead Publishing Limited, 2013

Published by Woodhead Publishing Limited, 2013

Published by Woodhead Publishing Limited, 2013

Published by Woodhead Publishing Limited, 2013

WHO Library Cataloguing-in-Publication Data, 43
wide spectrum activity, 253
wiping, 256
working shifts, 233
World Health Organisation (WHO), 43–4

X-radiations, 163–4
X-ray tube, 164
X-rays, 159, 163–4

Z-value, 271–2
'zero dead leg' valves, 31